# Well of Living Water

### Jeannine Williams

# Dedication

*I would like to dedicate this book in loving memory to my dad, Charles Baldwin, who was a wonderful Christian, loving dad, as well as one of my biggest encourages in life. He always encouraged me to persevere and not to give up. I'm thankful that the Lord gave me such an incredible dad. Sure do love and miss him!*

# Introduction

God, the Father, gave His only begotten Son, Jesus Christ, to be the Saviour of the world; He also gave us a personal *love letter*—the Bible—to be every Christian's guide through life on earth. It is my prayer that this book will encourage you to spend daily time with God in His Word, learning how to live a victorious Christian life that will glorify Him. May we be able to honestly say as the Psalmist said, "Thy word is very pure: therefore thy servant loveth it"—Psalm 119:140.

Mrs. Jeannine Williams

*But whosoever drinketh of the water that I shall give him shall never thirst; but the water that I shall give him shall be in him a well of water springing up into everlasting life.*
John 4:14

# Well of Living Water

John 4:6

*"Now Jacob's well was there. Jesus therefore, being wearied with his journey, sat thus on the well."*

Jesus, the Son of man, grew weary, as we see from this account of Him in the Gospel of John. It is a comfort to the Christian to know that He is "acquainted with grief" Isaiah 53:3, and understands our times of weariness. What is even more glorious to the Christian is that He not only understands, but He is a well of living water for the Christian's thirsty need. He is the water of refreshment and of abundant strength for each new day. He is the source of revival, renewing the Christian's soul upon the journey of life. Jesus Christ will quench the thirsty soul and help the weary. It is going to occur, this weariness in the journey, but drinking from the well of living water will nourish and strengthen the Christian to continue in the battle for the Lord. It is my prayer that this book will encourage you to spend daily time with God in His Word, sitting at His feet and learning from Him, for "He that dwelleth in the secret place of the most High shall abide under the shadow of the Almighty" –Psalm 91:1.

*Looking unto Jesus*
*Look up, not down*
*Look forward, not back*
*Look out, not in*
*Lend a hand*
*In His Name whose I am and whom I serve*

## Day 2

# Taking Time at the Well of Living Water

John 4:6

*"Jesus therefore, being wearied with his journey, sat thus on the well."*

When we, as Christians, become weary with our journey, we must go and sit awhile "on the well," which is Christ Jesus our Lord. He is our source "of living water" –John 4:10. Drinking of the water that He gives will satisfy our thirst and give us strength to continue on our journey of life in this world. Jesus said, "Whosoever drinketh of the water that I shall give him shall never thirst; but the water that I shall give him shall be in him a well of water springing up into everlasting life" –John 4:14. The Lord Jesus has the words of life, for He is the Word of Life as the Holy Spirit, through the Apostle John, wrote in John 1:1-2: "In the beginning was the Word, and the Word was with God, and the Word was God. The same was in the beginning with God."

Jesus became wearied in His journey; therefore, we should not think it strange or unseemly for His children to become wearied in their journey of life. Follow His example and take time to sit "on the well," which is to say, sit and learn from Him as Mary of Bethany did in Luke 10:39. It is easy to become "cumbered about much serving" like Martha did in Luke 10, but remember the words Jesus spoke to her, "one thing is needful: and Mary hath chosen that good part, which shall not be taken away from her" –Luke 10:42.

When the journey becomes wearisome, take time to get alone with the Lord; open the Bible and let Him speak to you. Jesus said, when being tempted of the devil, "It is written, Man shall not live by bread alone, but by every word that proceedeth out of the mouth of God" –Matthew 4:4. We are going to become weary in our journey, as our Lord Jesus was in His; but we will be refreshed, strengthened, and renewed when we take time daily to sit alone with the Lord of lords and King of kings.

# Receiving Spiritual Sight

Acts 9:8b, 17, 20

*"And Saul arose from the earth; and when his eyes were opened, he saw no man . . . And Ananias . . . said, Brother Saul, the Lord, even Jesus, that appeared unto thee in the way as thou camest, hath sent me, that thou mightest receive thy sight, and be filled with the Holy Ghost . . . And straightway he (Saul) preached Christ in the synagogues, that he is the Son of God."*

Dear Christian friend, when you encountered Christ at salvation, did your experience blind you to man? Is your vision singular for Christ? Saul of Tarsus saw Christ in His glory on the road to Damascus, and he preached Christ "straightway"—immediately—after he received his sight. Throughout his ministry he continued to focus on Christ. If our vision is consumed with Christ, we too will be able to sing praises to Him as Paul and Silas did, although they had been beaten and imprisoned — Acts 16:22-25. Focusing on Christ will give us boldness in our witnessing for Him.

Do you, dear Christian, see Christ when you are in the sick bed, or do you only see Him when you are in good health? Do you see Christ when you are in the storm or only when your life is going along smoothly and calmly? Do you see Christ when you are in heartache or only when all is going well? If our eyes are open and focused on Christ, we will be able to see Him everywhere –both on the mountain top and in the dark valley below. If we look closely, we will see His arms stretched out wide to us and, running into the circle of His embrace, we will find comfort, security, peace and endless love. Focus your sight upon Jesus Christ and, with His help, you will be able to climb otherwise impassible mountains. There will be oceans you will be able to forge and deserts you will be able to cross. See Christ! See His glory, His power, His ability, His strength, and His love, and you will be more than conquerors. "Look outward and be distressed. Look inward and be depressed. Look upward and be at rest." –Corrie ten Boom

## Day 4

# Believest Thou Me?

John 11:25-26

*"Jesus said unto her, I am the resurrection, and the life: he that believeth in me, though he were dead, yet shall he live: And whosoever liveth and believeth in me shall never die. Believest thou this?"*

Can you hear the voice of the Lord Jesus asking you today, "Believest thou this?" He has said, "I am the resurrection, and the life: he that believeth in me, though he were dead, yet shall he live." Believest thou this? He has said, "I will never leave thee, nor forsake thee" –Hebrews 13:5b. Believest thou this? He has said, "With God all things are possible" –Matthew 19:26. Believest thou this? He has said, "I am the bread of life: he that cometh to me shall never hunger; and he that believeth on me shall never thirst" –John 6:35. Believest thou this?

Are you reading the Word of God with a heart of belief, or are the words of Scripture just so many words on paper to you? The Devil does not want anyone to believe the Word of the Lord because he knows when we believe, we become "more than conquerors" –Romans 8:37. Therefore take up that shield of faith spoken of in Ephesians chapter 6, verse 16, and simply believe God.

The Lord Jesus gently rebuked the father of the demoniac child, saying to him, "If thou canst believe, all things are possible to him that believeth" –Mark 9:23. That man, as many of us do, had put the "if" in the wrong place when he said to the Lord Jesus, "If thou canst do anything, have compassion on us, and help us" –Mark 9:22. It wasn't a question of whether or not the Lord Jesus could do anything for him, but rather if the man could believe or not. Oh that we would just believe God and not doubt His Word! We do not need great faith, only faith the size of a grain of mustard seed. The Lord Jesus said if we had faith the size of a grain of mustard seed, we could move mountains –Matthew 17:20. Believest thou this?

# Pride Is Our Enemy

Proverbs 11:2

*"When pride cometh, then cometh shame"*

*Pride can cause us to think more highly of ourselves than we ought to think. Pride can cause us to quarrel with others, because "only by pride cometh contention" –Proverbs 13:10. The proud are not teachable because their hearts and minds have swelled with self-conceit. King Nebuchadnezzar's pride caused him to be dethroned: "When his heart was lifted up, and his mind hardened in pride, he was deposed from his kingly throne, and they took his glory from him" –Daniel 5:20. "A man's pride shall bring him low" –Proverbs 29:23, because "Pride goeth before destruction, and an haughty spirit before a fall" –Proverbs 16:18.*

If we are going to pattern ourselves after our Lord and Savior, Jesus Christ, then we must be careful not to let pride rule our hearts. Pride will only bring shame. Pride is able to destroy our testimony for the Lord, our relationships with our family and friends, as well as take our dignity from us. "The heart is deceitful above all things" –Jeremiah 17:9a; therefore, we should make it a daily practice to kneel before the Lord and ask Him to search our heart for any trace of pride that may be there. Diligently work at getting pride out of your life. Do not let pride make a fool of you.

*Day 6*

# Whole Heart

Psalm 119:2

*"Blessed are they that keep his testimonies, and that seek him with the whole heart."*

It has been said of some people, at one time or another, "Their heart just isn't in it. They aren't putting their whole heart into it." Is that true of you today, dear Christian? Are you seeking the Lord with your whole heart, or is your heart just not in it? Do you read God's Word with a hunger to know Him better, and diligently seek Him by daily searching the Scriptures to discover the truths of His Word? Do you enter into your prayer closet and say, like Jacob, "I will not let thee go, except thou bless me" –Genesis 32:26?

Blessed are those who seek Him with their whole heart. "For thus saith the LORD . . . ye shall seek me, and find me, when ye shall search for me with all your heart" –Jeremiah 29:10-13. Jacob received a new name and became a prince with God when he tenaciously sought the Lord for His blessing. We can expect to be blessed when we seek the Lord with our whole heart.

# Sing and Praise

II Chronicles 20:22

*"And when they began to sing and to praise, the Lord set ambushments against the children of Ammon, Moab, and mount Seir, which were come against Judah; and they were smitten."*

Oh, that we would sing and praise the Lord during our troubles instead of bemoaning them! Singing defeated the enemy—"they were smitten." We would be a more joyful and victorious people if we would sing and praise the Lord "continually" –Psalm 34:1. Trying to figure out the reason for our troubles can rob us of our joy and cause us to become self-absorbed in our thinking. If we would rise each day and acknowledge the hand of the Lord in our lives, we would be better able to lift up our voices unto Him in praise in whatever experiences that may come our way.

The Scriptures often tell us to sing: "Sing unto him, sing psalms unto him, talk ye of all his wondrous works" –I Chronicles 16:9; "Sing praises to God, sing praises: sing praises unto our King, sing praises" –Psalm 47:6; "Sing unto God, sing praises to his name" –Psalm 68:4a; "Sing, O barren, thou that didst not bear; break forth into singing, and cry aloud, thou that didst not travail with child" –Isaiah 54:1a. We can sing our cares away better than we can reason them away; therefore, let us sing unto the Lord. If we will sing in the morning, sing in the evening, and sing throughout the day, our troubles will become easier to bear; for "when they began to sing and to praise," the Lord gave them victory.

*Day 8*

# All Things Through Christ

Philippians 4:13

*"I can do all things through Christ which strengtheneth me."*

When we trusted Christ as our Savior our sin was made "white as snow." Through Christ we are able to get our daily walk as clean "as wool" –Isaiah 1:18. He has made it possible for us to become "dead indeed unto sin, but alive unto God through Jesus Christ our Lord" –Romans 6:11. Therefore, as Christians, we can do all things through Christ. We can resist the devil's temptations; we can obey the will of God, our Father; we can be holy in all manner of conversation –I Peter 1:15; we can return good for evil; we can love each other "with a pure heart fervently" –I Peter 1:22; we can "continue in the faith" –Acts 14:22b. We can do all things through Christ, because Christ has already done all things victoriously, and we are in Him.

When we, through Christ, resist the devil's temptations, it strengthens us to resist temptation again. When we understand that we must yield ourselves unto Christ in order that sin will no longer control us, and when we realize that Christ has all power in Heaven and in earth, then we can begin to have victory in our life and do all things through Christ.

# The Reality of God's Presence

Joshua 1:9

*"The LORD thy God is with thee whithersoever thou goest."*

Wherever we are, God is there. Whether we are busily going about our daily lives or sleeping soundly in our beds, God is there. "The eyes of the LORD are in every place, beholding the evil and the good" – Proverbs 15:3. As Christians, we may not be conscious of His presence, but in reality, He is there whether we are conscious of it or not. When God's presence becomes a reality to us we will be able to say, like the Psalmist, "Therefore will not we fear . . ." –Psalm 46:2, because the reality of His presence says, "God is there, and He has been there all the time." The reality of God's presence comforts and calms the fearful heart of the Christian.

Like Adam and Eve, we might try to hide from the presence of God, but we will find that we cannot. As He saw them eat of the forbidden fruit, He also sees our sins of disobedience, whatever they may be, because His presence is real. "Glory and honour are in his presence" –I Chronicles 16:27, and as we have a greater reality of God's presence, we will know more of His glory and honor. His continual presence will become our continual delight. As we put the Lord first in our lives and daily seek Him, the reality of His continual presence will grow as we reflect on the truth that the Lord our God is with us wherever we are.

# In His Presence

*In the presence of Jesus*
*Our hearts are made glad*
*In His presence*
*Our countenance no longer is sad*

*In the presence of Jesus*
*All heartaches will cease*
*In His presence*
*Our minds are at peace*

*In the presence of Jesus*
*Is the fullness of joy*
*Yes, in His presence for every*
*Man, woman, girl or boy*

*In the presence of Jesus*
*There are no tears or sorrow*
*In His presence*
*There is joy today and every tomorrow*

*In the presence of Jesus*
*We find the warmth of His smile*
*To tarry in His presence*
*Is always worthwhile*

*In the presence of Jesus*
*doubts and fears flee away*
*In His presence*
*His child should stay*

*In the presence of Jesus*
*He clamps tight our armor on*
*In His presence*
*We are able to face the dawn*

*In the presence of Jesus*
*Our faith is made strong*
*In His presence*
*Assurance continues on*

*In the presence of Jesus*
*Never seek to depart*
*In His presence*
*There is no end only a start*

## *Day 10*

# Operating on God's Speed

Psalm 27:14

*"Wait on the LORD: be of good courage, and he shall strengthen thine heart: wait, I say, on the LORD."*

Waiting, for most if not all of us, is difficult to do. We dislike waiting at traffic lights, elevators, or railroad crossings, especially when we are in a hurry. We may become agitated or impatient, and even go so far as to lose our Christian testimony by exhibiting behavior that is not Christ like. This impatience is obviously not of God, but centers around self and the world's society that we live in. The Bible says, "Wait on the LORD." God, the Father, and His Son, Jesus Christ, have never been in a hurry. They have always been right on time, because Their time frame has been perfectly planned from the beginning of Creation. Lazarus, a close friend of the Lord Jesus, lay dead in the grave four days. His sisters, Martha and Mary, were grief stricken. They had sent for the Lord Jesus, but He had not come "in time," and now Lazarus was dead. However, the Lord Jesus was perfectly aware of the situation and **His** arrival was timed with a perfect purpose and plan, for "This sickness [was] not unto death, but for the glory of God, that the Son of God might be glorified thereby" –John 11:4.

Waiting isn't easy, but when we wait in God's time, the Lord will be glorified. When we impatiently get ahead of His time, then unwanted trouble and mishaps often occur. How many of us could say, "If I had waited none of _____ would have happened." We can all fill in the blank with our own difficulties that have occurred by not waiting on the Lord. When we wait on the Lord we are allowing Him to work. We are acknowledging His superiority and sovereignty. We are yielding our will to His will and thereby declaring our dependency upon Him who is all knowing, all powerful, and Almighty! Remember, dear Christian friend, God only has our best interest in mind and He sees the big picture; therefore, "wait on the LORD . . . wait, I say on the LORD."

# Power to Be Bold

Acts 4:13

*"Now when they saw the boldness of Peter and John, and perceived that they were unlearned and ignorant men, they marveled; and they took knowledge of them, that they had been with Jesus."*

Peter and John did not have higher education, nor did they have "silver and gold"-Acts 3:6. They had something much greater—they had the power of the Holy Spirit. "Then Peter, filled with the Holy Ghost, said unto them, Ye rulers of the people, and elders of Israel, If we this day be examined of the good deed done to the impotent man, by what means he is made whole; Be it known unto you all, and to all the people of Israel, that by the name of Jesus Christ of Nazareth, whom ye crucified, whom God raised from the dead, even by him doth this man stand here before you whole"—Acts 4:8-10. It was the power of the Holy Spirit that gave Peter and John such boldness.

That same power is available to Christians today in the Person of the Holy Spirit who dwells in every believer. It is the Holy Spirit that gives us power to speak out boldly for Christ among our unsaved co-workers, neighbors and family members. Those nudges we get at times to go speak to a particular person, or to call someone, or to pray for someone are the gentle leading of the Holy Spirit within us. When we ignore or disobey those nudges, we grieve the Spirit; and the more we disobey His leading, the more we hinder Him and quench His power. It takes power to boldly witness, to be a testimony of Christ's character, to put to death the deeds of our flesh, and to walk in His Spirit. That power comes when we yield our will to the Father's will and obey His Spirit when He speaks to us about doing something. Don't let the devil rob you of God's power by fear and timidity; "Submit yourselves therefore to God. Resist the devil, and he will flee from you"—James 4:7. When we yield to the Holy Spirit, we will have power to be bold, and we will be used by God to do what only He is able to do through us.

## Day 12

# Not I, But Christ

Romans 12:3

*"For I say, through the grace given unto me, to every man that is among you, not to think of himself more highly than he ought to think; but to think soberly, according as God hath dealt to every man the measure of faith."*

Pride is a sin that is in every one of us by nature, for "Behold, I was shapen in iniquity, and in sin did my mother conceive me"—Psalm 51:5. Therefore, as Christians, we need to be aware of this prevalent and deadly sin that lies within us so that we may properly arm ourselves against it. Whatever talents we may have or however winsome our personality may be, we must remember that all we are, is "according as God hath dealt" to us. "There is none good but one, that is, God"—Mark 10:18. It may be that someone can sing and captivate the attention of those listening, while yet another has the ability to teach in such a way that their students achieve their highest potential scholastically. Someone else may have the great ability to cheer and encourage those around them and simply by their presence the day is brightened. Pride arises when we begin to think more highly of ourselves than we ought to think, to imagine that we gained all these abilities on our own, and forget that without Christ we can do nothing—John 15:5, and that we are nothing.

If we thought more about the power we have through Christ and His Holy Spirit dwelling in us, and how greatly we fail to appropriate that power in us, we would be more humble. ". . . whatsoever things are true, whatsoever things are honest, whatsoever things are just, whatsoever things are pure, whatsoever things are lovely, whatsoever things are of good report; if there be any virtue, and if there be any praise, think on these things"—Philippians 4:8. When we turn our thoughts toward Christ in such a way so that He has first priority in how we make decisions, as well as how we live our lives, then we will turn from prideful thoughts about ourselves. Humility is an element, or characteristic, of the Saviour's love, whereas pride is an element of our sinful flesh. Let's seek daily to fill our mind and our heart with the glories of Jesus Christ and His grace that He has given to us, so that we will not think more highly of ourselves than we should.

# Our Lifeline

I Thessalonians 5:17

*"Pray without ceasing."*

Prayer is not a daily exercise; it is a way of life. To pray without ceasing should become like the breath that we breathe—continually occurring day and night. Prayer is our lifeline to the Father and is what sustains our spiritual life. At times, prayer is a short, quick and sudden utterance, similar to the prayer of the Apostle Peter: "Lord, save me"—Matthew 14:30b. Sometimes prayer is being a long time alone with the Father, as was the Lord Jesus Christ, who "went out into a mountain to pray, and continued all night in prayer to God"—Luke 6:12. At other times it is continuing in prayer—or "praying through"—until the answer is confirmed in our hearts by the Holy Spirit. The Prophet Elijah continued in prayer when he "went up to the top of Carmel; and he cast himself down upon the earth, and put his face between his knees . . . And it came to pass . . . a great rain"—I Kings 18:42-45. Continual prayer is being in the childlike habit of turning to the Father, depending on Him for everything, and seeking His help for everything.

As Christians, we must be careful to guard against becoming independent from God, lest we begin to cease our praying. We must also be careful not to allow common sense to rule our thinking. Many times God's will is beyond the realm of common sense, "for [His] thoughts are not [our] thoughts, neither are [our] ways [His] ways, saith the LORD. For as the heavens are higher than the earth, so are [His] ways higher than [our] ways, and [His] thoughts than [our] thoughts"—Isaiah 55:8-9. Therefore, when our prayers "seemingly" go unanswered, we must be careful not to lean on our own understanding, but claim the promises of God's Word, believing that, if we call, He will answer. It is when we try to figure it out, and try to make sense out of it, that we become disillusioned and cease praying. As we daily grow more dependent upon the Lord and surrender our will to His, then prayer becomes a way of life to us, not merely a daily exercise, and we find ourselves praying about everything.

## Day 14

# Waiting for the Promise

Acts 1:4

*"And, being assembled together with them, [Jesus] commanded them that they should not depart from Jerusalem, but wait for the promise of the Father, which, saith he, ye have heard of me."*

There are many Christians who fail to receive the promises of God because they do not wait for them; therefore, some seem to live defeated, discouraged, and disillusioned lives. We must by faith, as by a key, open the door of God's promises—to fulfill any condition that is linked to a promise—and not become impatient. We must simply wait to receive the promise, for what He has promised, He will surely bring to pass, for "The LORD of hosts hath sworn, saying, Surely as I have thought, so shall it come to pass; and as I have purposed, so shall it stand"—Isaiah 14:24.

Every promise of God is worth waiting for; therefore, take the time to wait for God our Father to fulfill His promises. Joshua said at the end of his life that "not one thing hath failed of all the good things which the LORD your God spake concerning you; all are come to pass unto you, and not one thing hath failed thereof"—Joshua 23:14b. Following the resurrection of the Lord Jesus Christ, the disciples assembled together in Jerusalem in the spirit of prayer, waiting for the Father's promise—the Holy Spirit—and the promise came, and "they were all filled with the Holy Ghost"—Acts 2:4a. Let us take time daily to claim the promises of God and then wait for Him to fulfill them in our lives according to His perfect timing.

# Conquering the Blues

Psalm 95:1

*"O come, let us sing unto the LORD: let us make a joyful noise to the rock of our salvation."*

One of the most effective ways to "conquer the blues" is by singing. Singing always has a tendency to cheer and brighten our outlook on life, especially when our life is overwhelmed with pain, sorrow, or difficulty. This Psalm exhorts us to "sing unto the LORD" and "make a joyful noise unto the rock of our salvation"—Jesus Christ. There are many verses in the Scriptures that exhort us to sing unto the Lord: "Sing unto him, sing psalms unto him, talk ye of all his wondrous works"—I Chronicles 16:9. "Sing unto the LORD; for he hath done excellent things: this is known in all the earth"—Isaiah 12:5. Singing transfers our attention from the troubles we are experiencing to the "rock of our salvation"—Jesus Christ. Singing soothes our troubled spirit and puts us into a frame of mind to magnify the Lord and not our troubles, "for the LORD is a great God, and a great King above all gods. In his hand are the deep places of the earth: the strength of the hills is his also. The sea is his, and he made it: and his hands formed the dry land"—Psalm 95:3-5. "God is the King of all the earth: sing ye praises with understanding"—Psalm 47:7.

As Christians, singing unto the Lord can put us in a worshipful state of mind and spirit so that our hope is renewed, because when we sing unto the Lord we are reminded there is victory in Jesus: "O sing unto the LORD a new song; for he hath done marvelous things: his right hand, and his holy arm, hath gotten him the victory"—Psalm 98:1. Singing in the face of sorrow and pain may enable us to draw non-believers to the cross of Christ in order that they too may find true joy and peace in their life. It was when "Paul and Silas prayed, and sang praises unto God" that the jailer asked them what he must do to be saved—Acts 16:25-30. Let us remember to sing songs of praise unto the Lord in everything.

*Day 16*

# Turning Fear to Trust

Psalm 56:3

*"What time I am afraid, I will trust in thee."*

Fear is a real emotion. This Psalm teaches us that David, the sweet Psalmist of Israel, experienced times of fear. Everyone can be susceptible to periods of fear. There is much in this world that can make us afraid; therefore, we must understand it is a real emotion that can plague us in various ways. It may be fear of the unknown, fear of being alone, fear of people, fear of being hurt, and fear of any number of things. When we experience moments of fear, we must learn to say, like David, "What time I am afraid, I will trust in the Lord." The Lord understands our tendency to fear; therefore, He has given us abundant promises in His Word. He has promised to "cover thee with his feathers, and under his wings shalt thou trust: his truth shall be thy shield and buckler"—Psalm 91:4. When fear comes upon us, instead of yielding to it, let us rather seek God's promises, claim them for ourselves, and use them as a shield against our fears. God our Father "knoweth our frame; he remembereth that we are dust"—Psalm 103:14. He realizes that "the flesh is weak"—Mark 14:38b. Therefore, we must tell Him about our fears, then let Him guide us by His Spirit to His promises in the Scriptures. Saturating ourselves with the truth and promises of His Word will strengthen our faith and trust in Him, and it will cause us to lean upon Him rather than succumb to our fears.

"There is no fear in love; but perfect love casteth out fear: because fear hath torment. He that feareth is not made perfect in love"—I John 4:18. "God is love"—I John 4:16b; therefore, when fear comes upon us, let us seek the loving kindness of our Lord by prayer so that we will not yield to fear and let it torment us. Whenever we become afraid, let us trust in the Lord.

# Casting Burdens upon the Lord

Psalm 55:22

*"Cast thy burden upon the Lord, and he shall sustain thee: he shall never suffer the righteous to be moved."*

We have been given an outlet in which to unload our burdens, and that outlet is the Lord Himself. In providing an outlet for us He has also given His promise that He shall sustain: "He shall never suffer the righteous to be moved." Whatever our burden may be, we do not need to carry it alone; we can cast it upon the Lord. When we cast our burdens upon the Lord, we are demonstrating our trust in His Word, and it pleases Him; for we are told that "without faith it is impossible to please Him"—Hebrews 11:6. His shoulders are broad and strong and able to carry every burden that befalls us, and He is able to do so with the greatest of ease.

As parents try to ease the troubles of their children, so our Heavenly Father seeks to bear our burdens, that we may be sustained and buoyed up on His all-encompassing wings. We are more apt to cast our burdens upon the Lord if we "dwell in the secret place of the most High"—Psalm 91:1 –because it is there that we find solace, peace, strength, and help. Therefore, when the burdens do come we shall "abide under the shadow of the Almighty" rather than in the pits of worry and fretfulness. When we cast something, we are releasing our hold; therefore, when we "cast" our burdens upon the Lord, we are, in essence, flinging the burden into the only truly capable pair of hands. Do not continue to hold on to burdens which may lead to the sin of unbelief; rather, cast them upon Him who is able to sustain and keep you.

## *Day 18*

# Secret Place

Psalm 91:1

*"He that dwelleth in the secret place of the most High"*

Are you dwelling in the secret place where He speaks, "Peace, be still"? –Mark 4:39. The storms of life may howl and rage, but "in the secret place of the most High," the winds are calm and the air is peaceful; the still small Voice of comfort, of cheer, and of correction can be heard. It is while in the secret place during the storm of affliction that you may hear, "Be of good cheer; I have overcome the world"—John 16:33. Such wonderful words from the blessed Lord will dry the weeping eyes and cheer the overwhelmed heart, but if the secret place is neglected, how will the ear hear such words of comfort and how will the heart be so tenderly helped? In the secret place we are able to, so to speak, crawl up into our Heavenly Father's lap and nestle our head upon His broad shoulder. It is there that we can feel the strong arms of the Lord encircling us in a tender and firm embrace. The weights of tribulation, sorrow, and affliction are loosed and removed from off our shoulders and placed on His most capable ones. Our heavy hearts are freed to sing and rejoice; our feet have a lighter, surer step; and our weary hands are no longer weighed down. Dwelling in this secret place is like no other place. You may search for Him elsewhere, but it is in the secret place where He may be found.

# In the Secret Place of the Most High

*Dear Lord, you have been my confidant and friend*
*You have been my comfort and my joy*
*My heart sings knowing our friendship shall never end*
*But rather continue when you call me on to Glory*

*You have been my source of help and strength*
*In despair you are the lifter of my head*
*It is reassuring that you will go to any length*
*To battle the enemy in my stead*

*The secret place alone with you*
*Refreshes my spirit and my soul*
*It rebuilds my hope and trust and makes them new*
*With you I am complete and fully whole*

*When Satan comes and tempts me sore*
*To complain and doubt*
*Fleeing to my secret place I am able once more*
*To become victor with a joyous shout*

*Oh, death you haven't any sting*
*And grave you haven't any glory*
*Christ, our Salvation, rules over everything*
*He's not a child's fabled story*

*In my secret place will I continually dwell*
*That I may abide under the shadow of thy wings*
*So as long as I live, I may gleefully tell*
*How it is there that my heart joyfully sings.*

*Day 19*

# Arise and Shine for Christ

Isaiah 60:1

*"Arise, shine; for thy light is come, and the glory of the Lord is risen upon thee."*

As children of God, let us rise and shine with the light of Christ, "for God, who commanded the light to shine out of darkness, hath shined in our hearts, to give the light of the knowledge of the glory of God in the face of Jesus Christ" –II Corinthians 4:6. Shine with the love of Christ so that the world may see unconditional love. Shine with the joy of Christ so the world may see that His joy transcends every circumstance. Shine with the peace of Christ that the world may see unwavering trust in the Prince of peace. The Lord Jesus said, "I am the light of the world: he that followeth me shall not walk in darkness, but shall have the light of life" –John 8:12. "Let your light so shine before men, that they may see your good works, and glorify your Father which is in heaven" –Matthew 5:16.

We can shine the light of Christ by going the extra mile when it isn't required, by "turning the other cheek" and not retaliating, by giving to others, by loving our enemies, by blessing them that curse us, by doing good to those who hate us, and by praying for those who persecute us— Matthew 5:38-44. As children of God, the light of Christ dwells in us; therefore, we should make it our daily goal to arise and shine the light of Christ for the glory of God.

*Day 20*

# Growing in Grace and Knowledge of Jesus Christ

II Peter 3:18

*"But grow in grace, and in the knowledge of our Lord and Savior Jesus Christ. To him be glory both now and for ever. Amen."*

Grow in grace —not only in one grace, but in **all** grace. Grow in the grace of faith, determining to believe the truths of God's Word and His promises more strongly than before. Believe the Word of God with simplicity, sincerity, and consistency, having a fuller understanding that "without faith it is impossible to please him" —Hebrews 11:6a. Grow in the grace to love. Ask that the Savior's great heart of love would be made known to others through you. Seek for a deeper, fuller and more ardent love for our Almighty God, for lost sinners, for fellow Christians, and for your enemies. Grow in the grace of humility, becoming more conscious of your own nothingness, seeking to be humble, for "He must increase, but I must decrease" —John 3:30. Grow upward, drawing nearer to God in prayer and personal fellowship with Him. Grow in forgiveness. Release grudges and commit all hurt to the Heavenly Father, "forgiving one another, even as God for Christ's sake hath forgiven you" —Ephesians 4:32.

As you grow in grace, may God, the Holy Spirit, enable you to also grow in the knowledge of Jesus Christ. Grow in the knowledge of His death, His resurrection, His divine nature, His human relationship, and His wonderful intercession. An increasing knowledge of Christ will draw the heart toward Him in an ever-endearing love by more fully comprehending His great love for us. *"An increase of love to Jesus, and a more perfect apprehension of His love to us is one of the best tests of growth in grace"* —*Charles H. Spurgeon*. As believers it is imperative that we "grow in grace, and in the knowledge of our Lord and Savior Jesus Christ" so that we may bring glory to His Name.

*Day 21*

# Above the Earth and Heaven

Psalm 148:13bs

*"His name alone is excellent; his glory is above the earth and heaven."*

It isn't too difficult for us to comprehend that God's glory is above the earth, because the earth has been cursed with the sinfulness of mankind. We can look at the majestic grandeur of the Rocky Mountains, or watch the power of the ocean's waves swell and crest before they come crashing down upon the shore, and stand with awe as we realize that God's glory is above this wondrous creation of His.

The Scriptures tell us that His glory is above the earth **and Heaven**! Now our finite minds have trouble comprehending such a glorious truth, for this means that His glory is above the golden streets of Heaven, the pearly gates of Heaven, and above the beautiful foundation of Heaven that is made with various precious gems. If His glory is above Heaven, then that would mean that it exceeds the holiness of Heaven, the righteousness of Heaven, the purity of Heaven, and the wonder of Heaven. "When all the children of Israel saw how the fire came down, and the glory of the Lord upon the house, they bowed themselves with their faces to the ground upon the pavement, and worshipped, and praised the Lord, saying, For he is good; for his mercy endureth for ever" –II Chronicles 7:3. As children of God, let us take time to consider the glory of the Lord so that we too will worship and praise Him, for His glory is above the earth and Heaven.

# True Help

Isaiah 30:7

*"For the Egyptians shall help in vain, and to no purpose: therefore have I cried concerning this, Their strength is to sit still."*

Often times, as Christians, we are prone to turn to someone or something else for help other than God, our Father, and His Son, Jesus Christ, our Savior. If we have been deeply hurt by someone we may turn to a friend or close family member rather than turn to the Lord for solace and comfort. Then we wonder why their comfort did not satisfy or even help our hurting heart. Human comfort will always be lacking, "for vain is the help of man" –Psalm 60:11b; but God's comfort is never lacking.

When some people are struggling financially, their first inclination may be to turn to the aid of some government subsidy rather than to God. Government aid is never sufficient to meet all our need, but "God shall supply all your need" –Philippians 4:19a. Therefore, in trouble, in trial, in all of life, our strength is to "trust in the Lord with all [our] heart; and lean not unto [our] own understanding" –Proverbs 3:5. Once we do that, then we will be better able to practice Proverbs 3:6, which says, "In all thy ways acknowledge him, and he shall direct thy paths." We cannot expect too little from the world, and we cannot expect too much from God. Be still, or in other words, be calm, tranquil, and undisturbed, knowing that He is God, our true help.

## *Day 23*

# Truth

John 17:17

*"Sanctify them through thy truth: thy word is truth."*

So many, even born- again believers in Jesus Christ, at some point ask the question, "What really is truth?" We can know through this verse that God's Word is truth. The Lord Jesus said of Himself, "I am the way, the *truth*, and the life"—John 14:6a. In the beginning of the book of John we learn that Jesus Christ is the Word: "In the beginning was the Word, and the Word was with God, and the Word was God. The same was in the beginning with God. . . . And the Word was made flesh, and dwelt among us, (and we beheld his glory, the glory as of the only begotten of the Father,) full of grace and *truth*"—John 1:1-2, 14. The New Unger's Bible Dictionary states it this way: ***Words are the vehicle for the revelation of the thoughts and intents of the mind to others. Christ as the Word constitutes the complete and ultimate divine revelation. God has spoken with finality in "His Son".*** Therefore, according to God, "that cannot lie"—Titus 1:2, His Word is *truth*. The reason that many—non-believers and believers—question the truth of God and His Word is that they do not "search the scriptures"—John 5:39a. It was said of believers in Berea that "these were more noble than those in Thessalonica, in that they received the word with all readiness of mind, and *searched the scriptures daily*, whether those things were so"— Acts 17:11.

As Christians, it behooves us to study the Bible daily, for "faith cometh by hearing, and hearing by the word of God"—Romans 10:17. Going to church and listening to the preaching of the Word of God is good, but we also need to do as the Bereans did and study the Scriptures to be sure we are receiving the true Word of God from the pulpit. Someone once said that to know truth you would have to always have lived, and be alive now, and to always live. That exactly describes God Almighty and the Lord Jesus Christ. Let us be diligent to make time every day to study the Word of God so that we may not stray from the truth.

# A Sure Promise

Habakkuk 2:3

*"For the vision is yet for an appointed time, but at the end it shall speak, and not lie: though it tarry, wait for it; because it will surely come, it will not tarry."*

It may be that God has led you to a promise in the Scriptures and has given you the faith to claim it for yourself; however, it has not yet been fulfilled. "Wait for it; because it will surely come." "God is not a man, that he should lie; neither the son of man, that he should repent: hath he said, and shall he not do it? Or hath he spoken, and shall he not make it good?"—Numbers 23:19. What God has spoken is as good as done, even when the performance of the thing tarries; therefore, we must not let the devil steal, kill, and destroy our faith. It may simply be that God is trying our faith in order to deepen and strengthen His Word in us. The devil wants you to doubt, but listen to the words of Jesus as He spoke to the ruler of the synagogue, "Be not afraid, only believe"—Mark 5:36b, and apply them to your own situation. The situation may appear to be hopeless and impossible; but remember, "With God all things are possible"—Mark 10:27b. God has His timing for everything, and He is never one minute too late; He is always right on time. Though His promise to you tarries, wait for it; because it will surely come!

## *Day 25*

# In Thy Name

Psalm 89:16a

*"In thy name shall they rejoice all the day."*

It isn't in circumstances that we will rejoice all day long, because our circumstances can change in a moment. It isn't in our family and friends that we will be able to rejoice all day, because they may not always be there when we need them. It isn't in riches that we will be able to rejoice all the day, because in seconds we can lose everything and know the devastation of financial ruin. It isn't in our health that we will rejoice, because our health can fail instantly. It is only in the Name of the Lord that we can rejoice all the day. His Name is "Emmanuel, which being interpreted is, God with us"—Matthew 1:23b. There is never a time when He is not with us. It isn't in people, possessions, or property that we have cause to rejoice, but in the Lord Himself. "Although the fig tree shall not blossom, neither shall fruit be in the vines; the labour of the olive shall fail, and the fields shall yield no meat; the flock shall be cut off from the fold, and there shall be no herd in the stalls: Yet I will rejoice in the Lord, I will joy in the God of my salvation"—Habakkuk 3:17-18. While so many things change in our lives, the Lord remains the same; therefore, we are able to rejoice in the Lord all the day.

"His name shall be called Wonderful, Counsellor, The mighty God, The everlasting Father, The Prince of Peace"—Isaiah 9:6c. His Name is Wonderful—Rejoice! His Name is Mighty—Rejoice! His Name is everlasting—Rejoice! His Name is Prince of Peace—Rejoice! It is in the Name of the Lord that we can have confidence, strength, assurance, and help. "The name of the Lord is a strong tower: the righteous runneth into it, and is safe"—Proverbs 18:10. If you are not rejoicing, then begin to think on the Name of the Lord, and consider all that His Name means. It won't be long before you will be rejoicing, for in His Name we can rejoice all the day.

# All to God's Glory

I Corinthians 10:31b

*"Whatsoever ye do, do all to the glory of God."*

This portion of Scripture is saying that everything we do should be done to the glory of God. Doing all to the glory of God pleases and honors Him. Our motives behind what we do should never be to further our own selfish desires, but to magnify God. Therefore, if everything we do is done with God's glory in mind, then the smallest task we do is pleasing to the Lord. Ordinary daily tasks can change from being mundane to being grand when we do them with a desire to bring glory to God.

Reaching out to a fatherless child or a widow may seem simple; however, God's Word says, "Pure religion and undefiled before God and the Father is this, To visit the fatherless and widows in their affliction . . ."—James 1:27a. "God is no respecter of persons"—Acts 10:34; therefore, whether we are a CEO of a multi-million-dollar company or a janitor, both are the same in God's eyes. He desires that everything we do be done to His glory regardless of the job. Let's determine that whatever we do, we will do it all for God's glory.

*Day 27*

# Humble Yourself in the Sight of the Lord

James 4:10

*"Humble yourselves in the sight of the Lord, and he shall lift you up."*

To humble ourselves we must have an accurate perception of what we are –***nothing,*** and an appropriate understanding of who God is – ***ALMIGHTY!*** Humble yourself before God the Father and His Son, Jesus Christ. Humble yourself before Him who, by love, sent His only begotten Son to be the Savior of the world –John 3:16. Humble yourself before His holiness, His righteousness, His omnipotence, His omniscience. Give Him glory and honor and praise with an humble heart and bow low before Him. Humble yourself by submitting unto Him and resisting the devil –James 4:7. We have nothing whereof we may boast except it is in God Almighty.

When there was nothing, He was there; and by the breath of His mouth and the strength of His arm all creation was formed –Psalm 33:6 and Jeremiah 27:5. There is no power greater than His power. With love He draws mankind unto Himself. Humble yourself before the Lord, whose kindness far exceeds our understanding, whose thoughts are far above our thoughts, and whose ways are beyond finding out. Humble yourself by obedience to Him, surrendering to His will. Humility is our greatest asset and most closely resembles the character of our Lord and Savior, Jesus Christ. "Know ye that the Lord he is God: it is he that hath made us, and not we ourselves; we are his people, and the sheep of his pasture" –Psalm 100:3. Therefore, let us strive daily to humble ourselves in the sight of the Lord.

# The Lord's Lovingkindess

Psalm 143:8

*"Cause me to hear thy lovingkindness in the morning."*

"Thy lovingkindess is better than life" –Psalm 63:3; therefore, "cause me to hear thy lovingkindness in the morning." The lovingkindness of the Lord's voice will cheer the downcast, strengthen the weak, make glad the sorrowful, and rejoice the heart of the listener. The Devil may attack the Christian, resulting in despondency, discouragement, or even depression; however, when the tender lovingkindness of the Lord's voice is heard, the despondent heart is made glad, the discouraged one is encouraged, and depression is replaced with hope. It is with lovingkindness the Lord will speak: "In the world ye shall have tribulation: but be of good cheer; I have overcome the world" –John 16:33. "If we confess our sins, he is faithful and just to forgive us our sins, and to cleanse us from all unrighteousness" –I John 1:9. "As far as the east is from the west, so far hath he removed our transgressions from us" –Psalm 103:12.

The Devil thrills to torment and attack God's children; however, the tender lovingkindness of the Lord's voice enables the listener to resist the Devil and put him to flight. The Lord doesn't raise His voice or compete for anyone's attention; therefore, His voice will not be heard above the television, the radio, the computer or the cell phone. Shut off any distraction; then give your full attention to the Lord and say with the psalmist, "Cause me to hear thy lovingkindess in the morning." His voice will be your strength for the day.

**Day 29**

# Joyful in the Lord

Psalm 35:9

*"And my soul shall be joyful in the LORD . . ."*

Being joyful in the Lord of lords will turn any frown upside down and cast a brilliant glow upon a smiling face. A heart meditative upon the wonders of Almighty God will be joyful. "The Lord hath prepared his throne in the heavens; and his kingdom ruleth over all" –Psalm 103:19. He is higher than the highest, greater than the greatest, purer than the purest. "The Lord of hosts is his name . . . The God of the whole earth shall he be called" –Isaiah 54:5.

Be joyful in your King and sorrow will not consume you. Be joyful in your King and circumstances will not overwhelm you. Be joyful in your King and you won't believe the lies of the Devil. Be joyful in your King and you will "count it all joy when ye fall into divers temptations" –James 1:2. Be joyful in your King and you will "in every thing give thanks: for this is the will of God in Christ Jesus concerning you" –I Thessalonians 5:18. "The joy of the Lord is your strength" –Nehemiah 8:10d. The heart full of joy is a heart full of the Lord; therefore be joyful in your Lord!

# Redemption

Ephesians 1:7

*"In whom we have redemption through his blood, the forgiveness of sins, according to the riches of his grace."*

No longer do we stand maimed and ugly with sin before God the Father, but rather we are now seen as righteous and perfect through Christ and His blood "according to the riches of His grace" –grace that is unmerited, grace that gives us what we do not deserve, grace that is abundant and free. Once we have been saved, we possess all of Christ's glory and riches. The wealth of knowledge, of wisdom, of grace, of mercy, of forgiveness and of so much more now lies within our possession. Think of the great wealth we have in Christ! He owns the cattle on a thousand hills; He paves Heaven's streets with gold; He is preparing a place for us in our Father's house –"a mansion," the Bible says.

He never grows weary or even sleeps, and He has all power in Heaven and earth. So, why should we fret and worry when we have access to so much wealth? Do we need grace to continue? There is abundance in Christ. Have we grown weak? He is our strength; go to Him for needed strength. Are we in the heat of the battle for Him? He will fight for us. Is the heart dried up because of hurt? Flee to Christ; He will give the comfort needed and mend that which has been torn; but more than that, He will help us to once again love the one who has hurt us as though hurt never happened. All this and so much more is ours in Christ, when we seek first the kingdom of God and His righteousness—Matthew 6:33. Do not only receive redemption the day of your salvation, but grow in Christ and receive all His riches as a child of the King according to His grace.

**Day 31**

# The Lord Is My Help

Psalm 70:5b

*"Thou art my help and my deliverer; O Lord, make no tarrying."*

The Lord is my help and my Deliverer in the time of temptation: . . ."God is faithful, who will not suffer you to be tempted above that ye are able; but will with the temptation also make a way to escape, that ye may be able to bear it" –I Corinthians 10:13. The Lord is our help in every trial that we encounter, walking beside us the entire way. The Lord is a faithful help and strong Deliverer, One in whom we can always trust. He will not abandon any one of His children; rather, He will go before them. And in the very hottest battle, He will carry them. In any and all circumstances of life, the Lord is our help and our Deliverer. "God is our refuge and strength, a very present help in trouble" –Psalm 46:1.

# His Joy . . . Our Joy

John 15:11

*"These things have I spoken unto you, that my joy might remain in you, and that your joy might be full."*

The joy that the Lord Jesus Christ had was the result of His absolute surrender of Himself to the Heavenly Father, "for [He] came down from heaven, not to do [His] own will, but the will of him that sent [Jesus]"—John 6:38. Doing the will of the Father was His delight and joy, and it was His desire that our joy would be the same joy that He experienced. Joy comes from within; it is not dependent upon our health, our circumstances, or even in seeing God's work succeed. Joy comes from abiding in Christ, which is simply living a life of daily surrendering ourselves to the Father as Christ surrendered Himself.

When we begin to seek God Himself and not what He can do for us, then we are on the path toward knowing the fullness of joy that our Lord Jesus Christ knew. Joy is believing that the Father oversees every circumstance in our life and that "[our] life is hid with Christ in God"—Colossians 3:3b. The Lord Jesus said, "I am the vine, ye are the branches: He that abideth in me, and I in him, the same bringeth forth much fruit: for without me ye can do nothing"—John 15:5. We can only know the true joy of the Lord when our life is in sync with the life of Christ and we are surrendering ourselves unto the Father.

*Day 33*

# Behold! He's Coming

John 14:3b

*"I will come again, and receive you unto myself; that where I am, there ye may be also."*

Behold, Jesus is coming again! These words are the delight of every Christian, because Jesus, the Captain of our salvation, is going to return. Knowing that He is coming again will give us courage to fight against the fiercest temptations, boldness to stand for truth and right, resolve to persevere in our Christian life, strength when we become weary in our journey, and hope for every tomorrow. The Lord Jesus Christ said, "**I will** come again"; therefore, we can be sure that He **is** coming again!

When He comes we will not have time to get ready; we will have to **be ready** for His coming, because "the day of the Lord so cometh as a thief in the night" –I Thessalonians 5:2. Look up! He is coming again as He promised. We do not know when He is coming, because the Lord Jesus said, "But of that day and hour knoweth no man, no, not the angels of heaven, but my Father only" –Matthew 24:36. Turn your eyes heavenward and "watch therefore: for ye know not what hour your Lord doth come. . . . Therefore be ye also ready: for in such an hour as ye think not the Son of man cometh" –Matthew 24:42, 44. He is coming again!

# God Is All and Works in All

I Corinthians 12:6b

*"It is the same God which worketh all in all."*

God "worketh all" because He is all. He is **all** righteousness. He is **all** forgiveness. He is **all** love. He is **all** mercy. He is **all** grace. He is **all** compassion. Therefore, if we are going to take on any of His likeness, He will have to work them in us. "I will fetch my knowledge from afar, and will ascribe righteousness to my Maker" –Job 36:3. He who is all righteousness must work His righteousness in us. "Not by works of righteousness which we have done, but according to his mercy he saved us, by the washing of regeneration, and renewing of the Holy Ghost" –Titus 3:5. It was at our conversion, when we trusted in Christ by faith for salvation, that God began His work in us; and "he which hath begun a good work in you will perform it until the day of Jesus Christ" –Philippians 1:6b. He is able to work His righteousness, His forgiveness, His love, and every one of His characteristics in us. God is able to work all of Himself into all of His children, because it is He that "worketh all in all."

## Day 35

# The Lord Is . . .

Psalm 18:2

*"The Lord is my rock, and my fortress, and my deliverer; my God, my strength, in whom I will trust; my buckler, and the horn of my salvation, and my high tower."*

The Lord is—**MY ROCK!** He is my strong and sure foundation on which I may stand secure. "From the end of the earth will I cry unto thee, when my heart is overwhelmed: lead me to the rock that is higher than I" –Psalm 61:2. The Lord is—**MY FORTRESS!** He is a safe haven for all who will come unto Him. He will protect me against attacks from the enemy. The Lord is—**MY DELIVERER!** He shall deliver me from the hands of the enemy. Nothing and no one ever shall have dominion over Him; therefore, He shall always deliver me. The Lord is—**MY GOD!** "Know therefore this day, and consider it in thine heart, that the Lord he is God in heaven above, and upon the earth beneath: there is none else" –Deuteronomy 4:39. The Lord is all this and more to me personally! He is a personal God; therefore, as a Christian, I can confidently say, He *is* my God.

What about you, my friend? Have you trusted Christ as your personal Savior and Lord? If you have, then the Lord can be all these things to you too.

# My Lord, My All

O Lord my God, You are my hope
When the storms of life do rage
Or in the times of peaceful days
In You I have great confidence

Oh Lord my God You are my strength
When life's daily battle marches on
In Christ my weakened flesh is strong
In You I have all power

Oh Lord my God you are my help
When facing my tomorrows
That are filled with troubles and with sorrows
In You I will prevail

Oh Lord my God You are my Shepherd
In paths of righteousness You guide
Leading and directing, standing at my side
In You I shall not want

Oh Lord my God you are my song
That daily fills my heart with cheer
As well as puts to flight all fear
In You I have great joy

## *Day 36*

# Bring an Offering

Psalm 96:8

*"Give unto the LORD the glory due unto his name: bring an offering, and come into his courts."*

Give the Lord glory and bring an offering of praise when you go to Him in prayer. Do not go to Him without an offering. "Enter into his gates with thanksgiving, and into his courts with praise: be thankful unto him, and bless his name"—Psalm 100:4. Many times we experience a wide range of emotions that may cause us to be irritable, angry, discontent, and even depressed without knowing exactly what is the root problem. It just may be that we are not bringing our offerings of praise and thanksgiving to the Lord when we go to Him in prayer. In the weakness of our flesh we tend to be quicker to complain and murmur against our circumstances than to be thankful. "When the people complained, it displeased the LORD: and the LORD heard it; and his anger was kindled; and the fire of the LORD burnt among them, and consumed them that were in the uttermost parts of the camp"—Numbers 11:1. If we would "in every thing give thanks"—I Thessalonians 5:18a, we would complain less.

Think of circumstances in which you have complained; then go to God with a thankful heart and ask Him to help you to find something in those circumstances for which you may offer praise and thanksgiving unto Him. May we all make it a daily practice to "bring an offering" of praise and thanksgiving into the courts of prayer before our Heavenly Father. When we do, we will be more "joyful in the Lord"—Psalm 35:9a.

# It Is Done

Mark 9:3

*"Jesus said unto him, If thou canst believe, all things are possible to him that believeth."*

The Lord Jesus was in essence saying to this father of the demoniac son, "Believe I will answer and I will." The danger for most of us is that after we ask the Lord to do something, we do not believe it is done; therefore, we keep trying to help Him, as well as enlisting others to help Him, all the time wondering how He can do it. The language of faith is, "Commit thy way unto the LORD; trust also in him; and he shall bring it to pass"—Psalm 37:5.

Active faith means believing He will perform the requested action and that it is done. When we actively believe, we are able to thank and praise the Lord, even though our prayer has not yet been answered or what the Lord said would happen has not actually happened yet, because this kind of faith believes the promise of God.

"And it shall come to pass, as soon as the soles of the feet of the priests that bear the ark of the Lord, the Lord of all the earth, shall rest in the waters of Jordan, that the waters of Jordan shall be cut off . . . and they shall stand upon an heap. . . . And as . . . the feet of the priests that bare the ark were dipped in the brim of the water . . . the waters which came down from above stood and rose up upon an heap . . .and the people passed over right against Jericho"—Joshua 3:13, 15-16. They believed God; therefore, they did not wait on the bank of the river until the waters were parted, but stepped into the river believing it was done. The waters parted the moment they stepped into the river.

Many of us seem to have a passive faith, which means we possess the knowledge of God's promise with our minds, but that knowledge has not been cultivated and processed with our heart to actively believe and claim the promise. As a result, many times we must see in order to believe; however actively believing means we do not need to see the promise fulfilled in order to receive. God promised; therefore, it is as good as done.

## Day 38

# Fear Not

Revelation 1:17-18

*"Fear not; I am the first and the last: I am he that liveth, and was dead; and, behold, I am alive for evermore, Amen; and have the keys of hell and of death."*

Fear not! Jesus Christ is alive, and He is alive for evermore! He went through the doors of death and into the pits of hell for us, but they could not prevail over Him; "he is risen"! –Mark 16:6 "It is Christ that died, yea rather, that is risen again, who is even at the right hand of God, who also maketh intercession for us" –Romans 8:34; therefore, we need not fear. The devil would have us to believe we are defeated, and he is quite convincing at times, but we need not fear. Jesus Christ has prevailed, and it is Christ who has the keys of hell and death. He was crucified and He died, but He arose victoriously over death and hell and He is alive! Take courage and fear not! The devil knows we will cower if he is able to plant fear in our hearts; therefore, remember, Christ has already won the war. Our battles against the devil's temptations may be strong and they may seem long lasting, but we need not fear. The Captain of our salvation has defeated this wretched enemy. Listen to Him say, "Fear thou not; for I am with thee: be not dismayed; for I am thy God: I will strengthen thee; yea, I will help thee; yea, I will uphold thee with the right hand of my righteousness" –Isaiah 41:10. Follow close to Him and fear not! Stand strong in Jesus Christ and fear not!

# In the Wilderness with Christ

Luke 4:1

*"And Jesus being full of the Holy Ghost returned from Jordan, and was led by the Spirit into the wilderness."*

Do not despair, dear Christian, if you find yourself in the "wilderness." It is the Holy Spirit who leads us there. Jesus Christ, the Son of God, was "led by the Spirit into the wilderness." When the children of Israel were delivered from bondage in Egypt, they were led into the wilderness –Exodus 13:17-18. "Beloved, think it not strange concerning the fiery trial which is to try you, as though some strange thing happened unto you: But rejoice, inasmuch as ye are partakers of Christ's sufferings; that, when his glory shall be revealed, ye may be glad also with exceeding joy" –I Peter 4:12-13.

If our Lord Jesus Christ – the spotless, sinless One – was led into the wilderness, should we not also expect to be led there? It may be a place of hunger and of temptation, but take comfort; the Holy Spirit is our guide, and our Savior is our help. We may follow confidently if we follow closely to the Lord Jesus' side and combat the Devil, as He did, with the Holy Word of God. It may appear hopeless and seem that certain destruction will come, but remember, **the Spirit of God** is leading. Rest in Christ, follow His example, and, for the glory of God, deliverance will come.

## Day 40

# Living for Christ

II Corinthians 5:15

*"And that he died for all, that they which live should not henceforth live unto themselves, but unto him which died for them, and rose again."*

We are not our own; we have been "bought with a price" –I Corinthians 6:20b. Therefore, we should not live selfishly for ourselves, but we should live for our Lord Jesus Christ, who "laid down his life for us" –I John 3:16. It is our privilege to live for Him who died for us. May the love of Christ constrain us to live for Him. We who are saved owe so much to our Lord Jesus Christ. He has forgiven our sins and has covered us with His robe of righteousness. Now, when God the Father looks at us, He sees the righteousness of His Son, Jesus Christ, and we are "accepted in the beloved" –Ephesians 1:6b. He has written our names in His Book of life, and He is preparing a place in Heaven for us. There is no sting in death for those of us who are in Christ. "We are confident, I say, and willing rather to be absent from the body, and to be present with the Lord" –II Corinthians 5:8. Therefore, let us not live for self, but for Christ, and seek to please Him in every area of our life.

Let us fix our hearts upon the Lord with a constancy that will not be shaken. Let us resolve to honor Him with a determination that will not turn aside from serving Him. Let us press on in the work of the Lord without ever turning back to the beggarly elements of this world. He "died for all, that they which live should not henceforth live unto themselves, but unto him which died for them, and rose again." Then let us be bold to live for Christ in light of all that He has done for us.

*Day 41*

# The Lord Hears Our Murmurings

Exodus 16:8b

*"The Lord heareth your murmurings which ye murmur against him"*

God hears every discontented grumbling that we utter. We may speak with subdued voices, but He hears every word. Our murmurings have their origin in discontentment and unbelief. The Lord had so mightily released the children of Israel from the cruel bondage of the Egyptians and had miraculously made a way of escape from the Egyptian army through the Red Sea; however, their discontentment with the wilderness and their unbelief that their needs would be met, caused them to murmur against the Lord God Almighty. Because of their selfish desires and self-centered thinking, they quickly forgot the miracles God performed on their behalf. When we are absorbed with what *we* want, and those desires are not fulfilled, we become discontented and begin to murmur, for "out of the abundance of the heart the mouth speaketh" –Matthew 12:34b.

The children of Israel were also guilty of undervaluing their deliverance. If we are saved and are murmuring, then we too are guilty of undervaluing our deliverance from eternal damnation by the blood of Jesus Christ. When we murmur, we are murmuring against the Lord, the One who gave us eternal life. Murmuring reveals our discontentment, our unbelief, our self-centeredness, and undermines the power and glory of God. If we would focus our hearts and minds upon the Lord Jesus Christ, we would cease our foolish murmuring, because we would be awed by His amazing grace that saved such sinners as we are. Be certain that the Lord "heareth your murmurings which ye murmur against him."

## Day 42

# Singing Praises with Understanding

Psalm 47:7

*"For God is the King of all the earth: sing ye praises with understanding."*

The verse in our text begins, "For God is the King of all the earth"; therefore, for that reason, "Sing ye praises!" Ah, but the power of this command comes with the two words, "with understanding." Sing praises, understanding He is ALMIGHTY! He is Creator of all there is, seen and unseen. "All things were made by him; and without him was not any thing made that was made" –John 1:3. Sing praises, understanding there is no more sting in death, no more victory in the grave. The Lord Jesus Christ took our hell when He laid down His life for us and hung on Calvary's cross. Sing praises with understanding that God's grace has given us that which we ***do not deserve***—Heaven! "For by grace are ye saved through faith; and that not of yourselves: it is the gift of God" –Ephesians 2:8. Because of God's grace Heaven will be our home; we will walk the streets of gold; and "so shall we ever be with the Lord" –I Thessalonians 4:17. Sing praises with understanding the beauty of your home in Heaven; it is a mansion along stream frontage, and on streets paved with purest gold. More importantly, it is eternity with Jesus Christ our Lord. Sing praises with understanding that it is by His mercy we are kept from that which we ***do deserve***—Hell! "Not by works of righteousness which we have done, but according to his mercy he saved us, by the washing of regeneration, and renewing of the Holy Ghost; which he shed on us abundantly through Jesus Christ our Saviour" –Titus 3:5-6. If we have been redeemed, we will never see hell and our cry will never be, "I am tormented in this flame" –Luke 16:24. Sing praises! Sing praises ***with*** understanding! "Sing praises to God, sing praises: sing praises unto our King, sing praises. For God is the King of all the earth: sing ye praises with understanding" –Psalm 47:6-7.

# Accepted In Christ

Ephesians 1: 6

*"To the praise of the glory of his grace, wherein he hath made us accepted in the beloved."*

"Accepted in the beloved." Doesn't your heart beat wildly with the wonder of it all? Accepted in the beloved; perfect in Christ! It is not *we* who have accepted *Him*. Very clearly, the Bible says it is He who has accepted us! He "quickened" our hearts –made us alive unto Him. And, just as He did for Lydia in Acts 16:14, He opened our hearts on the day of our salvation that we would believe upon Him and receive Him for our very own.

Once we have been washed in His precious blood, we stand approved or accepted in Him. It is a truth that ought to cause our hearts to rejoice. Think on it, dear Christian; through Christ we are accepted into the very Holy presence of God where prayers are heard and answered. Now when Almighty God looks upon us He accepts us because He sees the righteousness of Christ and not our sinfulness. It isn't our goodness, but Christ's; it isn't our holiness, but Christ's; it isn't our perfection, but Christ's! Only by Christ does God, the Father, accept us with loving, open arms. *You* are "accepted in the beloved!" Let that thought saturate your mind, your heart and your soul, then praise Him for the glory of His grace which made us accepted in Him.

*Day 44*

# The Greatest Thing Is Love

I Corinthians 13:13

*"And now abideth faith, hope, charity, these three; but the greatest of these is charity [love]."*

Charity means the fullness of Christian love to our fellow man. This verse tells us that charity, or love, is greater than faith and hope. In Christianity it is generally assumed that the greatest thing a Christian could possess is faith; however, this verse says that love is greater than faith. The Lord Jesus said that the greatest commandment in the law was that we should "love the Lord [our] God with all [our] heart, and with all [our] soul, and with all [our] mind"—Matthew 22:37. He also said "the second is like unto it, Thou shalt love thy neighbor as thyself. On these two commandments hang all the law and the prophets"—Matthew 22:39-40. "Love is the fulfilling of the law"—Romans 13:10; therefore, if we would love as we should, we would be better able to fulfill the commandments that God and His Son, Jesus Christ, have given to us. Love is the greatest commandment for keeping all the commandments.

Love is greater than eloquent speaking, for "though [we] speak with the tongues of men and of angels, and have not [love], [we are] become as sounding brass, or a tinkling cymbal"—I Corinthians 13:1. Love is greater than prophecy, knowledge and faith, for "though [we] have the gift of prophecy, and understand all mysteries, and all knowledge; and though [we] have all faith, so that [we] could remove mountains, and have not [love], [we are] nfothing"—I Corinthians 13:2. Love is greater than abundant giving to the needy or even martyrdom, for "though [we] bestow all [our] goods to feed the poor, and though [we] give [our] body to be burned, and have not [love], it profiteth [us] nothing"—I Corinthians 13:3. "[Love] never faileth: but whether there be prophecies, they shall fail; whether there be tongues, they shall cease; whether there be knowledge, it shall vanish away"—I Corinthians 13:8. We must grow in our love for God and for others. We could not have any higher aspiration as a Christian than to love.

# Love Is Patient

I Corinthians 13:4

*"Charity [love] suffereth long"*

This kind of love is patient and not in a hurry; it is ready to do its work when the occasion arises. God and His Son, Jesus Christ, demonstrated this element of love toward us "in that, while we were yet sinners, Christ died for us"—Romans 5:8b. God loved, not because we were loveable, but because it was His nature to love, "for God is love"—I John 4:8b. God loved us in all our sinfulness and selfishness and wrong, and He expects His children to love one another in the same way. The Lord Jesus said, "This is my commandment, That ye love one another, as I have loved you"—John 15:12. Just think how disagreeable and unlovable we have been to God; yet He has loved us and continues to love us. When we are aware of "his great love wherewith he loved us"—Ephesians 2:4, then by His Spirit of love, we will seek to love others in the same way.

To patiently love others like God and His Son love us, we will have to cultivate it in our lives and maintain it by discipline. Remembering our failings and imperfections, and that "there is *none* righteous, no, not one"—Romans 3:10 will be a great help in doing so. Love understands and therefore waits. The Lord sometimes puts peculiar, disagreeable, and unlovable people in our lives to give us opportunities to practice patient love. Growth in this particular grace of love can be hindered when we become irritated and impatient; therefore, let's look to the Lord Jesus and dwell in His love so that His life and sweetness may be exhibited through us.

## Day 46

# Love is Kind

I Corinthians 13:4

*"Charity [love] . . . is kind"*

This is love in action. Our Lord Jesus' life was filled with acts of kindness as He "went about doing good"—Acts 10:38b. His greatest demonstration of love was on the cross of Calvary when He "lay down [his] life" for us —John 10:17b. No man took His life; He laid it down so that we could have a restored relationship with the Father through His shed blood. What an act of kindness—of love!

As Christians, God has given us the power and ability to bring happiness to those around us. By showing kindness we can make others happy. "Be kindly affectioned one to another with brotherly love; in honour preferring one another"—Romans 12:10. A kind word can make a huge difference in someone's life, for "a word fitly spoken is like apples of gold in pictures of silver"—Proverbs 25:11. "Recompense to no man evil for evil . . . If it be possible, as much as lieth in you, live peaceably with all men"—Romans 12:17a,18. Demonstrating any form of kindness to someone is the love of Christ in action.

# Love Is Generous

I Corinthians 13:4

*"Charity [love] envieth not"*

This is love being generous and not in competition with others so that we "let nothing be done through strife or vainglory; but in lowliness of mind . . . esteem other better than [ourselves]"—Philippians 2:3. Generous love does not possess a feeling of ill will or envy toward those who are in the same line of work, or who have the same talents as we have. Whatever work we are attempting to do, whatever talents we are attempting to use, there will be others doing the same kind of work, and possibly doing it better; love does not envy them. Love does not envy another's vocal talent; it is glad they have been given such talent to sing. Love prays that God would bless their voice and use them to touch hearts for His glory. Love does not envy another's wealth; it rejoices that God has blessed that person with such abundance, and it desires that God should give them even more if it would bring glory to Him.

To envy is to have the spirit of covetousness; however, if we yield ourselves to the Holy Spirit, allowing Him to love through us, we will not be discontent with our lot in life nor will we covet another's advantages, successes, or possessions. We will be secure in Christ and the purpose God has for our individual lives. When we strive to please God and surrender our desires to His, then we will be better able to love His way, which is without envy. A heart of abundant and generous love is something every Christian needs to desire and strive to acquire.

## Day 48

# Love Is Humble

I Corinthians 13:4

*"[Love] vaunteth not itself, is not puffed up."*

This is love retreating into the shadows. After we have done some act of kindness, something that helped, encouraged or blessed another, let's go back into "the shadows" and not say anything about it. Love does not need to boast. Love puts a seal upon our lips and "forgets" what we have done. Humble love is not motivated by any kind of reward, applause, or recognition that may be given; it is motivated by seeking to be a blessing to others without thinking of ourselves.  It is putting on, "as the elect of God . . . humbleness of mind, meekness"—Colossians 3:12 so that we may love for the glory of God and be satisfied that He sees what has been done. "Humble yourselves in the sight of the Lord, and he shall lift you up"—James 4:10.

Think of the many demonstrations of love we have received from our Heavenly Father and how often we fail to praise and thank Him, yet He continues to love us. Humble love seeks to do for others, though they may never show appreciation or say thank you; it simply does this to demonstrate love. Humble love would rather not be found out and rewarded for all the good deeds done, because love "vaunteth not itself, is not puffed up."

# Love Is Courteous

I Corinthians 13:5

*"Doth not behave itself unseemly"*

This is love being courteous and polite as seen in society. Love "doth not behave itself unseemly." It is being respectful and considerate of others. It is giving up a parking spot when coming upon it at the same time as someone else. It is seeing the need of another as more important than our own at the time. It is love in the little things. The secret to being polite is love, because love "doth not behave itself unseemly." To act unseemly is to be inconsiderate, ungentle, and unsympathetic to those around us, which is not love.

Judas Iscariot, one of Jesus' twelve apostles, betrayed Him; yet we see the gentleness with which the Lord Jesus responded when He asked Judas, "*Friend,* wherefore art thou come?"—Matthew 26:50. Such gentle love! Jesus Christ did not behave Himself unseemly even when it was justified. Courteous love simply cannot behave unseemly.

## Day 50

# Love Is Unselfish

I Corinthians 13:5

*"Seeketh not her own"*

Unselfish love does not look "on [our] own things, but every man also on the things of others"—Philippians 2:4. Our great Lord and Saviour demonstrated unselfish love: "when he was accused of the chief priests and elders, he answered nothing. Then said Pilate unto him, Hearest thou not how many things they witness against thee? And he answered him to never a word; insomuch that the governor marveled greatly"—Matthew 27:12-14. Christ's love for the others didn't require Him to answer back or think of Himself. The Lord Jesus knew they were witnessing falsely against Him; however, that didn't matter. It only mattered that He fulfill the will of the Father and, by unselfish love, lay down His life so that sinful man could be redeemed and restored unto the Father.

Unselfish love does not find it hard to give up anything, and nothing is hard to the one who unselfishly loves. "Seekest thou great things for thyself? Seek them not"—Jeremiah 45:5a; rather, "seek ye first the kingdom of God, and his righteousness"—Matthew 6:33a. "Take [Christ's] yoke upon you . . . and ye shall find rest unto your souls"—Matthew 11:29. Christ's way is to love unselfishly and to give of self for others, for the greatest happiness gained in life is not by having and getting things for ourselves, but by giving of ourselves to others, because love "seeketh not her own."

# Love Is Good Tempered

I Corinthians 13:5

*"[Love]is not easily provoked"*

This is love that is not quick to get angry, knowing that "a soft answer turneth away wrath: but grievous words stir up anger"—Proverbs 15:1. Many times we may give the excuse that a bad temper runs in the family, is a harmless weakness, and is not something to take very seriously when evaluating someone's character. But the Bible repeatedly condemns it as being one of the most destructive elements in human nature. "Be not hasty in thy spirit to be angry: for anger resteth in the bosom of fools"— Ecclesiastes 7:9. "Cease from anger, and forsake wrath"—Psalm 37:8a. "But now ye also put off all these; anger, wrath . . ."—Colossians 3:8. A bad temper can destroy a Christian's testimony, break up relationships, devastate homes, embitter hearts, and in general produce misery; however, if we would learn to love as we are instructed to love in God's Word, our tempers would be less inclined to flare up.

A bad temper can be fueled by many things, including anger, jealousy, pride, self-righteousness, touchiness, and sullenness. These are the characteristics of a dark and loveless heart. Any believer with such a temperament cannot be an effective witness for Jesus Christ. Such a temperament reveals an unloving nature with some sin that has not been dealt with. Therefore, it is not enough merely to deal with the bad temper; the root of the problem must be discovered in order to change one's nature and produce a more loving soul. We are made good tempered not by simply taking out the rancidness, but by putting in the sweet loving Spirit of Christ. This is done by surrendering ourselves more and more to the Holy Spirit. When the Holy Spirit of Christ has control of our spirit then we are sweetened, purified, and transformed into His loving nature. Neither will power nor time can change our temperament. We must yield our attitude to God's Holy Spirit and cooperate with Him in bringing about the needed change. Therefore, "let this mind be in you, which was also in Christ Jesus . . . For it is God which worketh in you both to will and to do of his good pleasure"—Philippians 2:5, 13. Love is the imitation of Christ; therefore, a person who truly loves "is not easily provoked."

## Day 52

# Love Is Sincere

I Corinthians 13:6

*"Rejoiceth not in iniquity, but rejoiceth in the truth"*

This is love which does not delight in exposing the weaknesses of others nor has joy when someone's faults have been discovered. Love does not believe any accusation without first getting at the truth. Love will probe for the truth; and if the truth uncovers the reality of the accusation, it does not rejoice. Love seeks to sincerely pray for those who have yielded to the temptation of sin and thereby fallen. Love says, "But for the grace of God, there go I."

Love sincerely seeks the truth of God's Word—not necessarily what we have been taught to believe, not in one church's doctrine or in another's, not in religion, but "in the truth." It is seeking the truth of Scripture so that we may "grow in grace, and in the knowledge of our Lord and Saviour Jesus Christ"—II Peter 3:18a. May we not rejoice in iniquity, but rejoice in the truth, and "above all things have fervent [love] among [ourselves]"—I Peter 4:8a.

# Love Unto the End

John 13:1

*"Now before the feast of the passover, when Jesus knew that his hour was come that he should depart out of this world unto the Father, having loved his own which were in the world, he loved them unto the end."*

The Lord Jesus Christ "came unto his own, and his own received him not"—John 1:11; yet, "he loved them unto the end." "He knew all men, and needed not that any should testify of man: for he knew what was in man"—John 2:24b-25; still, "he loved them unto the end." The Lord Jesus knew that Judas Iscariot was going to betray Him, that Peter was going to deny Him, that the other ten apostles were going to abandon Him, and that His "own," for whom He came, were going to crucify Him; yet, "he loved them unto the end." "Greater love hath no man than this, that a man lay down his life for his friends"—John 15:13. "Hereby perceive we the love of God, because he laid down his life for us"—I John 3:16a.

The love of God never fails; He loves each of His children unto the end. Because of His great love, Jesus bore our sins on the cross of Calvary and gave us redemption through His blood that He shed there. Many Christians have strayed from Him even after the glory of being saved, for the weakness of the flesh causes them to yield to temptation; however, He will pursue each one who has gone astray because He loves us unto the end.

We have been given a family on this earth. It is made up of imperfect spouses, parents, children, siblings, and extended family consisting of grandparents, aunts, uncles and cousins. None are perfect; all have faults. Love looks past the faults of family members and the hurts inflicted, recognizes our own faults, and therefore patiently loves one another. As Christians, we have the love of Christ within us through His Holy Spirit, and we can love our "own" unto the end by His Spirit.

## Day 54

# Love One Another Like Christ Loves

John 13:34

*"A new commandment I give unto you, that ye love one another; as I have loved you."*

The Lord Jesus Christ did not tell us to only love one another; He told us to love each other as He has loved us. Earlier in this same chapter the Lord Jesus Christ "began to wash the disciples' feet and to wipe them with the towel wherewith he was girded" –John 13:5b. Love is an action word, and the Lord Jesus demonstrated His love with action when He washed the disciples' feet. He washed the feet of Peter, the one who denied Him; He washed the feet of Judas Iscariot, the one who betrayed Him; and He washed the feet of each disciple who forsook Him. He demonstrated this act of love, knowing He would be betrayed, denied, and abandoned by those who declared they loved Him.  Knowing He was going to be put to death, He still loved us. "Hereby perceive we the love of God, because he laid down his life for us" –I John 3:16a. Jesus said, "Greater love hath no man than this, that a man lay down his life for his friends" –John 15:13, and "we ought to lay down our lives for the brethren" –I John 3:16b.

How well do we love one another? Jesus Christ loved us when we were not loveable. Do we only love those who love us in return? If so, then we do not love as Christ loved us. Christ doesn't love us for what He wants us to be; He loves us just as we are, "For he knoweth our frame; he remembereth that we are dust" –Psalm 103:14. Christ's love suffers long, is kind, gracious and merciful toward us. When we encounter someone who is unlovable, even cruel, let us look unto the Savior; He will give us the ability to be longsuffering, kind, gracious, and merciful. He has said, "love one another, as I have loved you; By this shall all men know that ye are my disciples, if ye have love one to another" –John

13:34b-35. He is love; therefore, let's seek Him and He will enable us to love as He loves.

# Our Help Is in the Name of the Lord

Psalm 124:8

*"Our help is in the name of the Lord, who made heaven and earth."*

Our help is in the name of the Lord because there is so much that encompasses His Name. Jesus' Name is the key to opening the vault to Heaven's bank: "Whatsoever ye shall ask the Father in my name, he will give it you" –John 16:23b. In the midst of a world full of terrors and evil workings, there is peace and rest in the Name of Jesus. The Lord Jesus Christ is our peace, our strength, our advocate, our shelter and our refuge in any and all times of trouble. The Apostle Peter and Apostle John called on the name of Jesus, asking that a lame man at the gate of the temple would receive healing. "Then Peter said, Silver and gold have I none; but such as I have give I thee: In the name of Jesus Christ of Nazareth rise up and walk. And he took him by the right hand, and lifted him up: and immediately his feet and ankle bones received strength. And he leaping up stood, and walked, and entered with them in to the temple, walking, and leaping, and praising God" –Acts 3:6-8. Whatever our need may be, our help is in the name of the Lord, who made heaven and earth.

## Day 56
# The Lord Is Round About His People

Psalm 125:2

*"As the mountains are round about Jerusalem, so the LORD is round about his people from henceforth even for ever."*

The Lord encompasses His children with His strength and His power. He is solid and unmovable. He is secure, a "present help in trouble" –Psalm 46:1b. We are enveloped in the power of His might, and therefore, we are able to stand in the day of adversity when we stand in His strength and power. We need "not be afraid for the terror by night; nor for the arrow that flieth by day; Nor for the pestilence that walketh in darkness; nor for the destruction that wasteth at noonday" –Psalm 91:5-6, for "the LORD is round about his people." He is unmovable; therefore, we have a sure help, a sure refuge, and a sure habitation "from henceforth even for ever."

When trouble comes, we do not have to despair; instead, like the psalmist, we only have to lift up our "eyes unto the hills, from whence cometh [our] help. [Our] help cometh from the LORD, which made heaven and earth" –Psalm 121:1-2. Whatever struggles we are going through, and though they may seem to be getting the best of us, we can take courage in the truth of God's Word: "As the mountains are round about Jerusalem, so the LORD is round about his people from henceforth even for ever."

# Ready to Pardon

Nehemiah 9:17

*". . . but thou art a God ready to pardon, gracious and merciful, slow to anger, and of great kindness, and forsookest them not."*

The heart of man does not find it easy to pardon someone who has caused hurt, and many times will not pardon until much later, if ever. However, the heart of God not only is *"ready to pardon"* His children, but He cleanses them. His children often grieve His heart with willful disobedience, pride, stubbornness, rebellion and by refusing to live for Him. However, He doesn't hesitate to pardon when we repent and seek His forgiveness: "If we confess our sins, he is faithful and just to forgive us our sins, and to cleanse us from all unrighteousness" –I John 1:9. "For he knoweth our frame; he remembereth that we are dust" –Psalm 103:14. The Lord is greatly grieved when His children demonstrate love for the world and self rather than for Him; yet He is ready to pardon when they acknowledge their sin unto him and do not try to hide their iniquities from Him. Whatever the sin, whether great or small, He is ready to pardon without respect of persons. This Lord whose name "is exalted above all blessing and praise" –Nehemiah 9:5b, and who is "Lord alone" –Nehemiah 9:6, is the same Lord who is ready to pardon!

## Day 58

# Strive Not Against Christ

Isaiah 45:9

*"Woe unto him that striveth with his Maker!"*

Man, in the flesh and by pride, has the audacity to strive with the One who created him, the One who fashioned him in the womb, the One who knows the number of hairs upon his head, and the One who laid down His very life so that man might be redeemed back to the Father in Heaven.

Child of God do not strive against your Maker! All that God the Father and His Son, Jesus Christ, does is right and holy, pure and perfect; there isn't any sin in them. Psalm 145:17 says, "The Lord is righteous in all his ways, and holy in all his works." Therefore, beware when you, as imperfect, unholy, unrighteous and impure flesh, should contend with Him. He says, "Woe unto him that striveth with his Maker!" Do not struggle against the Creator or debate your circumstances with Him. Rather, listen as He says, "Come unto me, all ye that labor and are heavy laden, and I will give you rest" –Matthew 11:28.

There is no situation that will ever be out of His reach to give you that hand of help and rest so needed when you are in the valley of temptation, the valley of indecision, the valley of sorrow, or the valley of death. Cease your striving with your Maker and simply REST in Him. He will carry you; let Him. Do not struggle against Him. He is the lifter of your head; do not turn away from Him. He is the very breath you breathe; do not resist Him. "In the world ye shall have tribulation," but in Christ you shall possess peace, for He has "overcome the world" –John 16:33.

# Renewed Mind

Ephesians 4:23

*"And be renewed in the spirit of your mind."*

Our goal as Christians should be to have the same mind that God's Son, Jesus Christ, had while He lived upon this earth for 33 years. Everyone who trusts Christ as Savior receives the Spirit of Christ. "Therefore if any man be in Christ, he is a new creature: old things are passed away; behold, all things are become new" –II Corinthians 5:17. The mind becomes new. The mind also becomes a battlefield, because Satan does not want to give up without a fight. Although he lost the battle over the soul at salvation, he will do all he can to win the battle of the mind for the duration of one's life. Therefore, "be not conformed to this world: but be ye transformed by the renewing of your mind, that ye may prove what is that good, and acceptable, and perfect, will of God" –Romans 12:2. Realize there is an adversary, the Devil, and he is seeking to devour the mind of every Christian. Therefore, "be sober, be vigilant" –I Peter 5:8, and be renewed in the spirit of your mind daily by keeping your mind focused on Jesus Christ. "Whatsoever things are true, whatsoever things are honest, whatsoever things are just, whatsoever things are pure, whatsoever things are lovely, whatsoever things are of good report; if there be any virtue, and if there be any praise, think on these things" –Philippians 4:8. If we keep our minds focused upon Jesus Christ and His goodness, we will be kept "in perfect peace" –Isaiah 26:3, and will become likeminded with Christ – thinking more highly of one another than we think of ourselves –Philippians 2:3, seeking to serve others with humility, and becoming obedient unto the Heavenly Father in everything. Meditating daily on the Word of God will help to renew the spirit of our mind.

## *Day 60*

# Blessed Are the Poor in Spirit

Matthew 5:3

*"Blessed are the poor in spirit: for theirs is the kingdom of heaven."*

Blessed are those who realize their great need spiritually. They recognize their unworthiness to come before ALMIGHTY GOD. Blessed are those who understand their great need for grace and mercy, and enter into the glorious realm of abundant grace and endless mercy through Jesus Christ, the Righteous. Blessed are all those who humble themselves "in the sight of the Lord" –James 4:10, bringing them to the sweetness of humility, realizing their great lack before the Creator of Heaven and earth. They humble themselves because they see the Lord, "sitting upon a throne, high and lifted up" –Isaiah 6:1, and realize their tremendous need before such a Great and Holy God. With Isaiah, they cry out, "Woe is me! For I am undone; because I am a man of unclean lips, and I dwell in the midst of a people of unclean lips: for mine eyes have seen the King, the LORD of hosts" –Isaiah 6:5.

Blessed are those who realize the great lack that can only be filled through the Redeemer, Jesus Christ, who is "without blemish and without spot" –I Peter 1:19, receiving His gift of redemption and eternal life. Blessed are those who find their happiness not in this world, but seek it from Christ through His Word daily. "They that are Christ's have crucified the flesh with the affections and lusts" –Galatians 5:24; therefore, they "seek those things which are above, where Christ sitteth on the right hand of God" –Colossians 3:1. Blessed are those who have set their affection "on things above, not on things on the earth" –Colossians 3:2.

Is this you, dear reader? Are you "poor in spirit" today? If so, remember these words the Lord Jesus Christ spoke, "Blessed are the poor in spirit: for theirs is the kingdom of heaven."

# It Is a Good Thing

Psalm 92:1-2

*"It is a good thing to give thanks unto the LORD, and to sing praises unto thy name, O most High: To shew forth thy lovingkindness in the morning, and thy faithfulness every night."*

It is a good thing to be thankful unto the Lord because "every good gift and every perfect gift is from above, and cometh down from the Father of lights, with whom is no variableness, neither shadow of turning"— James 1:17. He has also promised to provide food and clothing for us. The Lord Jesus said, "Therefore I say unto you, Take no thought for your life, what ye shall eat, or what ye shall drink; nor yet for your body, what ye shall put on. Is not the life more than meat, and the body than raiment? Behold the fowls of the air: for they sow not, neither do they reap, nor gather into barns; yet your heavenly Father feedeth them. Are ye not much better than they?"—Matthew 6:25-26. Give thanks unto the Lord for His promises and bountiful supply.

It is a good thing to sing praises unto the name of the Lord, for "the LORD of hosts is his name"—Isaiah 54:5a. He is not the Lord of only a few; He is the Lord of hosts! He is "sitting upon a throne, high and lifted up"—Isaiah 6:1b; therefore, sing praises unto Him. He is worthy of our songs of praise, and it is a good thing to sing His praises in the morning, in the afternoon, and in the evening. "O come, let us worship and bow down: let us kneel before the LORD our maker"—Psalm 95:6. Singing His praises will affect our hearts with joy, which will also affect the lives of those around us.

It is a good thing to diligently tell others of His loving-kindness and His faithfulness. His loving-kindness is made up of mercy and grace toward us, and His faithfulness is the fulfillment of His promises to us. When we take the time to meditate on all the mercies God has shown toward us and how He has been ever faithful toward us, we cannot help but be compelled to tell others. Let us daily give thanks unto the Lord, to sing praises unto Him, and to tell others of His loving-kindness and faithfulness, because it is a good thing to do.

## Day 62

# Cause Me to Know

Psalm 143:8

*"Cause me to know the way wherein I should walk."*

We will be better able to know the way we should walk by spending time listening to the Lord speak to us through His Word, by prayer, and through the preaching and teaching of His Word. When we spend time alone with Him, we get to know His likes and dislikes, His ways, His character, His very heart. The more we personally get to know our beloved Lord, the more we will know how to "walk in love" –Ephesians 5:2, to "Walk in the Spirit" –Galatians 5:16, to "Walk with all lowliness and meekness, with longsuffering, forbearing one another in love" – Ephesians 4:2. As we grow in our relationship with Him daily, we will become close personal friends. This close friendship with the Lord will fill our hearts with a greater desire to follow His commandments, such as, "Remember the sabbath day, to keep it holy" –Exodus 20:7, by "Not forsaking the assembling of ourselves together, as the manner of some is; but exhorting one another: and so much the more, as ye see the day approaching" –Hebrews 10:25. "See then that ye walk circumspectly, not as fools, but as wise" –Ephesians 5:15, so that He may cause us to know the way wherein we should walk.

# The Glory of His Coming

John 12:15

*"Fear not, daughter of Sion: behold, thy King cometh, sitting on an ass's colt."*

Fear not! Our King has come and is coming again! He took the sins of the world upon Himself when He hung upon Calvary's cross. The glory of His coming shined through His humility. As we read in our key verse, He came, "sitting on an ass's colt." He did not come riding upon the grandest steed, dressed in royal gala as an earthly king would; but He came regally with humility as King of kings –not of this world, but of that greater place, the Heavenly realm. His Kingship is of the most pure, most holy, and grandest kind. He did not need any earthly convincing, for His glory, in His humility, declared His Kingship. There is no need for us to have a troubled heart; He is coming again as He promised: "And if I go and prepare a place for you, I will come again, and receive you unto myself; that where I am, there ye may be also" -- John 14:3. What a glory that shall be, to be with Him, to see Him face to face and remain with Him always! All that occurs on this earth is temporal, and regardless of what may come, our hearts need never be troubled, for we have a sure promise in Christ.

*When all my labors and trials are o'er*
*And I am safe on that beautiful shore*
*Just to be near the dear Lord I adore*
*Will through the ages be glory for me*
Charles H. Gabriel

## Day 64

# Grieve Not the Holy Spirit of God

Ephesians 4:30

*"And grieve not the holy Spirit of God, whereby ye are sealed unto the day of redemption."*

As Christians we love the Holy Spirit of God that dwells in us and yet we so easily grieve Him with angry tempers, with unbelief, with disobedience, with unforgiveness, with dishonesty, and with a number of other characteristics of the flesh that could be named. Any of these acts of the flesh "grieve" the Holy Spirit of God, or in other words, cause the Holy Spirit to be sorrowful. These characteristics which grieve the Holy Spirit do not demonstrate the character of Christ in us, but rather the carnal state of our flesh. We need not despair but realize that there is hope of victory for us. "But thanks be to God, which giveth us the victory through our Lord Jesus Christ" –I Corinthians 15:57. Yielding to the sinfulness of our flesh shall always grieve the Holy Spirit, but yielding ourselves to God through the help of the Lord Jesus Christ will give us victory. Therefore, let us "put on the new man, which after God is created in righteousness and true holiness" –Ephesians 4:24, and we will not grieve the Holy Spirit of God. May we daily be conscious of our thoughts, conversation, and actions so we think, speak and act in such a way that will not grieve God's Holy Spirit.

# Valiant Through God

Psalm 108:13a

*"Through God we shall do valiantly."*

It is through God that we exist: "And the Lord God formed man of the dust of the ground, and breathed into his nostrils the breath of life; and man became a living soul" –Genesis 2:7. It was through God that Salvation [Jesus Christ] came to restore our fellowship with Him: "For God sent not his Son into the world to condemn the world; but that the world through him might be saved" –John 3:17. It is through God that we live and breathe: "God that made the world and all things therein . . . he giveth to all life, and breath, and all things; . . . For in him we live, and move, and have our being" –Acts 17:24-25, 28a. Because God is our maker, our Salvation, our sustenance of life, then we are able to do valiantly through Him.

Through God we can be valiant for truth and right by living according to His Word. Through God we can be valiant to walk in the Spirit and not in the flesh as we yield ourselves as servants to obey Him. Through God we can be valiant to continue walking upon the narrow path that leads to life–everlasting life—by fixing our heart upon the Lord. It is through God that we shall do valiantly; therefore, let us seek Him, look unto Him, and follow Him in every aspect of life.

## Day 66

# Hindered by Satan

I Thessalonians 2:18b

*"Satan hindered us"*

Since we are saved by grace, through faith in the Lord Jesus Christ, then we may be sure that Satan is going to try to hinder us. Satan will try to hinder our work for the Lord in whatever way he can; "be ye therefore wise as serpents, and harmless as doves" –Matthew 10:16b. "Satan himself is transformed into an angel of light" –II Corinthians 11:14b; therefore, we need to "be sober, be vigilant; because [our] adversary the devil, as a roaring lion, walketh about, seeking whom he may devour" –I Peter 5:8. In our work for the Lord, in our Christian character, in our daily living, Satan is going to attack us. He will attempt to attack us in our faith, our virtue, our integrity, our character. He will seek to hinder us from praying so that we, if possible, will miss God's blessing. When we attempt great things for God and believe great things from God, Satan is sure to do all he can to hinder us. We must not become discouraged when he hinders us. Remember, he hindered the Apostle Paul and others; and, just as they had victory, we also have victory in Jesus Christ. "Yea, and all that will live godly in Christ Jesus shall suffer persecution" –II Timothy 3:12; therefore, do not think it "strange concerning the fiery trial which is to try you, as though some strange thing happened unto you: But rejoice, inasmuch as ye are partakers of Christ's sufferings; that, when his glory shall be revealed, ye may be glad also with exceeding joy" –I Peter 4:12-13. We must not be alarmed if Satan hinders us, for we serve One who is more powerful than Satan: "greater is he that is in you, than he that is in the world" –I John 4:4b.

# According to Your Faith

Matthew 9:29

*"Then touched he their eyes, saying, According to your faith be it unto you."*

According to our faith, we can move mountains –Matthew 17:20. According to our faith, we can see "great and mighty things" –Jeremiah 33:3. According to our faith, we will receive –Matthew 21:22. God's Word is the believer's "check" that may be taken to the bank of Heaven and cashed for its full amount. God has said, many times, in His Word, "I will." But do we believe what He has said? The Lord Jesus put the question very plainly to these blind men, "Believe ye that I am able to do this?" –Matthew 9:28b. Are we able, as the blind men were, to answer as definitively, "Yea, Lord"? –Matthew 9:28b.

Our answers to prayer come according to our faith, not according to our presumption. The prayer that presumes God will answer according to the way *we* decide He should, in the time frame *we* determine He should, or in the way *we* envision He should, is not the prayer of faith. Faith takes a hold on God's promises and simply believes them, then rests confident in Him to answer however and whenever He thinks is best. Faith continues in prayer to discover God's will, then claims His promised answer. It does not say, "The answer did not come so it must not have been God's will." *"Praying through' might be defined as praying one's way into full faith, emerging while yet praying into the assurance that one has been accepted and heard, so that one becomes actually aware of receiving, by firmest anticipation and in advance of the event, the thing for which he asks"* –*Streams in the Desert*. May we pray as Hannah in I Samuel 1:10-17, as Elijah in I Kings 18:42-44, or as any number of God's saints we read about in the Bible. "According to your faith be it unto you."

**Day 68**

# God Is Thinking of You

Psalm 40:17a

*"But I am poor and needy; yet the Lord thinketh upon me."*

The Lord knows "the thoughts" that He thinks of you, and they are "thoughts of peace, and not of evil, to give you an expected end" – Jeremiah 29:11. Your present circumstances may be such that it would seem there is no one who is mindful of you, and that you are completely alone; however, take courage, because Almighty God is thinking of you. You may be "poor and needy," but the Lord is thinking of you. You may be experiencing overwhelming changes in your life, yet the Lord is thinking of you with thoughts that "are more than can be numbered" –Psalm 40:5, and if you "should count them, they are more in number than the sand" –Psalm 139:18.

When fear over certain life events seems to grip your heart, remember, the Lord is thinking of you. Take courage and find rest in the thoughts of the Lord toward you. Persevere in hard trials, knowing that you are in a multitude of the Lord's thoughts. Find comfort in knowing that the Lord is thinking of you. Whatever may happen, one thing is certain, the Lord is thinking of you.

# Inseparable Love of God

Romans 8:38-39

*"For I am persuaded, that neither death, nor life, nor angels, nor principalities, nor powers, nor things present, nor things to come, nor height, nor depth, nor any other creature, shall be able to separate us from the love of God, which is in Christ Jesus our Lord."*

If we have called upon the Name of the Lord for salvation, then there is nothing that can ever separate us from Him and His eternal love. Death cannot separate us, because He is life; therefore, death for the Christian simply means "to be absent from the body, and to be present with the Lord" –II Corinthians 5:8. Life cannot separate us from His love, because when we became new creatures in Christ through salvation, the fullness of eternal life was awakened in us and remains with us, because Christ never leaves us. The sinfulness of our flesh has been pardoned by His blood: "If we confess our sins, he is faithful and just to forgive us our sins, and to cleanse us from all unrighteousness" –I John 1:9. Therefore, as Christians, our sinful flesh cannot separate us from His love. "Thine, O LORD, is the greatness, and the power, and the glory, and the victory, and the majesty: for all that is in the heaven and in the earth is thine; thine is the kingdom, O LORD, and thou art exalted as head above all" –I Chronicles 29:11. Therefore, neither angels, nor principalities, nor powers, nor things present, nor things to come, nor height, nor depth, nor any other creature, shall be able to separate us from the love of God, which is in Christ Jesus our Lord. Nothing shall remove us from the sweet security of His eternal love. "My beloved is mine, and I am his" –Song of Solomon 2:16, so we can rest secure that we shall never be separated from the love of God in Christ Jesus.

## Day 70

# Our Sufficiency Is of God

II Corinthians 3:5

*"Not that we are sufficient of ourselves to think any thing as of ourselves; but our sufficiency is of God."*

Our sufficiency is of God because our entire dependency is upon Him. We are dependent upon Him for the health of our bodies, for the food we eat, for the air we breathe, for the clothes we wear, for the shoes on our feet, for the eyes to see, for the ears to hear, for the nose to smell, for the ability to do anything. We are not able to sufficiently care for our needs without God. We may be the one who goes to work to earn the paycheck; however, it is God who provides the job and gives the body strength and health to work so that we can earn a paycheck. We may be the ones that till the soil, plant the seeds, and bring in the harvest; however, it is God that provides the soil, creates the seeds, provides the water, and gives us bodily strength to till and harvest the crops. The most angelic voice, the strongest man, the greatest athlete, the wisest scientist, and the most beautiful woman are completely indebted to God because their talents are from Him. Not one thing that we do or have done could ever be accomplished by our sufficiency. Our sufficiency is of God. The Lord Jesus Christ said, "Without me ye can do nothing" –John 15:5. If we would remember that our sufficiency is of God, we would ascribe all the glory to Him and walk in humility.

# Being a Friend of God

John 15:14

*"Ye are my friends, if ye do whatsoever I command you."*

The Lord Jesus gave us a very clear measuring guide that would determine how good a friend we are to Him. His friendship toward us exceeds the relationship we have with our own family. How good a friend are we toward our Lord? He said, "Ye are my friends, if ye do whatsoever I command you." We can determine what kind of friend we are to our Lord by how well we follow all that He commands.

Some may be fair weather friends, only doing what the Lord commands as long as it is agreeable with them. Others may be temporal friends, only doing what the Lord commands for a short period of time. Still others may be devoted friends, desiring to do all that the Lord commands, because they are ever mindful of all that the Lord has done for them. The first and great commandment that He told us to follow was to "love the Lord thy God with all thy heart, and with all thy soul, and with all thy mind" –Matthew 22:37. "The second is like unto it, Thou shalt love thy neighbor as thyself" –Matthew 22:39. If we would be a friend of the Lord Jesus, then we must do whatsoever He commands us.

## Day 72

# God Is Jealous

Nahum 1:2

*"God is jealous."*

God is jealous. Why? Because He loves us. He is jealous of our time, of our thoughts, of our heart's affection. Simply put, God is jealous! He wants our greatest love and devotion to be given to Him — not to something or someone else. He wants our thoughts to be centered upon Him. He wants us to be aware of His presence from morning to evening. That is why He said to Moses, "I am the Lord thy God . . . Thou shalt have no other gods before me. Thou shalt not make unto thee any graven image, or any likeness of any thing that is in heaven above, or that is in the earth beneath, or that is in the water under the earth: Thou shalt not bow down thyself to them, nor serve them: for I the LORD thy God am a jealous God . . ." –Exodus 20:2-4. When the Lord is not the object of our deepest affection and devotion, He is jealous. He gave Himself for us; should we not give ourselves to Him?

Think of the pain our hearts would feel if our spouse spurned our love and gave their affections to someone other than ourselves. Our hearts would be overwhelmed with pain and grief, and jealousy would consume us. The same is true of God toward all who are His. He desires our whole heart and our attention. He does not want to compete for our attention and affection; nor is He going to force Himself upon us. He will call to us because He longs for our fellowship, but if we refuse or slight Him, we will distance ourselves from the fullness of His presence. There is a perfect illustration in Song of Solomon 5:1-6. He called but she made excuse and did not rise to go to him. When she finally did answer to his call, he had already departed. God is jealous! Make Him the center of your life, not just a fair- weather friend.

# Power for Christian Living

Psalm 119:133

*"Order my steps in thy word: and let not any iniquity have dominion over me."*

Here is a prayer that every Christian ought to pray daily. It is aligned with the prayer Jesus taught His disciples when He said, "After this manner therefore pray ye . . . Lead us not into temptation, but deliver us from evil"—Matthew 6:9a, 13a. The Word of God "is a lamp unto [our] feet, and a light unto [our] path"—Psalm 119:105. Therefore, we would do well to daily seek guidance from the Days of God's Word, for it is from His Word that He will order our steps. If we want to follow in the steps of our Saviour, then we need to follow Him through the four Gospels of Matthew, Mark, Luke, and John, understanding that is only a start, because He can be found throughout the Scriptures.

If we want to have power with God in our Christian living, then it is imperative that we "search the Scriptures; for in them [we] think [we] have eternal life: and they are they which testify of me [Jesus]"—John 5:39. The Psalmist did not simply want his steps ordered, but he wanted them ordered according to God's Word. It is in God's Word that we learn how to live for God and with our fellow man. Let us daily spend time reading, studying, and meditating on God's Word as we ask Him to order our steps.

**Day 74**

# Demonstrating Love

John 14:15

*"If ye love me, keep my commandments.*

How much we love the Lord is demonstrated by how well we keep His commandments. We demonstrate our love for the Lord by keeping His commandments. "He that hath my commandments, and keepeth them, he it is that loveth me"—John 14:21a. "For this is the love of God, that we keep his commandments: and his commandments are not grievous"—I John 5:3. The Lord Jesus said that the second greatest commandment is to love our neighbor as ourselves. "And now I beseech thee, lady, not as though I wrote a new commandment unto thee, but that which we had from the beginning, that we love one another. And this is love, that we walk after his commandments. This is the commandment, That, as ye have heard from the beginning, ye should walk in it"—II John 1:5-6. The Lord Jesus said, "By this shall all men know that ye are my disciples, if ye have love one to another"—John 13:35. The more we love the Lord, the more we will love others. The less we love others, the more we love ourselves. "If a man say, I love God, and hateth his brother, he is a liar: for he that loveth not his brother whom he hath seen, how can he love God whom he hath not seen?"—I John 4:20.

Love is patient. Love is kind. Love is humble. Love is not selfish—I Corinthians 13:4-6. Love doesn't do things through strife or vainglory, but in humility will esteem others better than themselves—Philippians 2:3. "Beloved, let us love one another: for love is of God; and every one that loveth is born of God, and knoweth God. He that loveth not knoweth not God; for God is love"—I John 4:7-8. If we are going to demonstrate our love to God, then we must keep His commandments and love one another.

# Hearing the Voice of the Lord

Mark 9:7

*"This is my beloved Son: hear him."*

The Lord Jesus has the words of life, for He <u>is</u> life. He has the words of wisdom, for He <u>is</u> wisdom. He has the words of peace, for He is the Prince of peace. So often He speaks, but we do not hear Him over the din of the television, the noise of the radio, or the constant communication with our family and friends. If we are going to hear Him we must put everything aside and sit at His feet with listening ears and an open heart. Lay aside daily distractions so that you may "hear Him."

Peter, James and John were up on the mountain alone with the Lord Jesus when they heard a voice saying, "This is my beloved Son: hear him." It is alone with the Lord Jesus and away from everyone that we will hear Him. It is with a still, small voice that He speaks and, as Elijah, we will not hear Him in the "whirlwind," the "earthquake," or the "fire." "The mild voice of Him who speaks from the cross, or the mercy-seat, is accompanied with peculiar power in taking possession of the heart." –Matthew Henry. Elijah didn't cover his face in contrite humility during the wind, the earthquake or the fire, but he did when he heard that powerful "still small voice" –I Kings 19:12-13. When we get alone with Him and hear Him, we too shall be overcome with the might of His glorious power and the depravity of our sinful flesh. Meet Him in the garden of prayer and hear Him. He is speaking; take time to "hear him."

## Day 76

# Giving Myself to Prayer

Psalm 109:4b

*"I give myself unto prayer."*

The goal for all Christians should be to make prayer an extension of their life –a goal that is attained by making prayer a high priority. Regardless of circumstances, pray! When in distress, pray! When in joy, pray! As Christians, in whatever situation we face, we must learn to give ourselves to prayer. The more we understand that prayer is our lifeline to God, that it sustains us in trouble, and that it increases our joy in the Lord, the more we will pray. Prayer enables us to function in the realm of the Holy Spirit in our day to day living. Prayer is vital for the Christian; therefore, we must learn to give ourselves to prayer. Prayer changes us, because it allows us to see the glory of the Lord when we declare our dependence upon Him.

In order to give ourselves to prayer we must increase our knowledge of the One to whom we are praying and search the Scriptures daily –see Acts 17:11b. We must also be on guard against "the wiles of the devil" –Ephesians 6:11, because he will do all he can to keep us from prayer. Spending time with the Lord and including Him in every aspect of our lives will lead us in making prayer the highest priority in our life. Make it your goal, if you haven't already, to give yourself to prayer.

## A Place of Rest

There is a place of peace and rest
Where the storm clouds roll away
It's a place I love the best
Where I'm prone to linger and extend my stay.

It's a place where I can get alone
With One who is mightier than all.
He sits upon the highest throne
And intently listens when I call.

Dwelling there with Him, just He and I,
My heart forgets the sorrow and the pain.
Being with the Lamb who was crucified,
I find pure joy in His Name.

Resort, dear friend of mine,
And seek your solace there.
It will please you to find
Such love and tender care.

*Day 77*

# Hope in His Word

Psalm 130:5b

*"And in his word do I hope."*

The lost sinner can hope in the Word of the Lord. Why? Because God said, "For whosoever shall call upon the name of the Lord shall be saved" –Romans 10:13. The widow and the fatherless can hope in His Word, because "he relieveth the fatherless and widow" –Psalm 146:9b. The dying Christian can hope in His Word, for we have the assurance: "Yea, though I walk through the valley of the shadow of death, I will fear no evil: for thou art with me; thy rod and thy staff they comfort me" –Psalm 23:4. The sorrowful can hope in His Word, "For I [God] have satiated the weary soul, and I have replenished every sorrowful soul" –Jeremiah 31:25. The Word of God, from Genesis to Revelation, permeates with hope because it is full of God's promises that cannot be broken. "God is not a man, that he should lie; neither the son of man, that he should repent: hath he said, and shall he not do it? Or hath he spoken, and shall he not make it good?" –Numbers 23:19. We should daily read the Bible and search its Days for the promises of God so that we may say with the Psalmist, "in his word do I hope."

# Glory in the Lord

I Corinthians 1:31

*"He that glorieth, let him glory in the Lord."*

Are you glorying in the Lord or, in other words, being boastful of Him?  Are you telling others of His greatness?  Are you telling Him how great He is?  Are you consciously recognizing that "it is he that hath made us, and not we ourselves; we are his people, and the sheep of his pasture" –Psalm 100:3b?  He is the Creator!  We live and breathe because He made us and He gives us the breath to breathe.  In Him is *all* power!  There isn't any weakness in Him!  He is our provider!  NOTHING is too hard for Him.  He fed the children of Israel in the wilderness. He fed the multitude with five loaves and two fish.  He healed the multitude of many sicknesses.  He is "the same yesterday, and to day, and for ever" –Hebrews 13:8; therefore, He is able to care for our needs today.  He provides the food on our tables, the clothes we wear, and the shoes on our feet.  "It is better to trust in the Lord than to put confidence in man. It is better to trust in the Lord than to put confidence in princes" –Psalm 118: 8-9.  Nothing in the flesh is worthy of glory, but everything in the Lord Jesus Christ is worthy of glory.  Therefore, "he that glorieth, let him glory in the Lord."

# Glorious King

Oh Thou most Glorious King

And most High God

Thou has given me of everything

As in thy steps I trod


When the early morning dew

Lies upon the ground

It is then I eagerly come to you

Knowing you'll always be found


Bowing myself at your feet

I share with you my joys and sorrows

Such fellowshipping is always sweet

And there are no thoughts for my tomorrows

# The Lord Is Personal

Exodus 15:2

*"The Lord is my strength and song, and he is become my salvation: he is my God . . ."*

The Lord is **my** strength, **my** song, **my** salvation, **my** God! He is a very personal God. I am weak, but in Christ, His strength becomes mine, and "I can do all things through Christ which strengtheneth me" –Philippians 4:13. When my heart is heavy because of sorrow or some other reason, in Christ, I can sing regardless of the circumstance, because "he hath put a new song in my mouth, even praise unto our God" –Psalm 40:3. "Weeping may endure for a night, but joy cometh in the morning" –Psalm 30:5b. I was born in sin and in iniquity, but He became my salvation when He quickened my heart and saved me out of all my trespasses and sins. He is my salvation from the wickedness of this world and from eternal damnation in hell. So many places in the Bible it is said that the Lord is mine, denoting that He is a very personal God, and, as a result, His children are very dear to Him. He is not strength, a song, or salvation to anyone but His own children. Rejoice that our God is a personal God. If you cannot say with full assurance that the Lord is **your** God, then call unto Him today and ask Him for His free gift of salvation that you may know this personal God and be able to call Him yours.

## Day 80

# An Excellent Spirit

Daniel 6:3

*"Then this Daniel was preferred above the presidents and princes, because an excellent spirit was in him; and the king thought to set him over the whole realm."*

As a young boy, Daniel was taken captive out of his homeland and was enslaved, as well as imprisoned; yet he maintained an excellent spirit before his captors and was preferred above dignitaries. His excellent spirit was a result of his faithfulness to God and his love for God in the midst of life's harsh trials. He never turned away from trusting in the Lord. He never allowed his circumstances to dictate His love for, his trust in, and his honor of his Almighty God. Like the psalmist, he could say, "My heart is fixed, O God, my heart is fixed: I will sing and give praise" –Psalm 57:7.

As Christians, we too may have an excellent spirit within us by "looking unto Jesus the author and finisher of our faith" –Hebrews 12:2a. If we would set our "affection on things above, not on things on the earth" –Colossians 3:2, and seek "first the kingdom of God and his righteousness" –Matthew 6:33a, then we could have an excellent spirit like Daniel. When God's "Spirit itself beareth witness with our spirit, that we are the children of God" –Romans 8:16, and we humble ourselves "in the sight of the Lord" –James 4:10, then we, through the power of God's Holy Spirit, will be able to develop an excellent spirit. As an excellent spirit was in Daniel, may an excellent spirit also be in us, that we would bring glory to God.

# My Health, My Countenance

Psalm 42:11

*"Why art thou cast down, O my soul? and why art thou disquieted within me? Hope thou in God: for I shall yet praise him, who is the health of my countenance, and my God."*

Charles Spurgeon once said, "The countenance is often a true index to the state of the mind." The questions King David asked –"Why art thou cast down, O my soul? and why art thou disquieted within me?"— clearly exhibit the fear and depression he was experiencing at the time. His countenance revealed how he felt. King David was able to quiet those fearful and despondent thoughts by focusing his thoughts on the hope that there is in God.

If we yield to fear and depression, our health will be affected, and our countenance will reveal what we are feeling. But, like David, we can conquer fear and depression by looking unto the Lord and being often in His Word. Our physical health may fail, but in God we can have a healthy countenance, for "though our outward man perish, yet the inward man is renewed day by day . . . For we know that if our earthly house of this tabernacle were dissolved, we have a building of God, an house not made with hands, eternal in the heavens" –II Corinthians 4:16b & 5:1.

As Stephen stood before his false accusers, and in the midst of impending death, those around him "saw his face as it had been the face of an angel" –Acts 6:15. Just before he was martyred, he "looked up stedfastly into heaven, and saw the glory of God, and Jesus standing on the right hand of God" –Acts 7:55.

The health of a person's countenance depends upon how healthy the heart and mind are in God. In this life we are going to have trials and sorrows, and our flesh is going to naturally turn to despair, fear, and despondency; however, the more we saturate our minds and our hearts with God and His Word, the healthier our countenance will be. May we all hope in God and praise Him, for He is the health of our countenance.

**Day 82**

# Fools Quarrel

Proverbs 18:6

*"A fool's lips enter into contention, and his mouth calleth for strokes."*

Contention is nothing more than quarreling; therefore, we are a fool if we quarrel with someone. "Only by pride cometh contention"—Proverbs 13:10a; therefore, we become a fool when we let our pride lead us into contentious arguments. As Christians let us imitate our Saviour who made people wonder "at the gracious words which proceeded out of his mouth"—Luke 4:22a. "He was oppressed, and he was afflicted, yet he opened not his mouth: he is brought as a lamb to the slaughter, and as a sheep before her shearers is dumb, so he openeth not his mouth"—Isaiah 53:7. May we follow the example of the Lord Jesus Christ and walk meekly and humbly with others so that we will not feel the need to vindicate ourselves or demand our own will and way. "A fool uttereth all his mind: but a wise man keepeth it in till afterwards"—Proverbs 29:11. As Christians, let us endeavor to turn away from foolishness and walk wisely.

# Looking Unto Jesus

Hebrews 12:2

*"Looking unto Jesus the author and finisher of our faith . . ."*

Looking unto Jesus, we will "behold the Lamb of God, which taketh away the sin of the world" –John 1:29. He is the One who "loved us, and washed us from our sins in his own blood" –Revelation 1:5. Looking unto Jesus, we will find "the peace of God, which passeth all understanding" –Philippians 4:7, and "a friend that sticketh closer than a brother" –Proverbs 18:24. The Lord Jesus is the Author of our salvation: "If thou shalt confess with thy mouth the Lord Jesus, and shalt believe in thine heart that God hath raised him from the dead, thou shalt be saved" –Romans 10:9.

The Lord Jesus Christ is also He that builds our faith when we continue looking unto Him. The Apostle Peter walked on the water while looking unto Jesus; however, "when he saw the wind boisterous, he was afraid" –Matthew 14:30. When he ceased to look unto Jesus and began to look upon the storm, fear gripped him; and it was then that he began to sink. In tenderness, the Lord reached down and lifted Peter to safety after Peter cried out for help. Peter may have turned his eyes away from seeing the Lord Jesus, but Christ's presence remained. "Storms" may rage during life, but the sweet presence of the Lord Jesus Christ is continual. We will see Him and our faith will be enlarged if we continue to look unto Him.

The Lord Jesus is also the Finisher of our faith and will lead us home to Heaven. Look unto Jesus and be saved; keep looking unto Jesus and grow in faith; and one day expect to worship Him by sight, face to face! He is the Author and Finisher of our faith.

**Day 84**

# Zealous for the Lord

Revelation 3:19

*"Be zealous"*

When we are zealous for the Lord we will desire to win souls for Christ–to "rescue the perishing and care for the dying." When we are led by true zeal, then knowledge, patience and courage will follow, because it is our zeal for the Lord that will cause us to attempt great exploits for Him. Zeal will enable us to be bold for Jesus Christ as we allow God's Holy Spirit to work in us. Zealousness is ignited, and its flame is kept burning as the Holy Spirit continues to work in us. However, if our inner life dwindles and our heart grows cold toward the things of God, we will not have zeal. But if we daily "draw near to God" –Psalm 73:28 by fervently praying and faithfully reading the Bible, then our hearts will burn with zeal to see God's "will be done in earth, as it is in heaven" – Matthew 6:10b.

Our zeal will be nurtured when we have a deep sense of gratitude. When we remember how Christ lifted us up out of "an horrible pit" –Psalm 40:2, then we will have an abundant desire to "spend and be spent" –II Corinthians 12:15 in order to boldly share with others what Christ has done for us. Our zeal will stimulate us to think of lost souls in an eternal hell, as well as believers in Christ who are enjoying Heaven's eternal glories. Zeal motivates us to work, because we realize the time is short; and we must devote time and energy to the work of the Lord for the glory of the Lord. As children of God let us be zealous for our Lord!

# Waiting in Prayer

Psalm 62:5

*"My soul, wait thou only upon God"*

Begin to wait upon God by waiting in prayer. To wait in prayer is to "be still, and know that [He is] God"—Psalm 46:10a. Take time to be silent in prayer, and in the silence allow the Holy Spirit to bring to your heart and mind a realization of the greatness of who God is: He is "a sun and shield: the LORD will give grace and glory: no good thing will he withhold from them that walk uprightly"—Psalm 84:11. Waiting on God in prayer in this way will allow the Holy Spirit within us to make "intercession for us with groanings which cannot be uttered"—Romans 8:26b. When we confess that we have failed Him He will extend His mercies to us and lovingly remove "our transgressions from us"—Psalm 103:12b. When we are lacking in some specific grace of God, such as patience, He will refine and perfect that grace in us as we wait on Him first in prayer. When we wait on God in this way, we will develop deeper dependency on Him and will cultivate greater confidence in Him. This will enable us to say with assurance, "Thou art great, and doest wondrous things: thou art God alone"—Psalm 86:10.

God longs to reveal Himself to us and to fill us with the knowledge of Himself. When we wait on God it provides the opportunity for Him to do this in His own divine time and way. Therefore, do not rush in your prayers: "Be not rash with thy mouth, and let not thine heart be hasty to utter any thing before God: for God is in heaven, and thou upon earth: therefore let thy words be few"—Ecclesiastes 5:2. Prayerfully "wait thou only upon God."

# Be Still and Know

Be still and know
In the crushing blows
Of heartache's woes
I am God

When the furnace heat does hotter grow
Then it's time
To be still and know
I am God

As the shadow of death
Consumes the valley so low
Pause to be still and know
I am God

Be still and know
As the billows roll
Upon life's tempestuous sea
I am God

When that dearest friend
Becomes thy foe
Be still and know
I am God

Be still and know
Though strength may flee
And thy body feeble be
I am God

He is the beginning and the end
And soon He's coming back again
Therefore be still and know
He is God!

# Nothing Is Impossible with God

Luke 1:37

*"For with God nothing shall be impossible."*

With God, NOTHING is impossible! He is able to fill the barren womb. He did so for Elisabeth, for Hannah, for Rachel, for Sarah; and He is still able to fill the barren womb. He made the womb; shall He not be able to fill it? He is able to open the blind eyes that they might see. He is able to open the deaf ears that they might hear. He is able to heal the sick, make the lame to walk, and raise the dead to life again. He is able to loose the tongue that the mute may speak. He is able to feed the multitudes with two small fish and five little loaves of bread –Matthew 14:19, and to send quail in abundance –Numbers 11:31. He has used the ravens to feed His servant –I Kings 17:4-6. He is able to walk on water to get to His children in the storm –Mark 6:48-50. "By the word of the Lord were the heavens made; and all the host of them by the breath of his mouth" –Psalm 33:6. He created the heavens and the earth, and all that exists were made by His hands. Therefore, NOTHING is impossible with God, the Creator, the Almighty!

*Day 87*

# Wisdom of God

James 1:5

*"If any of you lack wisdom, let him ask of God, that giveth to all men liberally, and upbraideth not; and it shall be given him."*

When we lack wisdom to make even the simplest decisions of everyday life we need not despair for we have been given a promise which, as our key verse says, if we lack wisdom, we can ask God for it. God is wisdom! Therefore, go to God and ask Him for the wisdom you need. He will never fail to answer! Proverbs, chapter 3, declares the great importance of wisdom; it far exceeds the revenue of silver or gold; it ranks higher than precious stones; it brings happiness, peace, prolonged life, riches and honor. We also learn that, "the Lord by wisdom hath founded the earth; by understanding hath he established the heavens. By his knowledge the depths are broken up, and the clouds drop down the dew" –Proverbs 3:19-20. "Wisdom is the principal thing; therefore get wisdom: and with all thy getting get understanding" –Proverbs 4:7. Regardless of the situation or circumstance, if you lack wisdom, go to God who "giveth to all men liberally."

# Pleasure in Distresses

II Corinthians 12:10

*"Therefore I take pleasure in infirmities, in reproaches, in necessities, in persecutions, in distresses for Christ's sake: for when I am weak, then am I strong."*

To take pleasure in our problems is contrary to our natural way of thinking. We are not naturally inclined to take pleasure in our physical or mental weaknesses—our "infirmities." It does not please us when someone accuses us of something, or expresses disapproval and disappointment with us. These are our "reproaches." When we are in need, or are being persecuted in some way, or in distressful circumstances, we do not normally find pleasure in them. The majority of us tend to complain, vent, or even whine when such instances occur in our lives. The Apostle Paul was able to take pleasure in them, and he was able to say, "Most gladly therefore will I rather glory in my infirmities"—II Corinthians 12:9b. How could he have that attitude? Because he was looking and listening to Christ. His focus turned from the "thorn in [his] flesh"—II Corinthians 12:7b to the sufficient grace and power of Christ which come to us in the weakness of our flesh.

George Matheson, a well-known blind preacher of Scotland in the 1800's, once said: "My God, I have never thanked Thee for my thorn. I have thanked Thee a thousand times for my roses, but not once for my thorn. I have been looking forward to a world where I shall get compensation for my cross; but I have never thought of my cross as itself a present glory." Our difficulties are not meant to destroy us; instead, they are meant to empower us with the power of Christ. They are meant to remove self-sufficiency so that we will find our sufficiency in Christ. When we begin to see our difficulties as stepping stones to blessings, we will "take pleasure in infirmities, in reproaches, in necessities, in persecutions, in distresses." God often allows difficulties in order to draw us closer to Him.

**Day 89**

# Soul-Joyful

Psalm 35:9

*"And my soul shall be joyful in the LORD: it shall rejoice in his salvation."*

Joy that is felt in our soul doesn't come from knowing **about** the Lord; it comes from **knowing** Him. When we begin to **know** the Lord, our soul becomes joyful in Him, and we experience "joy unspeakable and full of glory"—I Peter 1:8b. Studying the Bible and memorizing Scripture is necessary to grow in our knowledge of the Lord, but it is at His feet, in the stillness of His presence, without any distractions—that we begin to **know** Him—that He is God. He sweetly reveals Himself to us at those times, teaching us His power, His mercies, His love, His grace, His strength, His greatness that is "past finding out; yea, and wonders without number"—Job 9:10. Take some unhurried time today and every day to be still in the presence of the Lord. Do not allow the busyness of serving cause you to neglect that good part that the Lord Jesus told Martha would not be taken from her sister, Mary. Fill your soul with joy by spending time alone with God, listening to Him speak to you from His Word. Talk to Him and unburden your heart to Him. If we seek Him, we will find Him. It is He that fills us with joy.

# Sufficient Grace

II Corinthians 12:9

*"And he said unto me, My grace is sufficient for thee: for my strength is made perfect in weakness. Most gladly therefore will I rather glory in my infirmities, that the power of Christ may rest upon me."*

God's grace *is* sufficient. His grace has been promised to us, and it has been made a ready, sufficient supply for us. We can have great confidence that His grace will be sufficient for whatever the need may be. When life's burdens grow heavy, we must simply, by faith, claim His grace as a reality, and then we will find it *is* sufficient as He said.

God's strength *is* made perfect in weakness. "When I am weak, then am I strong" –II Corinthians 12:10b. It is when I am weak that the glory of God can be exalted, because it is then that I realize I can do nothing without Him, and I therefore declare my dependency on Him. My weakness reveals to me *my* utter helplessness and *God's* Almighty power.

When we experience the reality of God's grace being sufficient and His strength being made perfect in our weakness, then, like the Apostle Paul, we also will most gladly glory in our infirmities. We will find that our burdens and our weaknesses are bridges by which we may obtain more of Christ's glorious likeness, and have His power resting upon us.

*He giveth more grace when the burdens grow greater, He sendeth more strength when the labors increase; To added afflictions He addeth His mercy, To multiplied trials, His multiplied peace. When we have exhausted our store of endurance, When our strength has failed ere the day is half done, When we reach the end of our hoarded resources, Our Father's full giving is only begun. His love has no limit, His grace has no measure, His power no boundary known unto men; For out of His infinite riches in Jesus, He giveth, and giveth, and giveth again.* –Annie Johnson Flint

## Day 91

# The Lord Remains the Same

Hebrews 1:10-11

*"And, Thou, Lord, in the beginning hast laid the foundation of the earth; and the heavens are the works of thine hands: They shall perish; but thou remainest . . ."*

Life brings so many changes; however, for the child of God there is something that never changes – the presence of the beloved Savior, Jesus Christ. He is One that never changes. He is the same "yesterday, and today, and forever" –Hebrews 13:8. The earth and the heavens shall perish and change, but the glorious Lord remains the same! The earth and heavens "shall wax old as doth a garment" –Hebrew 1:11, but the sweet Lord Jesus remains the same. He is always present; and although His presence may not be recognized or realized, He is right there beside you. He is unseen, but He is within reach. Circumstances, moods and feelings, or other elements may hinder us from recognizing the presence of the Lord, yet His presence is the same. He remains. He is there all around you. He doesn't depend upon your mood, your feelings, your circumstances, or any other thing; His presence is real. He is real! He is "Emmanuel . . . God with us" –Matthew 1:23. These truths bring sweet comfort. Jesus Christ is with us and He never changes; therefore He is always with us. He is with us in joy and in sorrow; He is with us today and tomorrow, because He ever remains the same. He is there, a Holy presence and Divine. Take comfort today because the Lord remainest!

# Acknowledging God in All Our Ways

Proverbs 3:6

*"In all thy ways acknowledge him, and he shall direct thy paths."*

In all our ways that are joyful and pleasant, we are to acknowledge Him with thankfulness. The Lord is the origin of our joy and happiness; without Him we would not know seasons of delight. Recognize that "every good gift and every perfect gift is from above, and cometh down from the Father of lights . . ." –James 1:17, and acknowledge Him with heartfelt thanksgiving.

In all our ways that are unpleasant, uncomfortable, dark, and difficult, we are to acknowledge Him with submission. "God understandeth the way thereof, and he knoweth the place thereof" –Job 28:23. His thoughts toward us are "thoughts of peace, and not of evil, to give [us] an expected end" –Jeremiah 29:11. He knows what to give us and what to withhold from us; therefore, let's acknowledge Him in every trial and temptation by submitting to His will. When we are tried, we will come forth as gold –Job 23:10b.

His immutability is our security, for though we are constantly changing, He **never** changes; He is "the same yesterday, and to day, and for ever" –Hebrews 13:8. His grace will always be sufficient, His love eternal, and His forgiveness readily available. Acknowledge Him in life's joys and sorrows with thankfulness and submission; He is "the good shepherd" –John 10:11a. His ways are higher than our ways and His thoughts than our thoughts –Isaiah 55:9b. When we acknowledge Him in all our ways, then He will direct our paths.

**Day 93**

# Glorifying the Lord *in* the Fire

Isaiah 24:15

*"Wherefore glorify ye the LORD in the fires, even the name of the LORD God of Israel in the isles of the sea."*

Notice the little word *in*; we should glorify the Lord *in the fires.* We seem to find it easy to glorify the Lord when our finances are stable, when our family is well, when our business is progressing without trouble; however, it is *in* the fire that we are exhorted to glorify the Lord. We should glorify Him *in* our trials and honor Him by our faith in His perfect love and goodness that has permitted such trials to enter our life.

We glorify Him *in* our trials by walking in the Spirit of Christ, rooting ourselves in Christ, and establishing ourselves in the faith of Christ while all the time abounding in thanksgiving –Colossians 2:6-7. We should glorify the Lord in our fiery trials by exercising His sufficient grace while we wait for Him to deliver us from them if He so chooses. We should, like Christ, be "triumphing over them in it" –Colossians 2:15b. Real triumph is triumphing over sickness *in* it with a sweet spirit surrendered to His will; triumphing over difficult circumstances *in* them, trusting in the Lord to direct our steps; triumphing over death, by His grace, and committing to Him our souls to be carried safely to our final rest.

There is nothing so compelling and inspiring than to see someone so broken in their body, yet not in their spirit; or to hear the sweetest notes of praise coming from one so laden with troubles; or to witness pure and gentle love being expressed toward those who have inflicted horrid cruelty. All this is a great testimony of His wonderful grace when we glorify Him *in* the hard trials.

# Blessed by Trusting

Psalm 2:12

*"Blessed are all they that put their trust in him."*

We will be blessed, or happy, when we put our trust in the Lord. Worry and fretfulness are the result of doubts and lack of trust in the Lord, and can even lead to despondency. Those who continually yield to these doubts and fears rarely experience the joy of the Lord and His happiness in their lives.

If we are to have blessed, happy lives then we must anchor ourselves upon the Rock, Christ Jesus, and put our trust in Him. It was the Lord that said unto Noah, "Come thou and all thy house into the ark" – Genesis 7:1, signifying that the Lord was *in* the ark. Wherever the Lord leads us, whatever He asks of us, He will always go before us. As our Captain, He will steer us to safety. The Lord maneuvered the Ark around every possible obstacle and brought it to land safely upon Mount Ararat –Genesis 8:4. Our happiness comes when we trust in the Lord with *all* of our heart and do not lean on our own understanding –Proverbs 3:5-6. Noah had never seen rain or an ark, but he obeyed and built the ark by trusting in the Lord. Blessed are all they that put their trust in him.

**Day 95**

# The Lord Is My Strength

Psalm 27:1b

*"The Lord is the strength of my life."*

The Lord is my strength to courageously persevere, regardless of any physical weakness my body may have. He is my strength to overcome any spiritual battle that I may be fighting. He is my strength to conquer the devil's temptations, and my strength to walk through trials with grace. He is my strength to conquer my fears, because "perfect love casteth out fear" –I John 4:18. It is when I am weak that I find that the Lord *is* my strength, that His grace *is* sufficient, and that His strength **is** made perfect in my weakness. "Therefore I take pleasure in infirmities, in reproaches, in necessities, in persecutions, in distresses for Christ's sake: for when I am weak, then am I strong" –II Corinthians 12:10. I do not need to fear my weakness, because the Lord is the strength of my life.

# Believe in Me

John 14:1

*"Let not your heart be troubled: ye believe in God, believe also in me."*

Believe *in* Christ! Many believe *about* Jesus Christ, but He desires that we believe *in* Him. Believe that He *is* the Son of God, who *is* the Salvation of our souls. For if we will "confess with [our] mouth the Lord Jesus, and shalt believe in [our] heart that God hath raised him from the dead, [we shall] be saved"—Romans 10:9. Once we are saved let us believe that He *is* with us, by His Spirit, so that we will not "give place to the devil"—Ephesians 4:27.

Believe that He *is* holy, and that because we are saved through faith in Jesus Christ, then we ought to also strive to be holy. "For if the firstfruit be holy, the lump is also holy: and if the root be holy, so are the branches"—Romans 11:16.

The more we get to know our Lord Jesus, the closer our hearts will draw toward Him, and the greater our belief will be *in* Him. We get to know Him better when we spend time with Him. It is alone with Him that He reveals Himself to us by opening our understanding of the Scriptures. He becomes *real* to us, not as some mystical being out there somewhere, but as someone right beside us, listening to us and talking with us. "Believe also in me" said the Lord Jesus, not merely believe about Him.

## The Power of the Cross

Have you been to Jesus
For His cleansing power?
Have you sought His face
For one sweet hour?

Have you bowed your face
Kneeling before His throne?
His tender embrace
Have you ever known?

Have you confessed your sin
At the foot of His cross?
Has He entered in
Are you no longer lost?

He came to seek and to save
For the world He bled and died
All sin, He readily forgave
When He was crucified

He stands ready to forgive
All who call upon His Name
And because He ever lives
We in Christ will do the same

# No Confusion

Psalm 71:1

*"In thee, O LORD, do I put my trust: let me never be put to confusion."*

"God is not the author of confusion"—I Corinthians 14:33a; therefore, we must realize that when we become confused it is not from God. The devil would like to get us off track and out of step with the Lord and completely confused. He will attempt to do that by planting doubt in our minds when trouble comes, or when circumstances do not go according to *our* plans. We must not be "ignorant of his devices"—II Corinthians 2:11b, but ever be mindful that "God is our refuge and strength, a very present help in trouble"—Psalm 46:1.

We become confused when we stop "looking unto Jesus the author and finisher of our faith; who for the joy that was set before him endured the cross, despising the shame, and is set down at the right hand of the throne of God"—Hebrews 12:2. We open the door to confusion when we yield to fears, when we doubt God's love for us, His care for us, and His presence with us. We must remember that "the earth is full of the goodness of the LORD"—Psalm 33:5. Let's "praise the LORD for his goodness, and for his wonderful works to the children of men!"—Psalm 107:15b. King David said, "I had fainted, unless I had believed to see the goodness of the LORD in the land of the living"—Psalm 27:13. When our hearts and minds are filled with the praises of God's goodness, then our faith is strengthened in God who is our Help and our Deliverer, and we are less likely to be put to confusion.

**Day 98**

# Walking with the Lord

I Corinthians 15:58

*"Therefore, my beloved brethren, be ye stedfast, unmoveable, always abounding in the work of the Lord, forasmuch as ye know that your labour is not in vain in the Lord."*

Under inspiration of God's Holy Spirit, the Apostle Paul is urging Christians to be stedfast in the faith of the Gospel of Jesus Christ. Being stedfast means to be diligent, unwavering in our faith by determining that "[our] heart is fixed"—Psalm 57:7a on God Almighty. Stedfast Christians do not walk "in the vanity of their mind"—Ephesians 4:17b, but in the truth of the Gospel of Jesus Christ. They are not "carried about with every wind of doctrine, by the sleight of men, and cunning craftiness, whereby they lie in wait to deceive"—Ephesians 4:14, but they are firm in the sound doctrine of Jesus Christ. They "are not ignorant of [Satan's] devices"—II Corinthians 2:11 to deceive, but they walk stedfast by committing themselves firmly to the truth of the Word of God.

Christians are also exhorted in this verse to be unmovable in their faith. Unmovable Christians do not change their position in Christ because of society changes or any other kind of temporal changes. They are "always abounding in the work of the Lord" regardless of peer pressure, popularity, or opposition. As Christians, we can be unmovable because our hope is in the Lord Jesus Christ, and we know that our labour is not in vain in the Lord.

Finally, we are exhorted to abound in the work of the Lord. "Whether therefore [we] eat, or drink, or whatsoever [we] do, do all to the glory of God"—I Corinthians 10:31. Abounding in the work of the Lord means to be an extension of the life of Christ as He lived while on earth so that we may bring glory to Him and the Father. Therefore, we need to "pray always"—Luke 21:36a, to be "fishers of men"—Matthew 4:19b, to "love one another"—John 13:34a, and do so through the power of the Holy Spirit by yielding ourselves unto Him. Let us be diligent to be "stedfast, unmoveable, always abounding in the work of the Lord, forasmuch as ye know that your labour is not in vain in the Lord."

# Meditating on the Love of God

Psalm 63:5b-6

*"My mouth shall praise thee with joyful lips: When I remember thee upon my bed, and meditate on thee in the night watches."*

The greatest thing we can think on is "his great love wherewith he loved us"—Ephesians 2:4b. "For God so loved the world, that he gave his only begotten Son, that whosoever believeth in him should not perish, but have everlasting life"—John 3:16. The Lord Jesus said, "I lay down my life for the sheep. . . . No man taketh it from me, but I lay it down of myself. I have power to lay it down, and I have power to take it again. This commandment have I received of my Father"—John 10:15b, 18. "As the Father hath loved me, so have I loved you. . . . Greater love hath no man than this, that a man lay down his life for his friends"—John 15:9a, 13. Such great love God the Father and His Son, Jesus Christ, has for us! God so loved that He gave Jesus to us, and Jesus so loved that He gave His life for us.

If we would just think on this great love showed to us, we would never feel unloved again. When we remember God's great love for us, it will also put us in mind of His great mercies toward us and of His amazing grace given to us. His mercy keeps us from receiving what we deserve—Hell; and His grace gives us what we do not deserve—Heaven! When we think of our great God and Saviour in this way we cannot help but praise Him with joyful lips; therefore, let us take time each day to meditate upon the Lord and all He has done for us because of His great love for us.

**Day 100**

# Inherited Promise

Hebrews 6:12

*"That ye be not slothful, but followers of them who through faith and patience inherit the promises."*

It is by faith in God, who "cannot lie"—Titus 1:2, that we inherit the promises of God. God promised Abraham that he would be the father of many nations; however, his faith was tried for many years before his promised son, Isaac, was born. Abraham "staggered not at the promise of God through unbelief; but was strong in faith, giving glory to God; And being fully persuaded that, what he had promised, he was able also to perform"—Romans 4:20-21. When Abraham placed the matter into God's hands, and took his own hands off, then he was able to continue strong in faith, believing that what God had promised, He would do.

Our faith is increased and strengthened when we look unto the Lord Jesus, because He is "the author and finisher of our faith"—Hebrews 12:2a. It is the very trial of our faith that compels us to depend more upon the Lord and to keep looking to Him for the inherited promises. Abraham endured many trials of his faith, but he chose to believe God. "After he had patiently endured, he obtained the promise"—Hebrews 6:15. "God hath dealt to every man the measure of faith"—Romans 12:3b; therefore, in order for us to obtain God's promises, we must exercise the faith we have been given, and choose to believe God and rest on His Word.

# Rejoice, the Lord Is Risen as He Said

Luke 24:5-6

*"Why seek ye the living among the dead? He is not here, but is risen."*

These words should cause the heart of the child of God to beat with exuberant joy, for here it is in black and white in the very Word of God – that our blessed Savior is ALIVE! We indeed serve a RISEN Savior! He is not dead, but is alive, sitting at His rightful place by His Father in Heaven. He is also interceding for all that are His, for "he ever liveth to make intercession for them" –Hebrews 7:25. "It is Christ that died, yea rather, that is risen again, who is even at the right hand of God, who also maketh intercession for us"—Romans 8:34. He arose victorious over death and hell; corruption could not take hold of Him for He is incorruption.

Since Christ has risen, I have a glorious hope because of this promise: "When Christ, who is our life, shall appear, then shall ye also appear with him in glory"—Colossians 3:2. Take hold of hope today, dear Christian, that this life and its turmoil and tribulations will not last forever. One day the blessed Savior will call to us and we will go Home to Heaven, where we shall forever live with Him! Do not give way to despair; but rather, "look up . . . for your redemption draweth nigh"—Luke 21:28. We have power because of Christ and His resurrection, so we can look up today and rejoice that the Spirit of the risen Savior lives within our hearts!

## Day 102

# Having Holy Spirit Power

I Thessalonians 5:19

*"Quench not the Spirit."*

There are many ways in which we can quench the Spirit on a daily basis. First, it may be that we do not "rejoice evermore"—I Thessalonians 5:16. Usually when all is going well we rejoice; however, the moment something occurs to impede the order of our day we may be inclined to complain and become anxious. When we do not rejoice in everything, both good and bad, then we are quenching the Spirit that lives within us. Secondly, the Word of God teaches us that we can quench His Spirit if we do not "pray without ceasing"—I Thessalonians 5:17. The majority of Christians turn to God in prayer during a crisis, but only a few of us are meeting Him "in the secret place"—Psalm 91:1a daily to worship Him and to pray. When we fail to pray we are quenching the Holy Spirit of God. Then thirdly, we can quench the Holy Spirit by not being thankful "in everything"—I Thessalonians 5:18. We have, for the most part, become an unthankful people, unthankful for our family, our friends, our neighbors, and our co-workers. Many times we do not thank one another for a kindness shown, a gift given, or help given in a difficult situation. Our society, in general, has become a self-centered society; and when the focus is on self, our thoughts are not generally going to be of others; therefore, un-thankfulness becomes more and more the norm.

As Christians, our power to serve God and lead others to salvation in His Son, Jesus Christ, as well as to live the victorious Christian life, in general, comes from the Holy Spirit of God who lives within us. When we quench the Holy Spirit then our power decreases. The Lord Jesus said, "He that believeth on me, as the scripture hath said, out of his belly shall flow rivers of living water. (But this spake he of the Spirit, which they that believe on him should receive: for the Holy Ghost was not yet given; because that Jesus was not yet glorified.)"—John 7:38-39. When we do not rejoice, do not pray, and do not give thanks in everything, we are hindering the Holy Spirit's power in us. Let us seek the Lord's help so that we will not quench the Spirit and thus impede the work of the Lord.

# Stirred Up

II Timothy 1:6

*"Wherefore I put thee in remembrance that thou stir up the gift of God, which is in thee by the putting on of my hands."*

In essence the Apostle Paul is telling Timothy, "Remember, God has given you the Holy Spirit"; therefore, "stir up the gift of God" and be obedient unto Him when He encourages you to do something. "Grieve not the holy Spirit of God, whereby ye are sealed unto the day of redemption"—Ephesians 4:30. All who have received Christ as their Saviour have been given the Holy Spirit, and He lives in us. When we disobey Him, we grieve Him and hinder His working in and through us. However, we can stir up this gift that God has given by our obedience and surrendering the control of ourselves unto Him. We have been given the spirit of power so that we may courageously face difficulties. We have been given the spirit of love so that we may be carried through opposition. And we have been given the spirit of a sound mind so that we may not yield to fears that can put a stranglehold on us, but can "be bold as a lion"—Proverbs 28:1b. Therefore, when you feel the compulsion to call a brother or sister in Christ to encourage them, be obedient and make that call, for that is the Holy Spirit nudging you. When you are compelled to do something that would encourage or edify the brethren and glorify the Lord, then be obedient to that leading of the Holy Spirit who lives in you.

## Day 104

# The Destroyer

I Corinthians 10:10

*"Neither murmur ye, as some of them also murmured, and were destroyed of the destroyer."*

Murmuring, which is the expression of discontentment about something or someone in a subdued manner, is a destroyer. Murmuring greatly provokes the Lord, and it is in our best interest to learn from those who did murmur, because their stories were "written for our admonition"—I Corinthians 10:11b. It is a destroyer of joy when we focus on our discontentment and not on the Lord. The "joy of the LORD is your strength"—Nehemiah 8:10b; however, murmuring and complaining can overwhelm our spirit—Psalm 77:3.

Murmuring can also be a destroyer of peace. When discontentment dominates us we become dissatisfied, which leads to murmuring; therefore, we lack that inner peace that the Bible describes as a peace that "passeth all understanding"—Philippians 4:7b. Believing that God is in control of the events in our lives can put an end to murmuring, for Faith says, *God sent this; therefore, it must be good for me in order to glorify Him.*

May we seek to see God in every aspect of our lives so that we will not yield to murmuring and be defeated by the Destroyer—the Devil.

# God's Word Fulfilled

Luke 1:20

*"And, behold, thou shalt be dumb, and not able to speak, until the day that these things shall be performed, because thou believest not my words, which shall be fulfilled in their season."*

God's Word will be fulfilled in His perfect timing, regardless of whether or not we believe it; there ***will be*** a performance of those things which He has spoken. Every circumstance can look contrary to what He has said, but that doesn't matter, because God's Word is going to be fulfilled. "For all the promises of God in him are yea [yes], and in him Amen [so be it], unto the glory of God by us"—II Corinthians 1:20.

In the days of Noah "God saw that the wickedness of man was great in the earth, and that every imagination of the thoughts of his heart was only evil continually"—Genesis 6:5; therefore, "God said unto Noah, The end of all flesh is come before me . . . Make thee an ark of gopher wood . . . behold, I , even I, do bring a flood of waters upon the earth, to destroy all flesh . . . "—Genesis 6:13, 14, 17. Noah had never before heard of rain, let alone seen rain, because it had never rained upon the earth at that time; however, God said it was going to rain, so Noah began to obediently build the ark in preparation for this thing that was going to happen. The rain did not come for more than 100 years; however, just before it came, in God's appointed time, "The LORD said unto Noah, Come thou and all thy house into the ark . . . And the rain was upon the earth forty days and forty nights"—Genesis 7:1, 12.

We can be as sure today as Noah was in his day, that God's Word will be fulfilled in due season. It may be that you are in a situation just now that appears hopeless. God's Word says, "It is of the LORD's mercies that we are not consumed, because his compassions fail not. They are new every morning: great is thy faithfulness. The LORD is my portion, saith my soul; therefore will I hope in him"—Lamentations 3:22-25. Whatever God has spoken, believe that His Word will be fulfilled "in their season" regardless of contrary appearances.

## Day 106

# Waiting on God with Confidence

Psalm 25:20-21

*"O keep my soul, and deliver me: let me not be ashamed; for I put my trust in thee. Let integrity and uprightness preserve me, for I wait on thee."*

While we are waiting on the Lord to answer our prayers, it is possible for us to grow impatient, doubtful, and fearful that He is not listening. Therefore, we must do as the Psalmist did and plead with the Lord to "let integrity and uprightness" keep us from these shortcomings. To succeed in waiting on the Lord, we must surrender our will to the Father's will. When we have a singleness of heart toward God and a surrendered will to His, we can wait on Him with the confidence of a child and boldly claim the expected promise with calmness and joy. When our hearts are honest before the Lord, we will, with humility, "give unto the Lord the glory due unto his name"—I Chronicles 16:29a, seeking no glory for ourselves. Then we will be able to wait on Him with a fuller consciousness and greater confidence that only He is able to answer, that He desires to answer, and that He will answer according as He has promised. When we wait on the Lord in this honest and upright way, time no longer becomes a factor. We are able to confidently say, *Lord, I know You see that I am waiting and You will answer according to Your Divine time.* This confidence comes from fully surrendering to His will, resting in His Word, and waiting for His time, all while believing He **does** hear and He **will** answer. The closer we get to the Lord and the more we learn of Him the more we will, with confidence, wait on Him. "Let integrity and uprightness" keep you waiting on the Lord.

# Waiting on God in Faith

Psalm 27:14

*"Wait on the LORD: be of good courage, and he shall strengthen thine heart: wait, I say, on the LORD."*

"Be of good courage!" Remember upon whom you are waiting and take up "the shield of faith, wherewith ye shall be able to quench all the fiery darts of the wicked"—Ephesians 6:16. Before charging us to "wait on the LORD," the Psalmist said, "I had fainted, unless I had believed to see the goodness of the LORD in the land of the living"—Psalm 27:13. Waiting on the Lord will take faith; therefore be of good courage and **believe** that you are waiting on *the* God who only is able to help and will help. One of the things we will need when we wait on the Lord is a strong confidence that our waiting is not in vain. Many times while we are waiting we may not feel that God is at work, but we must remember that faith is not a feeling: faith is taking God at His Word. Therefore, as we wait, we must be frequently in His Word, for "faith cometh by hearing, and hearing by the word of God"—Romans 10:17. We are not going to be waiting on ourselves to see what we feel or what we can do; we are going to be waiting on God so that we will discover who He is and what He will do. Above everything, we must wait on God with the spirit of hopefulness because it is on God in His glory, His blessedness, His never-failing love that we are waiting. We will draw strength from being in the light of God's presence; therefore, let us "be of good courage, and he shall strengthen [our] heart; wait, I say, on the LORD."

## *Day 108*

# Waiting on God with Your Heart

Psalm 27:14

*"Wait on the LORD: be of good courage, and he shall strengthen thine heart: wait, I say, on the LORD."*

When we wait on the Lord, we must wait on Him with our heart. "Be of good courage, and he shall strengthen thine heart." Our waiting on God is dependent upon the condition of our heart, "for as he thinketh in his heart, so is he"—Proverbs 23:7a. We must differentiate between knowing with our mind and believing with our heart. Unfortunately many Christians suppose that abundant knowledge of God's Word is all that is necessary to becoming strong and steadfast; however, knowledge that is not cultivated and processed with the heart will produce little comfort and courage when the battles and trials come into our lives. We must have knowledge as well as the application of God's Word in our lives. We can know the promises of God, but it isn't the knowledge of our minds that helps us to wait on the Lord; it is the believing with our heart that helps us to wait on Him.

"Trust in the LORD with all thine heart; and lean not unto thine own understanding"—Proverbs 3:5. We gather knowledge from God's Word with the intellect of our mind, but it is with the heart that the Spirit within us directs us to love, trust, worship, and obey God. The heart must wait on God so that His Spirit can work love, trust, worship, and obedience in us. Therefore the condition of our hearts is essential to the cultivating of God's Word in us. We must be careful not to lean on our own understanding, but get before the Lord in quietness and humility and allow Him to search our hearts so that He can take what we have learned and make application of it in our lives. The more we wait on the Lord with our heart, the greater our faith in Him will grow. It is during these times of waiting on Him with our hearts that He reveals Himself to us and makes the knowledge we have attained from Scripture alive in our hearts so that He and His Word become real as life to us, and our love and desire for Him is enlarged. "Wait on the LORD . . . and he shall strengthen thine heart: wait, I say, on the LORD."

# Waiting on God for His Counsel

Psalm 106:13

*"They soon forgat his works; they waited not for his counsel."*

This was being said of the children of Israel, God's chosen people, as they were in the wilderness. God had delivered them out of the hand of Pharaoh. He had made a way for His people to cross the Red Sea and had victoriously defeated the Egyptian army. "He rebuked the Red sea also, and it was dried up: so he led them through the depths, as through the wilderness. And he saved them from the hand of him that hated them, and redeemed them from the hand of the enemy. And the waters covered their enemies: there was not one of them left"—Psalm 106:9-11. However, "they soon forgat his works; they waited not for his counsel."

This has been the sin of God's people throughout the generations. God meets a need and makes a way for us when it seems there is no way, yet when another need arises later on in our life, we tend to forget God's previous miraculous works and do not wait for His counsel. When the Lord Jesus taught His disciples to pray, He said, "After this manner therefore pray ye: Our Father which art in heaven, Hallowed be thy name. Thy kingdom come. Thy will be done in earth, as it is in heaven"—Matthew 6:9-10. As Christians, we are to carry out the Heavenly Father's will here on earth, and it is by prayer with an open Bible before us that we come to learn what His will is. Each child of God has been given the Holy Spirit and the promise that He "will guide [us] into all truth . . . and he will shew [us] things to come. He shall glorify me (Jesus): for he shall receive of mine, and shall shew it unto you"— John 16:13-14. His Spirit is available to guide us as we read God's Word, as we pray, in our Christian labors, in our daily living. But in order to receive His guidance and counsel, we have to patiently wait to hear from Him instead of forging ahead and making decisions without Him. God always works according to the counsel of His own will; therefore, we must take the time to ascertain the mind of God in whatever we do. The more that we seek His counsel and do His will, the more He will do His work for us and through us as He has promised. Therefore, we must take the time to wait on God for His counsel.

## Day 110

# Waiting on God Together

Isaiah 25:9

*"And it shall be said in that day, Lo, this is our God; we have waited for him, and he will save us: this is the LORD; we have waited for him, we will be glad and rejoice in his salvation."*

In this verse of Scripture there was a united waiting for God among His people, and the fruit of their waiting was an abundant joy that led them to say, "Lo, this is our God . . . this is the LORD."

It is this kind of waiting on the Lord that we need among Christian brothers and sisters in our churches. The importance of this collective waiting together is made clear, as twice in this verse it was said, "*we* have waited for him." Many churches would still have their doors open, and would not have had to shut down if the people had come together to pray and wait for God. In our day of fast food, instant this and that, many people have been led away from waiting on anything, including waiting on God. If we would come to the place as they did in this verse, and during times of trouble gather together to seek and to wait on God, then we too would be able to proclaim, "this is the LORD . . . we will be glad and rejoice in his salvation."

To wait on God in this way requires a more humble understanding of our utter helplessness and deep dependence upon God, as well as a deeper conviction that apart from God we can do nothing. It would require us to have a greater awareness and consciousness of His presence and His ability to care for our need however great it may be, and that without Him we are completely helpless. We must have a more concentrated consciousness of His high place of honor and of power so that we may confidently expect that He will, by His Spirit, show Himself mighty to take care of our pressing needs. Together, we must wait on God to demonstrate His glory and power and bring about our deliverance. "And it shall be said in that day, Lo, this is our God; we have waited for him, and he will save us: this is the LORD; we have waited for him, we will be glad and rejoice in his salvation."

# Alive in Christ

Romans 6:11

*"Likewise reckon ye also yourselves to be dead indeed unto sin, but alive unto God through Jesus Christ our Lord."*

As believers, we are alive "unto God through Jesus Christ"; therefore, the person we were before we came to Christ has been made new. So why do we continue to live and act like we did before we were saved? The answer is simple; we have not reckoned ourselves to be dead unto sin and alive unto God. As a result we do not yield ourselves unto God, but we continue to yield to the sins of our old nature. Once we "yield [ourselves] unto God, as those that are alive from the dead, and [our] members as instruments of righteousness unto God"—Romans 6:13b, then we will begin to have victory over our sinful nature. Can you imagine the number of wrecks there would be if no one yielded the right of way when entering an Interstate or highway? Well, the same is true of us as Christians with God; if we do not yield our right of way to Him, then we will continue to be defeated by our sinful nature. When we yield ourselves to God, "sin shall not have dominion over [us]: for [we] are not under the law, but under grace"—Romans 6:14.

It is by the grace of God that we overcome our sinful nature; therefore, when our old nature begins to rise up and wants to rule us, we need to stop and declare, out loud, if necessary, "Jesus, I belong to You! Live Your life through me as I yield myself unto You." If we have to yield ourselves to God a thousand times a day, then we must do so in order to gain the victory over our sinful nature and be alive unto God. It is not our effort that will gain the victory, but simply yielding ourselves to God and letting His Holy Spirit do the changing in us so that we can begin to imitate our Lord Jesus Christ, and have victory over our sinful nature.

## Day 112

# The Soul's Daily Refreshment

Hosea 14:5

*"I will be as the dew unto Israel: he shall grow as the lily, and cast forth his roots as Lebanon."*

Dew is refreshment to the earth that is formed when warmer temperatures of the day decrease during the night, producing droplets of water upon vegetation. This refreshing and renewing dew invigorates the vegetation and causes it to grow. To the Christian, time spent with the Lord brings refreshment to the soul, which is the reason He says, "I will be as the dew unto Israel." When the trials, temptations, and battles we face in our Christian lives become greater and greater, we need this spiritual refreshing and renewal more and more. This refreshment comes when we seek the presence of the Lord in prayer, in Bible reading, in study and in meditation upon God's Word.

Our physical strength weakens when we do not eat. Our spiritual strength weakens when we do not spend time with God. We cannot be sustained by an occasional meeting with the Lord; we must spend time alone with Him daily in order to refresh and renew our walk with Him and for Him. King David, the sweet psalmist of Israel, said, "Evening, and morning, and at noon, will I pray, and cry aloud: and he shall hear my voice" –Psalm 55:17. The Prophet Daniel "kneeled upon his knees three times a day, and prayed, and gave thanks before his God" –Daniel 6:10c.

The dew refreshes the vegetation on earth. Meeting with God refreshes us. Time spent with Him not only refreshes our spirit, but it also strengthens us to stand in the midst of great trials, temptations, and battles that we may experience. The Lord God Almighty will be as the dew to refresh us, so let us come unto Him and allow Him to "create in [us] a clean heart, and renew a right spirit within [us]"—Psalm 51:10. When our hearts are clean before Him, and our spirits are in harmony with His Spirit, then we can have a greater influence in the lives of others for the Lord Jesus Christ.

# The Freedom of Forgiveness

Matthew 6:14-15

*"For if ye forgive men their trespasses, your heavenly Father will also forgive you: But if ye forgive not men their trespasses, neither will your Father forgive your trespasses."*

An unforgiving spirit is a hindrance to our prayers, because it is sin, and "if I regard iniquity [sin] in my heart, the Lord will not hear me"—Psalm 66:18. It isn't that He **cannot** hear, but that He **will not** hear. He is a holy God, and our hearts need to be pure before Him in order for Him to fellowship with us in prayer. "Who shall ascend into the hill of the LORD? Or who shall stand in his holy place? He that hath clean hands, and a pure heart; who hath not lifted up his soul unto vanity, nor sworn deceitfully"—Psalm 24:3-4. "Truly God is good to Israel [and Christians], even to such as are of a clean heart"—Psalm 73:1; therefore, "purify your hearts"—James 4:8b of any unforgiveness toward anyone.

"If we confess our sins, he is faithful and just to forgive us our sins, and to cleanse us from all unrighteousness"—I John 1:9; therefore, consider today if your heart is pure before Him of any unconfessed sin—including unforgiveness. If there is someone you have not forgiven, "when ye stand praying, forgive, if ye have ought against any: that your Father also which is in heaven may forgive you your trespasses"—Mark 11:25. God will, by His Spirit, help you to forgive that person. When we harbor grudges and do not forgive, we are the ones who are affected the most, because it breaks our fellowship with our Heavenly Father and robs us of our peace and joy in the Lord. If we do not forgive others, then our Heavenly Father will not forgive us. If you want to know the undisturbed peace with God and joy in the Lord, then be quick to forgive others and cast those cares upon the Lord.

**Day 114**

# By My Spirit

Zechariah 4:6

*"Then he answered and spake unto me, saying, This is the word of the LORD unto Zerubbabel, saying, Not by might, nor by power, but by my spirit, saith the LORD of hosts."*

God does not need any of us in order to carry out His purposes; however, He graciously chooses to use us as His vessels to accomplish His work. It will never be by any might of our own strength, for the flesh, at its best, is weak. It will never be by any power of our own, because apart from Christ we can do nothing. It is by the Spirit of the Lord that His work will be accomplished through His people; therefore, we must remember, it will not be by our might, nor by our power that we will be able to successfully overcome Satan's attacks; rather, it will be by the Spirit of the Lord, for "the LORD said unto Satan, The LORD rebuke thee, O Satan; even the LORD that hath chosen Jerusalem rebuke thee: is not this a brand plucked out of the fire?"—Zechariah 3:2. By grace we were "plucked out of the fire"—saved—and it will be His grace, through faith in Christ, that will bring us Christian victory against the attacks of our enemy—Satan.

It is the Spirit of the Lord who works in us to accomplish anything for the Lord. Victory in Christ will come by the Holy Spirit; revival in our churches will come by the Holy Spirit; every work of the Lord, and for the Lord, will come by His Holy Spirit. May we humble ourselves before the Lord, submit ourselves to His Holy Spirit, and stop trying to do anything in our might or power so that He may accomplish His purposes through us. "Not by might, nor by power, but by my spirit, saith the LORD of hosts."

# Open Our Eyes

II Kings 6:17

*"And Elisha prayed, and said, LORD, I pray thee, open his eyes, that he may see. And the LORD opened the eyes of the young man; and he saw: and, behold, the mountain was full of horses and chariots of fire round about Elisha."*

This is the prayer that we, as Christians, need to pray, "Lord, open our eyes" in order that we may see the power of God and His glory all around us. Our enemy the devil would have us to believe we are outnumbered and are a defeated people; however, we must remember that "they that be with us are more than they that be with them" –II Kings 6:16. "If God be for us, who can be against us?" –Romans 8:31b May we see the multitude of our Lord's army all around us, ready for battle. May we see our Captain praying for us, that our faith would not fail –Luke 22:32. Our hope is in the Lord; therefore, let us pray that He would open our eyes to see that our strength lies in Him and His battalion. He will fight for us: "behold, God himself is with us for our captain" –II Chronicles 13:12a.

The enemy is seeking to weaken and to "wear out" God's people –Daniel 7:25 by a continual siege, so that from sheer weakness we let go of our victory cry. When the enemy attacks us we need to pray that the Lord will open our eyes, so that we may behold our Lord's army and be strengthened to press on, shouting the victory in Jesus Christ.

**Day 116**

# Time to Worship

Job 1:20

*"Then Job arose, and rent his mantle, and shaved his head, and fell down upon the ground, and worshipped."*

The time to worship the God of all gods is now—during all seasons of our life. Job had just received word that his entire wealth of livestock were either killed or stolen, and all of his children were dead. His heart was overwhelmed with grief and sorrow; however, he "fell down upon the ground, and worshipped." It was not a time to curse God; it was a time to worship Him. Job believed and trusted that God would do only what was ultimately for his good and God's glory; therefore, he was able to say, "Naked came I out of my mother's womb, and naked shall I return thither: the LORD gave, and the LORD hath taken away; blessed be the name of the LORD"—Job 1:21.

It is time to worship the Lord when everything would seem to indicate that God has left us, and Satan has gotten the upper hand. It is time to worship when our hearts are heavy with sorrow. It is time to worship when we do not understand the Lord's dealings with us. The Lord of Heaven and earth is too good to be unkind, and He loves us too much to be cruel. It was this God who "so loved the world, that he gave his only begotten Son, that whosoever believeth in him should not perish, but have everlasting life"—John 3:16. Thinking that God has dealt unjustly with us is a lie that the Devil wants us to believe. Be strong in faith, and follow the example of Job so that when overwhelming trials come, you also will be able to say, "Shall we receive good at the hand of God, and shall we not receive evil?"—Job 2:10b. Believing that our life is in the hand of the Lord, and that all He does is with the intention for our good, will help us to worship the Lord even in sorrow, as Job did.

# Being Led by the Right Way

Psalm 107:7

*"And he led them forth by the right way, that they might go to a city of habitation."*

The Lord will always lead His children by the right way. The way may be a path of difficulties, sorrows, and changes; but when God is leading, it is by the right way. When change occurs in our life, we may become anxious and inquire: "Why is this happening to me?" Yesterday light illumined the path, but today it is dark with clouds. Yesterday we had confidence in the future as we viewed it from the mountaintop, but today the future appears uncertain down in the valley below. Instead of a path of hope, it would seem to be full of fears and distress, causing us to wonder if this could possibly be God's plan and leading for our life. Though our faith may dim, and our hopes grow faint, we may be certain that our Lord is leading us forth by the right way if we are truly seeking His guidance. All these trials are for the testing and strengthening of our faith. "He knoweth the way that I take: when he hath tried me, I shall come forth as gold" –Job 23:10.

We may be led upon a stormy path, but our Lord is at the helm, traversing the waves for us. As we pray and seek His guidance, may we "listen" for His voice, as did the psalmist, so He can speak to our heart: "Be still, and know that I am God" –Psalm 46:10a. We must not think that our sorrows and difficulties are out of God's plan; rather, we need to understand that they are necessary parts of His plan, which is for our good, so that we may be molded into a better likeness of our Savior, Jesus Christ. "We must through much tribulation enter into the kingdom of God" –Acts 14:22b, remembering that He is leading us forth by the right way.

*O let my trembling soul be still, and wait Thy wise, Thy holy will! I cannot, Lord, Thy purpose see, yet all is well since ruled by Thee. –Charles Hadden Spurgeon*

**Day 118**

# Being Christ Minded

Philippians 2:2

*"Fulfill ye my joy, that ye be likeminded, having the same love, being of one accord, of one mind."*

"Let this mind be in you which was also in Christ Jesus" –Philippians 2:5. The very Creator God of Heaven took on Himself "the form of a servant . . . humbled himself, and became obedient unto death, even the death of the cross" –Philippians 2:7-8. It is His desire that we be of the same humble and obedient mind. Christ Jesus obeyed the Father even unto death and demonstrated humility when "he poureth water into a bason, and began to wash the disciples' feet" –John 13:5. His heart's love for the Father and for His redeemed led Him to obedience and to humility.

"If there be therefore any consolation in Christ, if any comfort of love, if any fellowship of the Spirit, if any bowels and mercies," we must "be likeminded, having the same love" –Philippians 2:1-2. "Let nothing be done through strife or vainglory; but in lowliness of mind let each esteem other better than themselves" –Philippians 2:3. Be of "one mind," that Christ and His Spirit can be evidenced in you and that His purposes can be accomplished through you. We will be of one mind, in Christ, when we seek to serve Him by serving others; when we make His will dearer to our hearts than our own will so that we will obey Him in all things. If we, the church today, are to have the power of Jesus Christ, then we must have the same love He had, be of one accord with Him, and be of His same mind.

# Trial of Our Faith

I Peter 1:6-7

*"Wherein ye greatly rejoice, though now for a season, if need be, ye are in heaviness through manifold temptations: That the trial of your faith, being much more precious than of gold that perisheth, though it be tried with fire, might be found unto praise and honour and glory at the appearing of Jesus Christ."*

We can learn from these verses that as children of God we are going to experience difficult times. However, the purpose of these trials of our faith is to refine us and make us become more like our Savior, Jesus Christ, so that we may bring glory to God. Trials compel us to "draw nigh to God"—James 4:8a. They help us learn to "trust in the Lord with all [our] heart"—Proverbs 3:5a. As we go through trials we learn that His grace is sufficient for us and that His strength is made perfect in our weakness—II Corinthians 12:9. Trials are designed to make us more conscious of our dependency upon Almighty God. He is ever trying to teach us that "without [Him we] can do nothing"—John 15:5b. We need Him for everything! Without trials we could not learn to trust in Him and our faith could not grow.

If you are in a trial of your faith today do not despair; rather, rejoice, and "count it all joy when ye fall into divers [various] temptations; Knowing this, that the trying of your faith worketh patience. But let patience have her perfect work, that ye may be perfect and entire, wanting [lacking] nothing"—James 1:1-4. God is teaching you to depend upon Him, and He is seeking to deepen your faith in Him. Remember that every trial is for our good and for God's glory. He is glorified and made glad when we lean upon Him and trust in Him.

# Faith—Unwavering

In dire straights and valleys low
Upon God's Word we can believe
Standing firm and confident --unwavering
In His time we shall receive

Though the answer coming tarries
And the tempter does all to deceive
God's Word will never fail
It's His promise we'll receive

So when it's answers that you need
It is upon His Word you must believe
And with boldness seek Him praying
For it is then you will receive

He is Alpha and Omega
The beginning and the end
Nothing is impossible
When we come unto Him

# A Bright Light

Matthew 5:14-16

*"Ye are the light of the world. A city that is set on an hill cannot be hid. Neither do men light a candle, and put it under a bushel, but on a candlestick; and it giveth light unto all that are in the house. Let your light so shine before men, that they may see your good works, and glorify your Father which is in heaven."*

In many instances our life is the only "Bible" that others will read; therefore, as a child of God, we need to let the light of Christ shine through us, for "In him [Christ] was life; and the life was the light of men"—John 1:4. As Christians we need to apply to our lives what we read in the Bible, doing "all things through Christ which strengtheneth [us]"—Philippians 4:13. It "is Christ in [us], the hope of glory"—Colossians 1:27b that enables us to "love [our] enemies, and do good, and lend, hoping for nothing again" and to be "merciful, as [our] Father also is merciful. Judge not . . . condemn not . . . forgive . . . Give . . . For with the same measure that ye mete withal it shall be measured to you again"—Luke 6:35-38. If we are born-again believers in Christ, then we have been given the Spirit of Christ; therefore, through the power of the Holy Spirit, the life of Christ can be lived through us.

The Lord Jesus Christ was never anxious. He did not waiver in His faith in God, the Father. He never had an unforgiving spirit. He did not have an unruly temper. He did "always those things that please him [God]"—John 8:29b. That life of Christ now lives in every believer; therefore, may the light of Christ shine through us by the power of the Holy Spirit so that others will see and glorify our Father in Heaven. May each of us allow the light of Christ's life to become an extension of His heart, His hands, His feet, His mind, His life to others around us by willingly turning from the old nature of our manner of life before salvation, to yielding to the leadership of the Holy Spirit in every aspect of our daily lives.

## *Day 121*

# Grace to Learn

Psalm 143:10a

*"Teach me to do thy will. . . . "*

It is not in human nature for Christians or non-Christians to follow the will of God. However, God gives grace to every Christian "both to will and to do of his good pleasure"—Philippians 2:13a. In order to learn to do His will we must surrender our will—that which our flesh desires—and "humble [ourselves] in the sight of the Lord"—James 4:10b. Then we must spend time with the Lord as did Mary, who "also sat at Jesus' feet, and heard his word"—Luke 10:39b. In order to learn the will of God, we must be taught the Word of God. The Lord Jesus is an excellent teacher. Many of us, however, are like Martha—"cumbered about much serving"—Luke 10:40, which hinders us from being alone with the Lord and learning His Word. We must not only want the Lord to show us His will, but we must also spend time with Him in order that we may learn how to live according to His will. May we take time daily to be with the Lord in prayer and meditating on His Word—the Bible—so that we may learn how to do His will.

# Acknowledging and Revealing

John 17:4

*"I have glorified thee on the earth: I have finished the work which thou gavest me to do."*

The Lord Jesus acknowledged and revealed the majesty and splendor of God with His life. He spoke of God's holiness and lived a holy life. He spoke of God's forgiveness and forgave by laying down His life on the cross of Calvary. He taught His disciples humility when He "began to wash the disciples' feet, and to wipe them with the towel wherewith he was girded"—John 13:5b.

In every facet of His life the Lord Jesus acknowledged and revealed God's glory. We, as Christians, should also acknowledge and reveal God's glory in our lives. We can only do this when we yield ourselves to the Holy Spirit and let Him reveal the holiness, love, humility, forgiveness, graciousness, and obedience of Jesus Christ through us. "Dearly beloved, I beseech you as strangers and pilgrims, abstain from fleshly lusts, which war against the soul; having your conversation honest among the Gentiles: that, whereas they speak against you as evildoers, they may by your good works, which they shall behold, glorify God in the day of visitation"—I Peter 2:11-12. May all of us acknowledge and reveal God's glory as long as we live on this earth.

**Day 123**

# Walking in the Light

Psalm 27:1

*"The LORD is my light and my salvation; whom shall I fear? The LORD is the strength of my life; of whom shall I be afraid?"*

Here is a personal assurance to every Christian—The LORD is *my* Light, *my* Salvation! We have the light of Christ within us, and His light dispels all the darkness of evil; therefore, the question is asked, "Whom shall I fear?" With Christ as *my* Light there is no one to fear, for "unto the upright there ariseth light in the darkness: he is gracious, and full of compassion, and righteous. . . . [We] shall not be afraid of evil tidings: [our] heart is fixed, trusting in the LORD"—Psalm 112:4, 7. "If I say, Surely the darkness shall cover me; even the night shall be light about me"—Psalm 139:11. Where Christ is, there is light, and His Light became our Light when we trusted Him as our Saviour.

The Lord doesn't just give light, He *is* Light. "This then is the message which we have heard of him, and declare unto you, that God is light, and in him is no darkness at all"—I John 1:5. The powers of darkness are not to be feared, because the Lord, our Light, has already defeated them. "Walk in the light, as he is in the light"—I John 1:7a, and we will have nothing and no one to fear.

# The Happiest People

Psalm 144:15b

*"Happy is that people . . . whose God is the LORD."*

We who have been saved by the blood of the Lamb should be the happiest people in the world; yet, so many Christians walk around defeated, depressed and discouraged. The devil, who is the Christian's enemy, has them right where he wants them. He didn't like losing the battle for their soul, so he will do all he can to keep them from living the glorious life in Christ. Satan is being much too successful, because many Christians are looking at their troubles in life rather than looking to God and His Son, Jesus Christ. "Happy is that people, whose God is the LORD," because He has freed them from the penalty of sin. "As far as the east is from the west, so far hath he removed our transgressions from us"—Psalm 103:12. At the day of salvation our sin was placed under the blood of Christ and we were given His righteousness. At that moment, God the Father accepted us "in the beloved"—Ephesians 1:6b. One of these days we are going to know Heaven as our eternal home, either at death or in the Rapture when "the Lord himself shall descend from heaven with a shout, with the voice of the archangel, and with the trump of God: and the dead in Christ shall rise first: Then we which are alive and remain shall be caught up together with them in the clouds, to meet the Lord in the air: and so shall we ever be with the Lord"—I Thessalonians 4:16-17. That truth alone should keep every Christian smiling and exceedingly happy. Therefore, if you are saved, remember that your eternal destination is Heaven where you will see your Saviour, Jesus Christ, face to face! The trials of this life are only for a moment, but the glories of Heaven will be for all eternity. Also, we can know the joy of the Lord here on earth if we will remember that we are "strangers and pilgrims on the earth"—Hebrews 11:13b and that God is our Lord. Let's persevere in the Christian race, for we will receive our eternal reward.

Secondly, "happy is that people . . . whose God is the LORD," because He has freed us from the power of sin. Sin has power over many Christians simply because they have not yielded themselves to the Lord. "Know ye not, that to whom ye yield yourselves servants to obey, his servants ye are to whom ye obey; whether of sin unto death, or of obedience unto righteousness?"—Romans 6:16. We become happy Christians when we yield ourselves unto the Lord, and we do that by resting in Christ. He will give us rest when we come to Him and yield ourselves to His power, His strength, His ability, His mercy, His grace, His love, His forgiveness, and His righteousness. Sin loses its power over us when we rest in all that Christ did for us on the cross of Calvary, surrender to His will and way, and live "by the faith of the Son of God, who loved [us] and gave himself for [us]"—Galatians 2:20b. Since we have been freed from the penalty and power of sin through Jesus Christ, then we can be truly happy, because the LORD is **our** God!

# Full of Power

Acts 6:5,8

*"And the saying pleased the whole multitude: and they chose Stephen, a man full of faith and of the Holy Ghost . . . And Stephen, full of faith and power, did great wonders and miracles among the people."*

To be full of the Holy Ghost is to be full of God's power, and this fullness of power will accomplish great wonders and miracles. Look at what the fullness of the Holy Ghost power accomplished through Stephen: 1. He was filled with wisdom and grace to respond well to His accusers: "And they were not able to resist the wisdom and the spirit by which he spake"—Acts 6:10. 2. The change in his countenance was clearly seen: "And all that sat in the council, looking stedfastly on him, saw his face as it had been the face of an angel"—Acts 6:15. 3. He was a bold witness for the Lord as we see in Acts 7:1-53. 4. He saw the glory of God: "But he, being full of the Holy Ghost, looked up stedfastly into heaven, and saw the glory of God, and Jesus standing on the right hand of God"—Acts 7:55. 5. He demonstrated a Christ-like love for his enemies: "And they stoned Stephen, calling upon God, and saying, Lord Jesus, receive my spirit. And he kneeled down, and cried with a loud voice, Lord, lay not this sin to their charge . . ."—Acts 7:59-60.

When someone is full of the Holy Spirit, then the character of Jesus Christ is predominate in that life. Stephen had surrendered his life to the will of God. As a result, the Holy Spirit controlled Stephen's actions and reactions toward his enemies, which empowered him to live the life of Christ before the people. The life of Stephen is a challenge for Christians today to be full of His power for the glory of God.

**Day 126**

# Working for Our Good

Romans 8:28

*"And we know that all things work together for good to them that love God, to them who are the called according to his purpose."*

"All things work together for good" means everything that occurs in the Christian's life—from the smallest event to the greatest hour of crisis, though it may not be good—is working for our good. The wonderful truth about this verse is that all things are presently working for good. Perhaps it is a delayed or cancelled flight; that dreaded diagnosis—*cancer*; that flat tire on the way to an appointment; whatever the "thing," it is at work right now in our life, for "all things work;" not working, not have worked, but presently working together for our good.

There is a higher plan and purpose that we do not see and may never know, but we can be sure that all things do work together for our good. God saw past Joseph's captivity to the thousands who were going to be in need because of a great famine that was going to come upon all the land—Genesis 41. Only God knows the "things" that will prepare us for His greater purpose and plan that He has for our lives. Therefore, when circumstances disrupt our day and possibly change the course of our life, remember that God is working them for our good. May we continue to look to God and accept and believe the fact that "all things work together for good to them that love God, to them who are the called according to his purpose."

# Sorrowing, Yet Always Rejoicing

II Corinthians 6:10

*"As sorrowful, yet alway rejoicing"*

In our Christian life we are going to experience heartache that brings sorrow; however, we can rejoice even in the midst of sorrow, because the Lord Jesus Christ is always there with us. "God hath said, I will dwell in them, and walk in them; and I will be their God, and they shall be my people" –II Corinthians 6:16c. He has promised to never leave us nor forsake us –Hebrews 13:5; therefore, in the midst of sorrow we are able to rejoice in Christ. Job experienced great sorrow when all ten of his children were killed, all of his livelihood was destroyed, and his body was covered with boils which caused him severe pain and discomfort; however, he said, "Naked came I out of my mother's womb, and naked shall I return thither: the LORD gave, and the LORD hath taken away; blessed be the name of the LORD" –Job 1:21.

As Christians, we will have sorrow, for "all that will live godly in Christ Jesus shall suffer persecution" –II Timothy 3:12, but through Christ, we will be able to rejoice in sorrow. Our rejoicing comes when we remember that our Saviour experienced sorrow while alive on earth, and therefore, understands our sorrow. We are able to take our sorrow to Him and share our heartache with Him. As a result, we receive comfort from Him, which will enable us to rejoice in Him at the same time our heart is sorrowing.

## *Day 128*

# I Shall Not Want

Psalm 23:1

*"The LORD is my shepherd; I shall not want."*

*I shall not want* [lack] any earthly thing because the Lord is my Shepherd. As a child of God I have been made an heir of God and a joint-heir with Christ –Romans 8:17; therefore, all that is the Lord's is now mine in Christ Jesus, who is my Shepherd. *I shall not want* [lack] my daily needs, for Christ instructed His disciples to pray, "Our Father. . . give us this day our daily bread" –Matthew 6: 10a-11; therefore, if we ask we will receive, because He is faithful to do as He has promised. *I shall not want* [lack] God's grace and glory, for "the LORD will give grace and glory: no good thing will he withhold from them that walk uprightly" –Psalm 84:11b. There is wonderful peace and security in this assurance, *I shall not want,* but it is known only to the sheep (those who have trusted Christ as Savior).

When we are united with Christ how can we lack when we have a right to all His riches? In Him we find rest, tranquility, refreshment, restoring mercies, guidance, peace in the midst of death, abundant blessings, great confidence and eternal security. His sheep have nothing to fear. According to your want –your need— will be your supply, for "the LORD is the portion of mine inheritance and of my cup: thou maintainest my lot" –Psalm 16:5. In all of life, we *shall not want*, but only if the Lord is our Shepherd.

# A Good Word

Proverbs 12:25

*"Heaviness in the heart of man maketh it stoop: but a good word maketh it glad."*

Fears, sorrows, and troubles weigh heavily upon the heart; however, when the Word of God is spoken, then received and applied by faith into the life of the hearer, the heart is made glad. When we see someone with a sad countenance, we can encourage that person with God's Word: "Let not your heart be troubled: ye believe in God, believe also in [Jesus]. . . . [He] will come again"!—John 14:1, 3b. "This same Jesus, which is taken up from you into heaven, shall so come in like manner as ye have seen him go into heaven"—Acts 1:11b. "When thou passest through the waters, I will be with thee; and through the rivers, they shall not overflow thee: when thou walkest through the fire, thou shalt not be burned: neither shall the flame kindle upon thee. For I am the LORD thy God, the Holy One of Israel, thy Saviour"—Isaiah 43:2-3a.

It may be that your own heart is stooped down with the cares of this life. Go to the Word of God and let ***Him*** speak ***His*** good Word to your heart so that you may be made glad. Listen to Him say, "I am the good shepherd, and know my sheep, and am known of mine. . . . My sheep hear my voice, and I know them, and they follow me: And I give unto them eternal life; and they shall never perish, neither shall any man pluck them out of my hand. My Father, which gave them me, is greater than all; and no man is able to pluck them out of my Father's hand"—John 10:14, 27-29. "These things I have spoken unto you, that in me ye might have peace. In the world ye shall have tribulation: but be of good cheer; I have overcome the world"—John 16:33. Our hearts may grow heavy at times, but the good Word of God will always make it glad.

## Day 130

# Leave It with the Lord

Job 5:8

*"I would seek unto God, and unto God would I commit my cause."*

It is easy for us to **take** our problems and concerns to the Lord, but many of us have a hard time **leaving** them with Him; we continue to hold on to them. In order to commit, or leave, something with the Lord we must release it completely and leave it with Him. If we get up off our knees and continue to worry and be anxious, then it is certain we did not leave the thing with the Lord. In order to be able to commit something to the Lord we must trust in Him. If we do not trust, we will not commit. We must exercise faith so that we may be able to say as did Job, "Naked came I out of my mother's womb, and naked shall I return thither; the LORD gave, and the LORD hath taken away; blessed be the name of the LORD"—Job 1:21. We must search the Scriptures for His promises, and then we must apply them to our lives by faith so that we can experience the truth of His Word. "For who in the heaven can be compared unto the LORD? Who among the sons of the mighty can be likened unto the LORD?. . . O LORD God of hosts, who is a strong LORD like unto thee? Or to thy faithfulness round about thee?. . . The heavens are thine, the earth also is thine: as for the world and the fullness thereof, thou hast founded them. . . . For the LORD is our defense; and the Holy One of Israel is our king"—Psalm 89:6, 8, 11, 18.

Our part is to take our concerns to the Lord and trust Him to work. Once we have done that, then He will do "great things and unsearchable; marvelous things without number"—Job 5:9. He works His part when we accomplish our part. When we can come away from the throne of grace with renewed faith and a glowing countenance, as Hannah did after she sought the Lord concerning her barren womb, then we can also expect great and marvelous things when we have sought the Lord and have left our cares and concerns with Him.

# Understanding and Knowing God

Jeremiah 9:23-24

*"Thus saith the LORD, Let not the wise man glory in his wisdom, neither let the mighty man glory in his might, let not the rich man glory in his riches: But let him that glorieth glory in this, that he understandeth and knoweth me, that I am the LORD which exercise lovingkindness, judgment, and righteousness, in the earth: for in these things I delight, saith the LORD."*

Wisdom, strength, and riches all come from God, for "every good gift and every perfect gift is from above, and cometh down from the Father of lights, with whom is no variableness, neither shadow of turning"—James 1:17. The question is, How well do we understand and know this truth? Any ability we may have, any wisdom, any wealth, any and all things come from God alone, for "In the beginning . . . All things were made by him; and without him was not any thing made that was made"—John 1:1a, 3. God provides the air we need to breathe, the materials we need to properly clothe ourselves, the food to eat, the ability to work and provide a living, shelter for us to live in—whether it be a house, an apartment, or mobile trailer. We may have purchased the house we live in; however, it was the Lord who provided the job and gave us the strength of body to work the job in order to earn the money to pay for the house or any other item, whether big or small.

Let us search the Scriptures so that we may better know the Lord our God and His Son, Jesus Christ, for "He hath made the earth by his power, he hath established the world by his wisdom, and hath stretched out the heavens by his discretion"—Jeremiah 10:12. Searching the Scriptures will give us a better understanding and knowledge of God's abundant resources and provisions for us, which will lead us to glorify Him, and in so doing, be a delight to Him. Therefore, "Let not the wise man glory in his wisdom, neither let the mighty man glory in his might, let not the rich man glory in his riches: But let him that glorieth glory in the LORD."

## Day 132

# Expectations and Beyond

Acts 12:5

*"Peter therefore was kept in prison: but prayer was made without ceasing of the church unto God for him."*

Prayer is the link that connects us directly to God, Who does "exceeding abundantly above" our expectations—Ephesians 3:20. The Apostle Peter was in prison, "but prayer was made without ceasing of the church unto God for him." "And, behold, the angel of the Lord came upon him . . . And his chains fell off from his hands. . . . And he went out . . . past the first and the second ward . . . unto the iron gate that leadeth unto the city; which opened to them of his own accord: and they went out, and passed on through one street"—Acts 12:7-10. Peter was freed from prison because of the prayers of fellow Christians. Prayer is our bridge to cross over every gulf of impossibility, because "with God all things are possible"—Matthew 19:26.

*Beware in your prayers, above everything, of limiting God, not only by unbelief, but by fancying that you know what He can do. Expect unexpected things, above all that we ask or think. Each time you intercede, be quiet first and worship God in His glory. Think of what He can do, of how He delights to hear Christ, of your place in Christ; and expect great things.*—Andrew Murray

Prayer can open to us all that God can do and above all we think He can do. He told King Solomon, "Ask what I shall give thee"—I Kings 3:5. Whether we are in sorrow, in joy and gladness, in extreme danger, in financial troubles, in uncertainty about some decision to make, prayer is our open door to God's abundant ability to work beyond our expectations.

# Glorious Rest

Isaiah 11:10

*"And in that day there shall be a root of Jesse, which shall stand for an ensign of the people; to it shall the Gentiles seek: and his rest shall be glorious."*

The rest that we have in our Lord Jesus Christ is a glorious rest. His rest is more than a refreshing ten-minute nap that can renew our strength so that we are better able to continue our duties of the day. It is more than a good night's rest that enables us to begin a new day energetically. The rest of our Lord is more than a two-week vacation designed to restore and renew our minds and our bodies. His rest is glorious, because it is full and complete. It encompasses the mind, the soul, and the body so completely that we experience a peace "which passeth all understanding" –Philippians 4:7.

His rest shall be glorious, but we must come unto Him to experience that rest. The Lord Jesus said, "Come unto me, all ye that labour and are heavy laden, and I will give you rest" –Matthew 11:28. He will give us rest from our fears, rest from our anxieties, rest from our labors, and rest from our battle against the devil's attacks. Whatever the circumstance, the Lord will give us rest when we come unto Him. The longer we experience His rest, the more glorious it becomes. His rest is complete. His rest is beyond our ability to fully comprehend it. Come unto Him and begin to experience this rest that He gives. His rest shall be glorious.

*Day 134*

# Christian Power

II Timothy 1:7

*"For God hath not given us the spirit of fear; but of power, and of love, and of a sound mind."*

God did not give the Christian the spirit of fear, which stems from the natural man, "for the Lord shall be [our] confidence, and shall keep [our] foot from being taken"—Proverbs 3:26. As Christians, we can have power over our old nature: "if any man be in Christ, he is a new creature: old things are passed away; behold, all things are become new"—II Corinthians 5:17. Therefore, we can have power over fearfulness, a bad temper, over timidity, over the sins of the flesh—whatever they may be—because every believer in Christ has the Holy Spirit of Christ living in them. It is by the Holy Spirit that we can become conquerors of our old nature so that the flesh no longer controls us. The more we tell our flesh "No" to whatever it lusts after, the more we will begin to say "Yes" to the ways of the Holy Spirit as He directs us. When we disobey the Holy Spirit, He is quenched and the fullness of His power in us is restricted so that our power over sin is hindered. "For they that are after the flesh do mind the things of the flesh; but they that are after the Spirit the things of the Spirit"—Romans 8:5.

As Christians, we are also given the Spirit of love, which can enable us to love others as Christ loves us. Therefore, by the power of the Holy Spirit in us, we can love all people, whether friends or enemies, because God has not given us the spirit of fear, but of love so that we can "love [our] enemies, do good to them which hate [us], bless them that curse [us], and pray for them which despitefully use [us]—Luke 6:27-28. The amount of God's power that is utilized in us depends on whether we yield to our flesh or to the Holy Spirit. We do not have to live in fear, anxiety, and the old nature, because God has given us the spirit of power, love and a sound mind.

# Made Perfect in Love

I John 4:18

*"There is no fear in love; but perfect love casteth out fear: because fear hath torment. He that feareth is not made perfect in love."*

"Whosoever shall confess that Jesus is the Son of God, God dwelleth in him, and he in God. And we have known and believed the love that God hath to us. God is love; and he that dwelleth in love dwelleth in God, and God in him"—I John 4:15-16. The very essence of God is love, and His love is perfect, because He is perfect. It cannot be otherwise. As Christians, we can be made perfect in God's love, because the Spirit of God lives in us. We can be made perfect in love when we believe and begin to comprehend how much God loves us. This occurs when we are "persuaded, that neither death, nor life, nor angels, nor prinicpalities, nor powers, nor things present, nor things to come, nor height, nor depth, nor any other creature, shall be able to separate us from the love of God, which is in Christ Jesus our Lord"—Romans 8:38-39.

"If we love one another, God dwelleth in us, and his love is perfected in us. Hereby know we that we dwell in him, and he in us, because he hath given us of his Spirit"—I John 4:12b-13. "He must increase, but [we] must decrease"—John 3:30 in order that His love may be perfected in us. We must daily seek to walk in humility, or as the Apostle Peter wrote, "be clothed with humility"—I Peter 5:5b. When we get dressed for the day, let us also "dress" our hearts with humility so that the love of God will be better perfected in us. The more we yield ourselves to God's Spirit living within us, the more His love can be perfected in us. The more His love is perfected in us, the more we will love others, regardless of how they may treat us. When we grow more in love with God, our Father, and His Son, Jesus Christ, our Saviour, "[we] will not be afraid what man can do unto [us]"—Psalm 56:11, for we will be filled with God's love. It was the fullness of God's love that gave David the assurance to speak those words in Psalm 56:11. We must make it our daily prayer and devotion that God's love will fill our hearts so that His love will be made perfect in us.

*Day 136*

# Declaring the Works of the Lord

Psalm 107:22b

*"Declare his works with rejoicing."*

Declare the Lord's works of healing, His works of restoring the wayward, His works of deliverance; and declare all His works with grateful praise and joy. Everyone has been in trouble of one sort or another, and most, if not all, of us can give testimony to the fact that when we "cried unto the LORD in [our] trouble . . . he delivered [us] out of [our] distresses"—Psalm 107:6.

May we be faithful to declare His deliverance with joy and tell everyone how He *has* heard and answered. When your health is poor, go to the Lord, and when you are healed, thank Him, as did one of the lepers who "fell down on his face at his feet, giving him thanks"—Luke 17:16a. Do not be as the other nine lepers who did not return to thank the Lord. Thank the Lord, then go and declare His works of healing with rejoicing, so that He will be praised and others will be encouraged and challenged to also seek the Lord in prayer. The Lord is constantly working on our behalf in one way or another; therefore, declare His works with rejoicing! "The LORD hath done great things for us; whereof we are glad"—Psalm 126:3.

# My Walk

I Corinthians 3:3

*"For ye are yet carnal: for whereas there is among you envying, and strife, and divisions, are ye not carnal, and walk as men?"*

As Christians, when we exhibit envy, strife, and divisions, we are still walking in the ways of our old nature, which the Bible says is "carnal." *Carnal* simply means to be in the flesh, which is acting according to our selfish desires and motives and not according to the Spirit of Christ. The question that the Apostle Paul asked the Corinthian church is one we need to ask ourselves today: Are we yet carnal and walking as men? Are we envious of one another? Are we at strife with others? Are there divisions among us? "As ye have therefore received Christ Jesus the Lord, so walk ye in him"—Colossians 2:6. "If ye then be risen with Christ, seek those things which are above, where Christ sitteth on the right hand of God. . . . Mortify therefore your members which are upon the earth; fornication, uncleanness, inordinate affection, evil concupiscence, and covetousness, which is idolatry: For which things' sake the wrath of God cometh on the children of disobedience: in the which ye also walked some time, when ye lived in them. But now ye also put off all these; anger, wrath, malice, blasphemy, filthy communication out of your mouth. . . . Put on therefore, as the elect of God, holy and beloved, bowels of mercies, kindness, humbleness of mind, meekness, longsuffering; forbearing one another, and forgiving one another, if any man have a quarrel against any: even as Christ forgave you, so also do ye. And above all these things put on charity, which is the bond of perfectness"—Colossians 3:1,5-8,12-14.

We have to turn away from our fleshy, selfish nature and turn toward the nature of the Lord Jesus Christ who now lives in us. Ask Him to think His thoughts through you, to speak His gracious words through you, to be an extension of Himself through you. Honestly examine your Christian walk. Be willing to forsake the flesh and its ways and to walk as Christ and not as men by yielding yourself to Him.

**Day 138**

# He Knows Me Because He Formed Me

Jeremiah 1:5

*"Before I formed thee in the belly I knew thee; and before thou camest forth out of the womb I sanctified thee, and I ordained thee a prophet unto the nations."*

Before the Lord formed us, He knew us. He knew our shortcomings, our failings, our weaknesses, our strengths, our personality, and all there is to know about us. He knew us, because He was the One who formed us. He saw "[our] substance, yet being unperfect . . . when as yet there was none of them"—Psalm 139:16. The color of our hair, the color of our eyes, the shape of our head, and the height of our body were determined by the Lord when He formed us. As He ordained Jeremiah to be a prophet, He has also ordained each of His children for a particular service in His work. Whatever the service may be, it is all significant in order to carry out the plans He ordained for each one of us. Each of us is "fearfully and wonderfully made"—Psalm 139:14a! The Lord our God has a plan for each of us who are His; therefore, may we strive to follow after Him so that we may accomplish the work He has for us to do.

# Walking in the Spirit

Galatians 5:16

*"This I say then, Walk in the Spirit, and ye shall not fulfill the lust of the flesh."*

In the realm of the Spirit there is God's abundant grace, which is the cultivator of spiritual fruit. When walking in the Spirit, love dispels the dark clouds of anger, hatred, and malice; joy outshines despair and depression; and peace supersedes conflicts and contentions. Faults of others are, by grace, overlooked and the Spirit enables the heart to forgive as Christ forgave. The manifestations of the flesh are no match for the power of the Spirit. Therefore, we Christians are challenged to "walk in the Spirit."

Walking in the Spirit requires daily surrendering the will of man to the will of God. Yielding to God requires disdaining everything that would oppose Him. "What? Know ye not that your body is the temple of the Holy Ghost which is in you, which ye have of God, and ye are not your own? . . . Therefore glorify God in your body, and in your spirit, which are God's" –I Corinthians 6:19-20. "And they that are Christ's have crucified the flesh with the affections and lusts" –Galatians 5:24. Walking in the Spirit glorifies God and exhibits the power that dwells within us. There can never be a "day off" or a letting down of our guard, for the flesh is weak and the Devil is cunning; therefore, "walk in the Spirit, and ye shall not fulfill the lust of the flesh."

**Day 140**

# Full of Praise

Psalm 71:8

*"Let my mouth be filled with thy praise and with thy honour all the day."*

If our mouths were filled with the praises of God, there would not be any room for complaining, slandering, gossip, criticism, or for any torrent of angry words to one another. In order for our mouths to be full of God's praises, our hearts must be full of Him, "for out of the abundance of the heart the mouth speaketh"—Matthew 12:34b. Our thoughts must be filled with His glory, His goodness, His mercies, His love, His benevolence, His grace, His creation, His beauty, His forgiveness, and any other characteristic from an inexhaustible list describing our Lord and Saviour, Jesus Christ.

If we were to think more about His honor throughout the day, we would be more prone to speak His praises. How can we praise someone we know so little about, or spend so little time with? The more time we spend in prayer and in the reading of Scripture, the more we will come to know our Lord. When we know Him better, we will love Him more; and when we love Him more, we will desire to speak His praises. Begin to make it a practice today to fill your mouth with the praises of God and honor Him all day long.

# Shout of Triumph

Psalm 47:1

*"O clap your hands, all ye people; shout unto God with the voice of triumph."*

As Christians we can shout triumphant praises unto God, because in the very center of our troubles, "God is our refuge and strength, a very present help in trouble"—Psalm 46:1. In the midst of life's troubled times we have a place of safety, a place of protection, and a place of rest. Cancer may come, but Christians have God Almighty who is "a shield for [us]; [our] glory, and the lifter up of [our] head"—Psalm 3:3. Therefore, clap your hands and shout unto God with the voice of triumph, for "the LORD of hosts is with us; the God of Jacob is our refuge"—Psalm 46:11. It may seem that everything in our lives is collapsing all around us, but God sees, and He is with us. Whether we experience financial ruin, death of those closest to us, or severe personal illness, we have the Almighty God with us; He will never leave us nor forsake us. "For this God is our God for ever and ever: he will be our guide even unto death"—Psalm 48:14. Clap your hands in praise and shout unto God with the voice of triumph.

We must not let the devil rob us of our joy in the Lord, our triumph in adversity, and our victory in Jesus Christ. We serve the living God who "is the King of all the earth" and sits "upon the throne of his holiness"— Psalm 47:7a, 8b. "Great is the LORD, and greatly to be praised in the city of our God, in the mountain of his holiness. Beautiful for situation, the joy of the whole earth, is mount Zion, on the sides of the north, the city of the great King. God is known in her palaces for a refuge"—Psalm 48:1-3; therefore, clap your hands and shout triumphant praises unto God. The devil is a defeated foe. Let's look unto the Lord and shout with triumph for the victory we have in Jesus Christ!

**Day 142**

# Knowledge

I Corinthians 8:1b

*"Knowledge puffeth up, but charity edifieth."*

Knowledge can make us proud, but charity—love—will help us to build up one another. When a person increases in knowledge, there may be a tendency to become proud; however, knowledge without proper application becomes foolishness and makes us nothing, for "though I have . . . all knowledge . . . and have not charity, I am nothing"—I Corinthians 13:2. A great proof of ignorance is revealed when people become conceited because they have increased in knowledge. It is possible to have a wealth of knowledge but not use it to good purpose. Satan can tempt us to become proud of possessing great knowledge just as certainly as he tempts others to various kinds of sinfulness.

"The fear of the LORD is the beginning of wisdom: and the knowledge of the holy is understanding"—Proverbs 9:10. Knowledge alone will only puff us up, but when we couple knowledge together with the wisdom of God, we will receive understanding. When we fear, or revere, the Lord, we become teachable; and the more we reverence God, the more we will practice hiding His Word in our hearts and applying it to our lives.

"Charity never faileth: but . . . whether there be knowledge, it shall vanish away"—I Corinthians 13:8. When we only have knowledge, then we do not have much, because knowledge does not last. It is always changing and becoming outdated and possibly could become irrelevant and unusable. Therefore, may we not seek knowledge for the sake of having knowledge, but seek to know the love of God so that His love will flow through us to others.

# Love Is an Action

John 3:16

*"For God so loved the world, that he gave his only begotten Son, that whosoever believeth in him should not perish, but have everlasting life."*

John 10:15

*"As the Father knoweth me, even so know I the Father: and I lay down my life for the sheep."*

Love is an action word. God *gave* His only begotten Son, because God *loved* the world. The Lord Jesus expressed His love for fallen man by *laying* down His life. No man took His life; He voluntarily laid it down—John 10:18. Love is seen through our actions. An act of kindness—whether it is an encouraging word, a hug, or some other gesture—demonstrates our love for someone.

When we obey and do what God commands us, then we are demonstrating our love for Him, because the Lord Jesus said, "If ye love me, keep my commandments"—John 14:15. The greatest commandment He gave us is found in Matthew 22:37: "Thou shalt love the Lord your God with all your heart, and with all your soul, and with all your mind." The second greatest commandment He gave us was to love our neighbor as ourselves—Matthew 22:39. We can say we love God, but our actions will prove to what extent we actually love Him and whether or not we love our neighbor as ourselves. It is easy to love those that love us, but when we love our enemies and demonstrate it with sincere actions, then we are showing God that we love Him, because we are following His commandment which says, "Love your enemies, do good to them which hate you"—Luke 6:27. Love is not simply a word; it is an action.

## Day 144
# Love Does Not Need a Reason to Love

Romans 5:8

*"But God commendeth his love toward us, in that, while we were yet sinners, Christ died for us."*

God loved us when there was no reason to love us. Since Adam and Eve sinned against God in the Garden of Eden, everyone has been born a sinner, for "that which is born of the flesh is flesh"—John 3:6. "Behold, I was shapen in iniquity; and in sin did my mother conceive me"—Psalm 51:5. Here the Psalmist is tracing his sin back to its original corruption and making confession. "We are all as an unclean thing, and all our righteousnesses are as filthy rags; and we all do fade as a leaf; and our iniquities, like the wind, have taken us away"—Isaiah 64:6; however, God loved us and gave us His Son, Jesus Christ. Since "there is none righteous, no, not one"—Romans 3:10, then there is no one who can ever stand before Him righteously apart from Jesus Christ. Yet God loved us, and does love us so much that He gave us His Son so that we could have eternal life.

As Christians, "we [only] love Him, because he first loved us"—I John 4:19; therefore, we love because He loved us. We have the ability to love others—whether friend, stranger, or enemy—because God and His Son loved us. It is through the Holy Spirit that we are able to accomplish this. The more we yield to the Holy Spirit, the more He enables us to love others—those who are easy to love and those who are difficult to love. In order to enlarge our love toward Christ our hearts must grow in love with Him. God did not need a reason to love us; He simply loved us because He is love. We have His love in the person of His Holy Spirit living in us; therefore, real love does not need a reason to love someone. The more we are filled with Christ and His love, the more we will love Him, and love others.

# Healthy Countenance

Psalm 42:11

*"Why art thou cast down, O my soul? and why art thou disquieted within me? Hope thou in God: for I shall yet praise him, who is the health of my countenance, and my God."*

Our hope in God will give us a healthy countenance. When our hope lies in God, then our face will reveal the assurance we feel in our hearts, the peace that hoping in God brings, and the joy we have in Him. However, "Hope deferred maketh the heart sick"—Proverbs 13:12a. When we are sick at heart our eyes will not have that joyful shine; our faces will no longer glow with exuberant smiles; and our faces may even have a pallor appearance. God is the health of our countenance; therefore, when our hope in God is rooted in believing His Word, by standing without wavering, on His promises, and remembering that He never changes, then our countenance will be healthier. Jesus Christ is "the same yesterday, and to day, and for ever"—Hebrews 13:8.

In this life we are going to battle times of doubt and despondency because we, like King David, are made of sinful flesh, and "[our] adversary the devil, as a roaring lion, walketh about, seeking whom he may devour"—I Peter 5:8. The devil is going to do all that he can to make us doubt the Living God with all manner of lies. ". . . there is no truth in him. When he speaketh a lie, he speaketh of his own: for he is a liar, and the father of it"—John 8:44. Therefore, when doubts, fears, and uncertainties arise, seek God; remember all He has done; read the Scriptures every moment you can; hope in Him, and praise Him. He is the health of our countenance, and our God!

**Day 146**

# Throne of Grace

Hebrews 4:16

*"Let us therefore come boldly unto the throne of grace, that we may obtain mercy, and find grace to help in time of need."*

The throne of grace has been made available to every born-again believer through Jesus Christ, for "the veil of the temple was rent in twain [torn in two] from the top to the bottom"—Matthew 27:51a when Jesus was crucified on the cross of Calvary and "yielded up the ghost"—Matthew 27:50. The rending of the veil signified that Christ, by His death, opened the way for every believer to go to God at the throne of grace.

At the throne of grace we are given what we do not deserve—mercy—which is a form of love granted to us, although we are unworthy and undeserving. "To the praise of the glory of his grace, wherein he hath made us accepted in the beloved"—Ephesians 1:6; therefore, "we may obtain mercy, and find grace to help in time of need"—Hebrews 4:16.

Do you need help to forgive someone who has horribly hurt you? It is at the throne of grace that you will find God's grace to enable you to forgive. Whatever need we may have, it is at the throne of grace that we will find God's grace to help us. We may need grace to love those who are hard to love, to walk in humility, to be content, to stop complaining, to rejoice always, to turn the other cheek, to go the extra mile, to keep looking at Jesus and not at our storm, to be patient, to be kind, to die to our will and live to God's will for our life. The Lord Jesus Christ opened the way for us to go to God's throne of grace; therefore, it is necessary that we go so that we will find the grace we need to help us in the time of need.

# Resisting Our Adversary

I Peter 5:9

*"Whom resist stedfast in the faith, knowing that the same afflictions are accomplished in your brethren that are in the world."*

Realize who your real adversary is and resist him: "The devil, as a roaring lion, walketh about, seeking whom he may devour"—I Peter 5:8b. He is our adversary as well as a deceiver, an accuser; and he desires to cause conflict between husbands and wives, family members, co-workers, friends, and Christian brethren. The more dysfunctional a family is, and the more there is a lack of unity between people, then the more the devil is pleased. If you are going to fight against anyone, then fight against the devil by submitting "yourselves therefore to God. Resist the devil, and he will flee from you"—James 4:7.

Pride is one of our greatest enemies and the devil's greatest instrument for breeding discord among people; therefore, humility is a powerful way to resist the devil. "Humble yourselves in the sight of the Lord, and he shall lift you up"—James 4:10. It is impossible to resist the devil when we are filled with pride. The Lord Jesus said, "I beheld Satan as lightning fall from heaven"—Luke 10:18b. Isaiah, inspired by the Holy Spirit, wrote, "How art thou fallen from heaven, O Lucifer, son of the morning! How art thou cut down to the ground, which didst weaken the nations! For thou hast said in thine heart, I will ascend into heaven, I will exalt my throne above the stars of God: I will sit also upon the mount of the congregation, in the sides of the north: I will ascend above the heights of the clouds; I will be like the most High"—Isaiah 14:12-14. The devil is full of pride, and he wants God's people to be full of pride. He was cast out of Heaven because of pride; therefore, when we are prideful, we are associating ourselves with the devil's ways, which makes it difficult to resist him. Realize the tactics of our enemy, the devil, and resist him stedfast in the faith.

**Day 148**

# Divine Thoughts

Psalm 139:17

*"How precious also are thy thoughts unto me, O God! How great is the sum of them!*

He who is high and lifted up is thinking about you and me. He who sits high above the heavens and the earth is thinking about His children. His thoughts of mercy, of love, of kindness, of graciousness are all being directed toward us. He thinks about what we are made of; dirt and His thoughts toward us are of mercy. "For he knoweth our frame; he remembereth that we are dust"—Psalm 103:14. He thinks of His creation that He made in His image, and His thoughts are of love and peace combined with mercy and grace. "For I know the thoughts that I think toward you, saith the LORD, thoughts of peace, and not of evil, to give you an expected end"—Jeremiah 29:11. "Grace be with you, mercy, and peace, from God the Father, and from the Lord Jesus Christ, the Son of the Father, in truth and love"—II John 1:3. As a child of God we are never out of His thoughts, for He is always thinking of us.

When we are going through hard trials, God is thinking of us. When we are walking through the valley of the shadow of death, God is thinking of us. When we are being sorely tempted by the devil, God is thinking of us. When we have yielded to temptation and fallen, God is thinking of us. When we are bewildered and uncertain about life's circumstances, God is thinking of us. When we are sorrowful, God is thinking of us. When we are on the mountaintop and rejoicing, God is thinking of us. We are continually on God's mind and, therefore, in His thoughts. How precious are His thoughts unto me! The sum of them is so great they cannot be numbered!

# Growing as a Christian

I Peter 2:2

*"As newborn babes, desire the sincere milk of the word, that ye may grow thereby."*

As Christians, do we hunger for the Word of God with as much earnestness as a newborn baby hungers for milk? How often are we opening the Bible and reading its pages? Newborn babies require multiple feedings each day so that they will be adequately nourished and will grow physically. The Christian's nourishment and spiritual growth is derived by daily reading the Bible. If a newborn baby isn't fed adequately it will not grow sufficiently. The same is true of Christians; if Christians do not read the Bible, they will not grow sufficiently spiritually. When the Apostle Paul described the Christian who does not grow as being carnal, he said, "And I, brethren, could not speak unto you as unto spiritual, but as unto carnal, even as unto babes in Christ. . . . For ye are yet carnal: for whereas there is among you envying, and strife, and divisions, are ye not carnal, and walk as men?" –I Corinthians 3:1, 3.

It is the Holy Spirit through the Word of God that teaches us how to conduct ourselves as Christians; how to live peaceably with all people, how to represent Christ to those who do not know Him, and how to love one another. If we are not reading the Word of God daily we will not grow; therefore, "as newborn babes, desire the sincere milk of the word, that ye may grow thereby."

**Day 150**

# Wait Only Upon God

Psalm 62:5

*"My soul, wait thou only upon God; for my expectation is from him."*

When we begin to understand and comprehend how completely dependent we are upon the Lord God who created all things, we will be more likely to wait on Him. We will begin to wait on the Lord when we realize that He **will** "supply all [our] need"—Philippians 4:19a. God is the Creator of everything as well as the Sustainer of all. "Behold the fowls of the air: for they sow not, neither do they reap, nor gather into barns; yet your heavenly Father feedeth them. Are ye not much better than they?"—Matthew 6:26. He will provide for us.

Wait on Him to strengthen you in your time of weakness. "Hast thou not known? hast thou not heard, that the everlasting God, the LORD, the Creator of the ends of the earth, fainteth not, neither is weary? there is no searching of his understanding. He giveth power to the faint; and to them that have no might he increaseth strength. Even the youths shall faint and be weary, and the young men shall utterly fall: But they that wait upon the LORD shall renew their strength; they shall mount up with wings as eagles; they shall run, and not be weary; and they shall walk, and not faint"—Isaiah 40:28-31.

Wait on Him for instruction when you need help to make wise and appropriate decisions. "Shew me thy ways, O LORD; teach me thy paths. Lead me in thy truth, and teach me: for thou art the God of my salvation; on thee do I wait all the day. . . . Let integrity and uprightness preserve me; for I wait on thee"—Psalm 25:4, 5, 21. Foolish decisions are made in times of pride and haste.

When we wait on the Lord for everything in our lives, we will experience sweet rest, joy and blessings. "The LORD is good unto them that wait for him, to the soul that seeketh him"—Lamentations 3:25; therefore, "Wait on the LORD . . . wait, I say, on the LORD"—Psalm 27:14.

# Grace and Truth

John 1:14

*"And the Word was made flesh, and dwelt among us, (and we beheld his glory, the glory as of the only begotten of the Father,) full of grace and truth."*

Jesus Christ, the only Begotten Son of God the Father, is full of grace and truth. Being full of grace means He was fully accepted by God the Father and therefore, completely qualified to plead our cause unto Him. When we received Christ as our Saviour we became "accepted in the beloved. In whom we have redemption through his blood, the forgiveness of sins, according to the riches of his grace"—Ephesians 1:6b-7. Grace is God's unmerited favor, which gives us what we do not deserve—an open door to Heaven and access to the Father—and it could only come by Jesus Christ, who is full of grace.

Jesus Christ is full of truth, because He is the truth—John 14:6. Therefore, since He is the Word that was made flesh, we can believe every promise we read in the Bible, which is the Word of God. As Christians, we do not have to doubt and fear, because we have the Spirit of truth, "whom the world cannot receive, because it seeth him not, neither knoweth him: but ye know him; for he dwelleth with you, and shall be in you"—John 14:17. It is by God's grace through faith in Jesus Christ that the lost can be saved. His grace is sufficient for every Christian, and His truth will be our guide through life.

**Day 152**

# Watch and Pray

Matthew 26:41

*"Watch and pray, that ye enter not into temptation: the spirit indeed is willing, but the flesh is weak."*

The Lord Jesus exhorted us to watch and pray so that we would not enter into temptation. He knows our flesh is weak, which is why He said, "the spirit indeed is willing, but the flesh is weak." Therefore, as Christians, we need to be diligent to follow the exhortation to watch and pray so that we do not yield to temptation. Satan knows how and where to attack our weaknesses. The disciples, in their weakness, forsook the Lord Jesus. One denied knowing Him, while another betrayed Him. Every person is susceptible to the same weaknesses. With cunning and deception Satan will tempt us; therefore, it is necessary to be continually on guard against his devices.

The admonition to "watch" simply means to be alert, awake, and on guard against our enemy—Satan. Our power to flee temptation and to escape Satan's subtle devices is by prayer. As we pray let us ask the Father to keep us from becoming spiritually drowsy; to be still and allow the Holy Spirit to guide our praying; and to be fervent in prayer. The devil wants to steal our joy, kill our effectiveness to labor for the Lord, and destroy our Christian testimony; therefore it is necessary for every Christian to watch and pray. May we pray as Jesus taught His disciples: "lead us not into temptation, but deliver us from evil: For thine is the kingdom, and the power, and the glory, for ever Amen"—Matthew 6:13.

# Faith in the Name of Jesus

Acts 3:16

*"And his name through faith in his name hath made this man strong, whom ye see and know: yea, the faith which is by him hath given him this perfect soundness in the presence of you all."*

It is by faith in the name of Jesus Christ that we are made strong. "Peter said, Silver and gold have I none; but such as I have give I thee: In the name of Jesus Christ of Nazareth rise up and walk"—Acts 3:6. This man had never been able to walk, but he was healed by faith in the name of Jesus Christ of Nazareth. It is through faith in His name that we receive anything—whether it is salvation, healing, strength, power, rest, or joy. Through faith in the name of Jesus Christ we have power over our sinfulness. Through faith in the name of Jesus Christ we become "joint-heirs with Christ"—Romans 8:17b so that the riches of Heaven become ours, and we can receive all things through faith in His name.

There is power in the name of Jesus. "And when they had set them in the midst, they asked, By what power, or by what name, have ye done this? Then Peter, filled with the Holy Ghost, said unto them . . . Be it known unto you all, and to all the people of Israel, that by the name of Jesus Christ of Nazareth, whom ye crucified, whom God raised from the dead, even by him doth this man stand here before you whole"—Acts 4:7-10. There is hope in the name of Jesus. There is healing in the name of Jesus. There is strength in the name of Jesus. There is joy in the name of Jesus. Whatever the need may be, we can find it in the name of Jesus Christ.

**Day 154**

# Delighting and Doing

Psalm 40:8

*"I delight to do thy will, O my God: yea, thy law is within my heart."*

As believers, we have the Holy Spirit of God living in us. Therefore, doing the will of God can become our delight when we surrender ourselves unto the Holy Spirit's guidance. "Let not sin therefore reign in your mortal body, that ye should obey it in the lusts thereof. Neither yield ye your members as instruments of unrighteousness unto sin: but yield yourselves unto God, as those that are alive from the dead, and your members as instruments of righteousness unto God. For sin shall not have dominion over you: for ye are not under the law, but under grace"—Romans 6:12-14.

The more we love someone, the more we delight to please them. The same is true with the Christian and the Lord. The more we love Him, the more we will delight to do His will, because doing His will is going to please Him. May it be said of us that we delight to do the Lord's will.

# He Hath Said

Hebrews 13:5c

*"For he hath said . . ."*

Have you ever thought of the great blessing in the phrase, "He hath said"? He has said, "I am the way, the truth, and the life"—John 14:6a. "I am with you alway, even unto the end of the world"—Matthew 28:20b. "All that the Father giveth me shall come to me; and him that cometh to me I will in no wise cast out"—John 6:37. "Come unto me, all ye that labour and are heavy laden, and I will give you rest"—Matthew 11:28. "I am the resurrection, and the life: he that believeth in me, though he were dead, yet shall he live: And whosoever liveth and believeth in me shall never die"—John 11:25. "I will come again"—John 14:3b. Think of the great comfort there is in all that He has said! He is the truth; therefore, all that He says *is* true: "[God's] word is truth"—John 17:17b. As Christians, when we worry and fear, we are either not believing what the Lord has said, or we do not know what He has said.

We cannot be comforted by what He has said when we do not know Him; therefore, we need to "make [our] calling and election sure"—II Peter 1:10a, for He has said, "My sheep hear my voice, and I know them, and they follow me"—John 10:27. The devil wants to plant doubt and fear in our hearts, but the more we know what the Lord has said, the more confident we will be in Christ, and the less we will yield to doubt and fear. "Whither shall I go from thy spirit? Or whither shall I flee from thy presence?"—Psalm 139:7. The more we learn what He has said, the more our faith in Christ will be strengthened, and our hearts will be comforted.

**Day 156**

# Commanding Deliverance

Psalm 44:4

*"Thou art my King, O God: command deliverances for Jacob."*

When we are in the middle of strong trials and testings, and we are being tempted by the devil in every way, our only deliverance is by turning to the Lord, our God and our King. "The LORD is my rock, and my fortress, and my deliverer" –Psalm 18:2a. He is able to command our deliverance; therefore, let us go to Him for victory. "Thanks be to God, which giveth us the victory through our Lord Jesus Christ. Therefore, my beloved brethren, be ye stedfast, unmoveable, always abounding in the work of the Lord, forasmuch as ye know that your labour is not in vain in the Lord" –I Corinthians 15:57-58. The devil desires to defeat us, but our King has already victoriously defeated the devil; therefore, we can claim the victory in Jesus Christ our King. Our God will command our deliverance through the victory He has already won. Our King did not win the victory for Himself alone, but for all of His children; therefore, remember that you have victory in Christ for every struggle you may encounter in this life. He is our King, our God, and He will command our deliverance. Therefore, shout the victory in Jesus Christ!

# To Will and to Do

Philippians 2:13

*"For it is God which worketh in you both to will and to do of his good pleasure."*

God works in us a will to do what pleases Him. Those desires to serve Him, those thoughts of how we can better witness for Him, the longings in our souls to be more like Jesus Christ all come from the grace of God. But the willing desire is not enough; we must also *do*, and God works in us "both to will and to do of his good pleasure." Because we are born sinners, we are not able to keep the law of God, regardless how hard we try. Every New Year there are many "New Year's resolutions" made that are soon put aside, because many people find it too hard to follow through and *do*. The good intentions are there along with the desire; however, the follow through—the *doing*—is a struggle. Even as believers in Jesus Christ our sin nature hinders us at times from doing the will of God, because "the flesh lusteth against the Spirit, and the Spirit against the flesh: and these are contrary the one to the other: so that ye cannot do the things that ye would"—Galatians 5:17.

To *will* and to *do* God's good pleasure requires a heart surrendered to Him. Many people who have the will to serve the Lord do not follow through with the service, because their hearts are not fully surrendered to Him. The desires of our flesh and our fearfulness are both hindrances to **doing** the will of the Lord. It is God's grace—unmerited favor—that enables us to do anything. It is the grace of God that saves us; and it is the grace of God that works in us to desire and to **do** His will. When we humble ourselves in the sight of the Lord and obey Him, then we will begin to realize that our desire to serve the Lord comes from Him, and it is He who performs the work through us. Surrendering ourselves to be an extension of the feet, hands, mouth, and heart of Jesus Christ will better enable God's grace to work in us "both to will and to do" anything for Him.

*Day 158*

# Daily Exercise

Psalm 37:1

*"Fret not thyself because of evildoers, neither be thou envious against the workers of iniquity."*

To fret is to be constantly worried and distressed. As Christians we need to remember that we "are dead, and [our] life is hid with Christ in God"—Colossians 3:3. Therefore, the grace of God that saves us will also keep us in the peace of Christ so that His nature can be manifested through us. We can live in His peace and walk in His peace by keeping our "minds stayed on [Him]"—Isaiah 26:3. "Whatsoever things are true, whatsoever things are honest, whatsoever things are just, whatsoever things are pure, whatsoever things are lovely, whatsoever things are of good report; if there be any virtue, and if there be any praise, think on these things"—Philippians 4:8.

The Lord has given us some exercises that we should practice daily to keep us from fretting and to help us rest in the peace of God. First, "Trust in the LORD, and do good"—Psalm 37:3a. Second, "Delight thyself also in the LORD"—Psalm 37:4a. Third, "Commit thy way unto the LORD"—Psalm 37:5a. Fourth, "Rest in the LORD, and wait patiently for him"—Psalm 37:7a. These are daily exercises that will deepen our awareness of the peace of God in our lives and help us to stop worrying.

# I Will Not Sin with My Tongue

Psalm 39:1

*"I said, I will take heed to my ways, that I sin not with my tongue: I will keep my mouth with a bridle, while the wicked is before me."*

It is so easy for us to sin with our tongue, because even though "the tongue is a little member . . . the tongue is a fire, a world of iniquity . . . and it is set on fire of hell" –James 3:5-6. How easy it is for our tongues to speak lies, to speak unkindly, to speak pridefully, to speak slanderously, and even to speak maliciously, for the simple reason that we originate from sin. Because of our sinful nature, it is needful for us to take heed to our ways so that we will not sin with our tongue. "Out of the abundance of the heart the mouth speaketh" –Matthew 12:34b; therefore, we should also take heed to keep our hearts clean and right before God, so that we do not sin with our tongue. "Let no corrupt communication proceed out of your mouth, but that which is good to the use of edifying, that it may minister grace unto the hearers" –Ephesians 4:29. It would be better to remain silent than to sin with our tongue. As the old saying goes, "If you can't say something nice, don't say anything at all."

We need to remember that the unsaved are watching our lives and listening to our conversations, and some would turn our words, if they could, to our disadvantage. We should also remember that children are listening to us and will imitate what they hear. Every day we should take heed to our ways and keep our mouths with a bridle so that we sin not with our tongue.

*Day 160*

# The Light of Christ Remains

Job 37:21

*"And now men see not the bright light which is in the clouds: but the wind passeth, and cleanseth them."*

The clouds may obscure the light of the sun on certain days, but they do not remove the sun from its place; for when the clouds move on, the sun is still there, shining in brilliance and warmth. The clouds of our life, whether they are clouds of sorrow or of sin, may seem to hide the favor of our Saviour's presence, but He has never left: He is still there, caring for His own. Do not moan if the clouds of trouble have entered your life. Remember that clouds bring a refreshing, a healing, and a quenching rain upon a parched ground. Without the "clouds" we would be barren in the identification of our Lord's sufferings, and His character would not be as fully manifested in us. "Men see not the bright light which is in the clouds," but we may be certain that our Lord is there; He is in the clouds. "And God said, This is the token of the covenant which I make between me and you and every living creature that is with you, for perpetual generations: I do set my bow in the cloud, and it shall be for a token of a covenant between me and the earth" –Genesis 9:12-13.

The cloud of sin may hinder our fellowship with the Lord, but He has not removed Himself from us. Our Lord loves us too much not to chastise us if we have yielded ourselves to sin, "for whom the Lord loveth he chasteneth, and scourgeth every son [person] whom he receiveth" – Hebrews 12:6. His purpose for chastening us is to lead us to repentance and full fellowship with Him once again. If we could see the clouds from Heaven's viewpoint, we would see the light of God's beauty shining in them. Since we cannot, then may we remember that the clouds (those in our lives as well as in the sky) are continually moving and passing before God's cleansing wind.

# Either Salt Water or Fresh

James 3:12

*"Can the fig tree, my brethren, bear olive berries? either a vine, figs? so can no fountain both yield salt water and fresh."*

As no fountain can yield both salt water and fresh, neither can children of God serve Christ and the world. "No man can serve two masters: for either he will hate the one, and love the other; or else he will hold to the one, and despise the other. Ye cannot serve God and mammon" –Matthew 6:24. If we are in Christ, then we are a new creature; "old things are passed away; behold, all things are become new" –II Corinthians 5:17b; therefore, we should look different, act different, speak differently, and in all areas of our life be different from the world. "The disciples were called Christians first in Antioch" –Acts 11:26c, because their conduct, speech, appearance, and their way of living so closely mirrored the life of the Lord Jesus Christ. This should be our goal as Christians today, to be so identified with Christ that we would stand out as peculiar to the world.

We should strive to be like Christ in His holiness, His purity, His compassion, His love, His gentleness, His goodness, His humility, His obedience to the Father, and His service to mankind. "Submit yourselves therefore to God. Resist the devil, and he will flee from you. Draw nigh to God, and he will draw nigh to you" –James 4:7-8. "Love not the world, neither the things that are in the world. If any man love the world, the love of the Father is not in him" –I John 2:15. A doctor can perform an operation without sterilizing the instruments, but the end result will be sick patients; and Christians, who do not separate themselves from the world's ways, will have a weak Christianity. No fountain can yield both salt water and fresh, and no Christian can be worldly and Godly at the same time.

*Day 162*

# Enriched by Christ

I Corinthians 1:5

*"That in every thing ye are enriched by him, in all utterance, and in all knowledge."*

As Christians, we are enriched by Christ. In other words, our lives have been enhanced and improved by Him. When we received Christ as our Saviour His Holy Spirit came to dwell within us. By His power we have the ability to live and be like Christ. For "if any man be in Christ, he is a new creature: old things are passed away; behold, all things are become new"—II Corinthians 5:17. Therefore, in Christ and by His Spirit, the way we speak can be improved and enhanced. We have the ability, through Christ, to "be gentle unto all men"—II Timothy 2:24b— gentle in our manner of speaking so that as it was true of Christ it can also be true of us, that people will wonder at the "gracious words" which proceed out of our mouth—Luke 4:22b. As Christians we should "speak evil of no man, to be no brawlers, but gentle, shewing all meekness unto all men"—Titus 3:2.

In order for us to be enriched by him in everything we say, we must fill our hearts with His Word, because whatever our hearts are full of, that is what we will speak of. If our hearts are full of anger and bitterness toward others, then most likely we will speak evil of them. If our hearts are full of discontentment and un-thankfulness, then we are probably going to complain. If our hearts are full of Christ and His goodness, His mercies, His faithfulness, His love for us, then we will most likely speak of Him and all that He has done for us. We can lose every earthly possession, but if our hearts are full of Christ, then we can speak joyfully of our situation with thankfulness. Jesus Christ makes the difference in our lives; therefore, we must fill our hearts and our minds with Him so that the things we say and do will reveal that we are His people and that in everything we are enriched by Him.

# The Lord Will Perfect

Psalm 138:8

*"The LORD will perfect that which concerneth me: thy mercy, O LORD, endureth for ever: forsake not the works of thine own hands."*

It is the Lord who has made us; therefore, He knows our innermost heart, whether or not it is clean and pure. Because His mercies "are new every morning"—Lamentations 3:22,23a, He **will** perfect that which concerns us. He will perfect any part of our Christian lives which we still have not surrendered to His control. God will bring to our lives whatever is needed to perfect the image of Christ in us. It may be by trials or by heartache of some kind. Because He knows our heart, and our innermost thoughts, He knows what circumstances will help us to become more like our Saviour, Jesus Christ. Nothing that occurs in our Christian life happens by chance, but by the very Omniscient leading of our Heavenly Father so that Jesus Christ may be greatly glorified. "He knoweth the way that [we] take: when he hath tried [us], [we] shall come forth as gold"—Job 23:10.

"The LORD said unto Satan, Hast thou considered my servant Job, that there is none like him in the earth, a perfect and an upright man, one that feareth God, and escheweth evil?"—Job 1:8; however, God allowed all the trials to come into Job's life so that Job would be made even more perfect. We find in the later chapters of Job that the hardships Job went through were designed to extract the pride that dwelt in his heart. "Now no chastening for the present seemeth to be joyous, but grievous: nevertheless afterward it yieldeth the peaceable fruit of righteousness unto them which are exercised thereby"—Hebrews 12:11. The Lord, in His mercy and love perfected Job, and He desires to perfect us.

*Day 164*

# Believe to Receive

Mark 11:22,24

*"And Jesus answering saith unto them, Have faith in God. . . . Therefore I say unto you, What things soever ye desire, when ye pray, believe that ye receive them, and ye shall have them."*

Believing is receiving, and yet so often, as Christians, we fail to believe. It is human nature to want to see before believing; however, Jesus said, "believe that ye receive." Many of us tend to think that we cannot believe because we do not have great faith, which is a lie of the devil. Jesus said, "If ye have faith as a grain of mustard seed . . . nothing shall be impossible unto you"—Matthew 17:20. A grain of mustard seed, the Lord Jesus said, "is less than all the seeds that be in the earth: but when it is sown, it growth up, and becometh greater than all herbs"—Mark 4:31b-32a. When our faith is "sown"—exercised—then it will grow and become greater, for it is not great faith that we need in order to believe; but rather, faith in our great God.

"Be not afraid, only believe"—Mark 5:36b were the words that Jesus spoke to the ruler of the synagogue. Our human tendency is to fear, but we must not let fear keep us from believing. If we become afraid, remember to look up and say, "What time I am afraid, I will trust in thee"—Psalm 56:3. George Mueller, the great man of faith in the 1800's, said, "The only way to learn strong faith is to endure great trials." Trials of our faith, though they are never pleasant, do help us to exercise our faith in Almighty God. May we make it a daily practice to believe God so that we may receive fully all that He desires us to have. When we believe, we will receive.

# Solution to Our Troubles

John 2:2-3,5

*"And both Jesus was called, and his disciples, to the marriage. And when they wanted wine, the mother of Jesus saith unto him, They have no wine. . . . His mother saith unto the servants, Whatsoever he saith unto you, do it."*

Our lesson from this portion of Scripture is threefold. When we have trouble, we need to first, invite the Lord Jesus to come and help; second, tell Him about our trouble; and third, follow His instructions. If Jesus had not been invited to the wedding, He would not have been there to help in their time of need. Invite Jesus Christ into every area of your life. Whatever our trouble, we must not try to solve it on our own. If we do, we will utterly fail to experience the peace that only the Lord Jesus can give.

Tell the Lord Jesus about your trouble and how you are hurting. He understands, for He is "acquainted with grief"—Isaiah 53:3b. If you are having financial troubles, tell Him. If you are struggling in your marriage, tell Him. If you have a problem of any size, tell Him. "For we have not an high priest which cannot be touched with the feeling of our infirmities . . . Let us therefore come boldly unto the throne of grace, that we may obtain mercy, and find grace to help in time of need"—Hebrews 4:15-16. "Humble yourselves therefore under the mighty hand of God, that he may exalt you in due time: Casting all your care upon him, for he careth for you"—I Peter 5:6-7.

After you have invited Him into your life and shared with Him your trouble, follow His instructions and do what He tells you to do. The Lord Jesus told the servants, "Fill the waterpots with water." And they filled them "to the brim. And he saith unto them, Draw out now, and bear unto the governor of the feast. And they bare it"—John 2:7-8. They did as He instructed, and they witnessed "this beginning of miracles"—John 2:11a. Obeying Jesus' instructions always helps to solve our issues and glorifies Him. There is no problem too difficult for Him to solve; therefore, invite Him in and tell Him all about your troubles. Then follow His instructions and look for His miraculous workings and glorify Him.

# Come Unto Christ

Come unto Christ and rest dear soul
In all life's toil and strain
When labors become so heavy laden
Come and rest in Jesus name

Careful and troubled with much serving
Will only cause your heart distress
It is when you come unto Christ dear soul
that you find comfort and sweet rest

Whether early morn, or noon, or night
Come unto Him and be at rest
For in quietness and confidence
Your strength is fully blessed

It's not the busiest life that serves the Lord so well
But the soul who finds that secret sweet
And trusting in God's Word
does come to worship at His feet

# Strong in the Grace of Jesus Christ

II Timothy 2:1

*"Be strong in the grace that is in Christ Jesus."*

Grace is that unmerited favor of God the Father that He gave us through His Son, Jesus Christ. When we got saved, the sin in us that separated us from the Father was forever removed through the sinlessness of Christ. In II Timothy 2:1, the Apostle Paul challenged Timothy (as well as Christians down through the ages) to be strong in that grace. This grace of God takes us through any kind of suffering and brings us out victors in Christ if we will look unto its Source –Christ Jesus, our Lord and Savior. Jesus Christ has already suffered for us and rose victorious over all that the Devil hurled at Him.

How much we turn the handle of a water spicket determines how much water will flow from the faucet. The same is true of the Christian and grace. We all, as His children, are given grace whether we live for Him or not. However, the more we abide and rest in Christ, the more we will be able to exercise the grace He freely gives. The following is a story told by Mrs. Charles Spurgeon.

*At the close of a dark and gloomy day, I lay resting on my couch as the deeper night drew on; and though all was bright within my cozy room, some of the external darkness seemed to have entered into my soul and obscured its spiritual vision. Vainly I tried to see the hand which I knew held mine, and guided my fog-enveloped feet along a steep and slippery path of suffering. In sorrow of heart I asked, "Why does my Lord thus deal with His child? Why does He so often send sharp and bitter pain to visit me? Why does He permit lingering weakness to hinder the sweet service I long to render to His poor servants?"*

*These fretful questions were quickly answered, and through a strange language; no interpreter was needed, save the conscious whisper of my heart. For a while silence reigned in the little room, broken only by the crackling of the oak log burning in the fireplace.*

*Suddenly I heard a sweet, soft sound, a little, clear, musical note, like the tender trill of a robin beneath my window. What can it be? Surely no bird can be singing out there at this time of the year and night. Again came the faint, plaintive notes, so sweet, so melodious, yet mysterious enough to provoke our wonder. My Friend exclaimed, "It comes from the log on the fire!" The fire was letting loose the imprisoned music from the old oak's inmost heart! Perchance he had garnered up this song in the days when all was well with him, when birds twittered merrily on his branches, and the soft sunlight flecked his tender leaves with gold. But he had grown old since then, and hardened; ring after ring of knotty growth had sealed up the long-forgotten melody, until the fierce tongues of the flames came to consume his callousness, and the vehement heart of the fire wrung from him at once a song and a sacrifice. Ah, thought I, when the fire of affliction draws songs of praise from us, then, indeed, we are purified, and our God is glorified! Perhaps some of us are like this old oak log, cold, hard, insensible; we should give forth no melodious sounds, were it not for the fire which kindles around us, and releases notes of trust in Him, and cheerful compliance with His will. As I mused, the fire burned, and my soul found sweet comfort in the parable so strangely set forth before me. Singing in the fire! Yes, God helping us, if that is the only way to get harmony out of these hard apathetic hearts, let the furnace be heated seven times hotter than before."*

So, as Christians are challenged in II Timothy 2:1, let us "be strong in the grace that is in Christ Jesus" and allow Him to perfect His grace in us.

# He Is at Work

Psalm 37:5

*"Commit thy way unto the LORD; trust also in him; and he shall bring it to pass."*

Roll the entire burden of life onto the Lord, and let Him carry it for you. "Cast thy burden upon the LORD, and he shall sustain thee: he shall never suffer the righteous to be moved"—Psalm 55:22. He will make provision for the need, whatever it may be. When we commit something to Him, then we must believe He is at work, and that He *will* work on our behalf, regardless of any contrary circumstances. When we believe He is at work, He takes our anxieties and replaces them with His sweet peace. When we "trust in the LORD with all [our] heart"—Proverbs 3:5, it will not matter that He does not seem to be working, for faith does not require sight. Our expectancy that He is at work on our behalf will enable the Holy Spirit to accomplish the very thing we have committed to the Lord. Release any hold you may have over a matter, place it in the capable hands of Almighty God, and trust Him to provide. He will work, and if we have truly committed our ways to Him, then we may rest assured He is at work on our behalf. He will bring it to pass.

# He Is Alive

Mark 16:6

*"And he saith unto them, Be not affrighted: Ye seek Jesus of Nazareth, which was crucified: he is risen; he is not here: behold the place where they laid him."*

The Lord Jesus is alive! "He is risen, as he said"—Matthew 28:6b. "Now when Jesus was risen early the first day of the week, he appeared first to Mary Magdalene, out of whom he had cast seven devils. . . . After that he appeared in another form unto two of them, as they walked, and went into the country. . . . Afterward he appeared unto the eleven as they sat at meat . . . So then after the Lord had spoken unto them, he was received up into heaven, and sat on the right hand of God"—Mark 16:9, 12, 14a, 19. The devil did not have power over Him, and death was powerless against Him, for Jesus Christ is "the resurrection, and the life"—John 11:25. "His soul was not left in hell, neither his flesh did see corruption. The Lord Jesus Christ—God's Lamb that was perfect and without blemish or spot—I Peter 1:19—took our sin upon Himself and went to hell for us. If He had not done this, we would have had to go to hell and pay our own penalty for sin. This Jesus hath God raised up"—Acts 2:31b, 32a.

Take courage today in your circumstances, because this risen Saviour of ours "ever liveth to make intercession for [us]"—Hebrews 7:25b. He is praying for us that our "faith fail not"—Luke 22:32b. "For there is one God, and one mediator between God and men, the man Christ Jesus"—I Timothy 2:5. Our circumstances may seem hopeless, but there is hope in Jesus Christ. He is alive! Look to Him. Rejoice in Him. Keep looking to Him and not at the stormy circumstances of life. He is, "the way, the truth, and the **life**"—John 14:6a.

# Triumphant in Christ

II Corinthians 2:14a

*"Now thanks be unto God, which always causeth us to triumph in Christ."*

God will always cause us to be triumphant in Christ, even though many of life's circumstances are so rough that they toss us to and fro like the waves of the sea. When the disciples were in the ship that was "in the midst of the sea, tossed with waves . . . Jesus went unto them, walking on the sea" –Matthew 14:24-25. The Lord Jesus walked on the water to demonstrate that His followers cannot go where He cannot come. He is able to always come to our aid, regardless of any difficult situation we face or what remote place we might be; and because of this truth, God can always enable us to triumph in Christ!

Jesus Christ is life everlasting, and in Him there is no death. Therefore, even when we "walk through the valley of the shadow of death" –Psalm 23:4, in Christ we can be triumphant. The Lord is always available to us whenever we need Him, for He "shall neither slumber nor sleep" –Psalm 121:4; therefore, we may be triumphant in Christ. In our weakness He is our strength; in our sorrow He is our comfort; in our uncertainty He is our wisdom; in all of life He is our sustenance. Jesus Christ is "he that liveth, and was dead." He is "alive for evermore," and He has "the keys of hell and of death" –Revelation 1:18; therefore, regardless of life's circumstances, we can be triumphant in Christ.

## Day 170

# Heavenly Benefits

Psalm 103:2

*"Bless the LORD, O my soul, and forget not all his benefits."*

The Lord has given us a greater benefit package than any job or insurance agency could ever give us. Life insurance policies are designed to help with expenses and to give a sense of security in the event of a loved one's death, but God gives us the benefit of eternal life through Jesus Christ. "For God so loved the world, that he gave his only begotten Son, that whosoever believeth in him should not perish, but have everlasting life"—John 3:16. We have been given security in death through Jesus Christ, because we have been given eternal life with Him. "For we know that if our earthly house of this tabernacle were dissolved, we have a building of God, an house not made with hands, eternal in the heavens"—II Corinthians 5:1. Everyone who has called upon the Name of the Lord has this great benefit that God has given.

The Lord's benefit package is quite extensive as we see in the following verses of Psalm 103. He "forgiveth all thine iniquities"—verse 3a. When we confess any sin that we commit, "he is faithful and just to forgive us our sins, and to cleanse us from all unrighteousness"—I John 1:9b. The benefit package continues. He heals all our diseases; He redeems our life from destruction; He blesses us with His loving kindness; He is merciful and gracious to us, and He is slow to get angry with us—Psalm 103:2-8. Whatever the status of your life is today, remember God's benefit package and bless the Lord.

# Speaking Out for Christ

Psalm 81:10b

*"Open thy mouth wide, and I will fill it."*

As Christians it is our privilege and our duty to be witnesses for Christ by telling others of His power to save. We are not required to be eloquent speakers or even highly educated. We are simply instructed to open our mouth, be willing vessels for our Lord to use to tell others of the hope that lies within us. The Holy Spirit of God within us will give us the words to tell others how to be saved from eternal death to eternal life through Jesus Christ. The Lord doesn't just ask us to open our mouth, but He asks us to open our mouth wide, or in other words, to "be ready always to give an answer to every man that asketh [us] a reason of the hope that is in [us] with meekness and fear"—I Peter 3:15b.

We will be ready witnesses for Christ when we, like the Apostle Paul, remember that we are "debtor both to the Greeks, and to the Barbarians; both to the wise, and to the unwise"—Romans 1:14. We will be bold witnesses for Christ when we are "not ashamed of the gospel of Christ: for it is the power of God unto salvation to every one that believeth; to the Jew first, and also to the Greek"—Romans 1:16. We came to Jesus Christ because someone told us the wonderful news of salvation; therefore, we must do the same by opening our mouth and telling others how they too may come to know Him and be saved. When we open our mouth for Christ, God will fill it.

**Day 172**

# Taking Hold

Hebrews 11:8

*"By faith Abraham, when he was called to go out into a place which he should after receive for an inheritance, obeyed; and he went out, not knowing whither he went."*

Abraham did not know where he was going, but he knew God had called him to go. He took hold of the promise, but more importantly, he took hold of the One who had promised. By faith, Abraham kept looking to the One who knew the way and who saw the path. Abraham believed God; therefore, he acted on that belief and he went as God had instructed him.

God has called many Christians to "go out" in obedience to His call upon their lives; however, because of fear and doubting they did not obey and go. When we fear the unknown and do not trust in the Lord that "his way is perfect" and that "he is a buckler to all them who trust in him"—II Samuel 22:31, then we will be more likely to disobey and not go as He has directed. "The fear of man bringeth a snare: but whoso putteth his trust in the LORD shall be safe"—Proverbs 29:25. The way may never be as we imagine, and our circumstances may not turn out the way we expected them to, but we can, by faith, simply take hold of the One who has called us to go. When we believe God and obey Him, though the way may not be easy, we will receive the blessing and reward that God has prepared for us.

# Standing Fast

Philippians 4:1

*"Stand fast in the Lord"*

Standing fast in the Lord is a place of security. It will keep us from being "carried about with every wind of doctrine" –Ephesians 4:14b, because we are anchoring ourselves to Christ. The lack of popularity, the ridicule and jeering we may receive from the world, even possible scorn and reproach from other believers, will not be able to turn us away from the Lord when we are standing unmovable in Him. When it is in Christ that "we live, and move, and have our being" –Acts 17:28a, then we will stand fast in Him.

We will stand fast in the Lord when we have the same mind "which was also in Christ Jesus" –Philippians 2:5a: the mind of humility, the mind to serve others, and the mind to glorify God, our Father. When we "do all things without murmurings and disputings" –Philippians 2:14, "rejoice in the Lord alway" –Philippians 4:4a, "and have no confidence in the flesh" –Philippians 3:3, we will be able to stand fast in the Lord.

*Day 174*

# Kept

Psalm 121:5

*"The LORD is thy keeper: the LORD is thy shade upon thy right hand."*

It is the Lord who keeps us. If He did not keep us, we would not be kept. He is our Protector from evil, our Attendant in trouble, and our Guard against sin. "He will not suffer [our] foot to be moved: he that keepeth thee will not slumber"—Psalm 121:3. Therefore, He is our Keeper by day and by night, and in every situation. If we "will lift up [our] eyes unto the hills, from whence cometh [our] help," then we can be assured that "[our] help cometh from the LORD, which made heaven and earth"—Psalm 121:1-2. Whatever the trouble may be, let us remember that it is the Lord who will keep us safe in His hands.

*Day 175*

# Jealous for Our Love

Zechariah 1:14

*"So the angel that communed with me said unto me, Cry thou, saying, Thus saith the LORD of hosts; I am jealous for Jerusalem and for Zion with a great jealousy."*

God is jealous with a great jealousy for those that are His. When someone asked Jesus what was the greatest commandment in the law, He answered, saying, "Thou shalt love the Lord thy God with all thy heart, and with all thy soul, and with all thy mind"—Matthew 22:37. God doesn't want only a portion of our love; He wants us to love Him with all our heart, soul and mind. Think a moment about His love for us: "God so loved the world, that he gave his only begotten Son, that whosoever believeth in him should not perish, but have everlasting life"—John 3:16. "Behold, what manner of love the Father hath bestowed upon us, that we should be called the sons of God"—I John 3:1a. The more we comprehend His great love for us, the more we will grow in love with Him, for "we love him, because he first loved us"—I John 4:19.

God is jealous as a husband or wife would be if they were not their spouse's only love. Many times it would seem that God has to compete for our love and attention. Is God competing for your love? Is there something or someone that you have a greater love for than the Lord God Almighty? Some people put their children or grandchildren before God. Others have a prized possession that attracts all their attention and time. Let us examine our hearts and consider if we are making the Lord jealous. If we are, we should ask the Lord to show us how to love Him with all of our heart, soul and mind.

## *Day 176*

# Faith in Contrary Circumstances

Matthew 14:22, 24

*"And straightway Jesus constrained his disciples to get into a ship, and to go before him unto the other side, while he sent the multitudes away. . . . But the ship was now in the midst of the sea, tossed with waves: for the wind was contrary."*

Faith is strengthened in the midst of storms. Faith is simply believing God and taking Him at His Word. It is not a matter of believing **about** Him, but **believing** Him. It believes He is Almighty, and that He is "Lord alone; [He] hast made heaven, the heaven of heavens, with all their host, the earth, and all things that are therein, the seas, and all that is therein"—Nehemiah 9:6. Faith believes the Lord has all power in Heaven and in earth –Matthew 28:18. Faith says, "Thine, O LORD, is the greatness, and the power, and the glory, and the victory, and the majesty: for all that is in the heaven and in the earth is thine; thine is the kingdom, O LORD, and thou are exalted as head above all"—I Chronicles 29:11. Faith believes that "He delivereth and rescueth, and he worketh signs and wonders in heaven and in earth, who hath delivered Daniel from the power of the lions"—Daniel 6:27. Faith believes that if God delivered Daniel, (and He did), He will deliver us from our troubles.

It is in our troubles that we realize our weaknesses and inabilities and begin to understand our need and dependency upon the Lord. There is no trouble too difficult for the Lord to take care of. The devil would like us to believe to the contrary, and so he comes to us in our trouble and speaks all sorts of lies, such as; "There's no way your God can deliver you from this." But remember, the devil is the father of lies—John 8:44. So be strong in the Lord during times of temptation and turn to the Scriptures, for "faith cometh by hearing, and hearing by the word of God"—Romans 10:17. The Lord allows troubles to come into our lives to strengthen our faith and deepen our walk with Him. Rest assured that He will be with you in the trouble and will deliver you. Therefore, "be not afraid, only believe"—Mark 5:36, and your faith will stand strong in the midst of your troubles.

# Clean Inside and Out

Matthew 23:24-25

*"Ye blind guides, which strain at a gnat, and swallow a camel. Woe unto you, scribes and Pharisees, hypocrites! For ye make clean the outside of the cup and of the platter, but within they are full of extortion and excess."*

As Christians, we spend much time and effort on our outward appearance. Like these scribes and Pharisees, we make our outward appearance clean, but do we give as much attention to the person we are on the inside? While our outward appearance is clean, our hearts may not be clean. Are we more concerned about how we look to people than about how God sees us? We would do well to remember: "the LORD seeth not as man seeth; for man looketh on the outward appearance, but the LORD looketh on the heart"—I Samuel 16:7b. David didn't look much like a king, but his heart was fervent toward the Lord.

Many times people look right on the outside, but their hearts are filled with jealousy, anger, unforgiveness, bitterness, gossip, and other sins of the flesh. It is human nature to think of self. When our hearts are filled with jealousy and anger, we are thinking of ourselves. Jealousy stems from wanting what someone else has, whether talent or possessions, and desiring to have it ourselves. Anger has its root in pride, and can rise up in us because something doesn't go according to our way, or someone doesn't do something according to our way. There is a tendency to withhold forgiveness, thinking we would never do what someone has done to us. In this way, we are thinking more highly of ourselves than we should. The root of our unclean hearts usually always stems from selfish pride.

As Christians, we need to spend more time on keeping our hearts clean and pure before the Lord. We need to take time daily to "groom" our hearts as well as our appearance. "Draw nigh to God, and he will draw nigh to you. Cleanse your hands, ye sinners; and purify your hearts, ye double minded"—James 4:8. We need to continue to keep our outward appearance clean, but we also must take time to make sure our hearts are clean.

## *Day 178*

# Hope in the Word of God

Psalm 130:5

*"I wait for the Lord, my soul doth wait, and in his word do I hope."*

The circumstances that presently encompass our lives may be bleak, but the promises of God will give us hope. Our prayers may seem to go unanswered, but God has promised to answer when we call; therefore, do not lose hope, but wait for the Lord; He will answer in His time.

Sin may seem to control us; however, there is hope in God's Word: "If we confess our sins, he is faithful and just to forgive us our sins, and to cleanse us from all unrighteousness" –I John 1:9. "We are more than conquerors through him that loved us" –Romans 8:37. There may be prodigals in our homes; however, there is hope in the Word of God. He gave us promises to claim by faith. We are able to take those promises to Him in prayer, then with confidence wait for the Lord to work. "And the peace of God, which passeth all understanding, shall keep your hearts and minds through Christ Jesus" –Philippians 4:7 when we hope in the Word of the Lord and bring everything to Him in prayer.

How can we have this blessed hope when we do not know the promises of God? It is by searching, by reading, and by studying the Word of God that we will find His promises upon which we may hope. God has given us a sweet love letter, an instructional guide book for life, called the Bible –His Word. Therefore, let us be diligent to read it, study it, memorize it, and get to know it well.

# Confident We Will Receive

I John 5:14-15

*"And this is the confidence that we have in him, that, if we ask any thing according to his will, he heareth us: And if we know that he hear us, whatsoever we ask, we know that we have the petitions that we desired of him."*

We can be confident to expect answers to our prayers when they are based on unwavering faith in the One to whom we are praying and in full submission to His will concerning a matter. Many will tack the phrase "if it be Your will" onto the end of their prayers, hoping His will *is* their will without taking time to find out what His will is. We need to be careful to examine our hearts to find out if we are truly submitted to God's will regardless of what it may be so that we may sincerely say as the Lord Jesus Christ said, "nevertheless not my will, but thine be done"—Luke 22:42.

It is the Holy Spirit that teaches us inwardly, and it is He, in us, who leads us to pray according to the will of God, because "we know not what we should pray for as we ought: but the Spirit itself maketh intercession for us with groanings which cannot be uttered. And he that searcheth the hearts knoweth what is the mind of the Spirit, because he maketh intercession for the saints according to the will of God"—Romans 8:26-27. Therefore, when we are uncertain of God's will, we should submit ourselves unto the Spirit's control and continue in prayer until "the peace of God rules in [our] hearts"—Collosians 3:15a regarding the will of God in a matter.

Unless we are led by the Holy Spirit in prayer, we will pray amiss; and therefore, we can ask, but we may not receive. When we pray according to the will of God, led by His Spirit, then we can have confidence that what we are praying for, we will receive.

**Day 180**

# Command Ye Me

Isaiah 45:11

*"Thus saith the LORD, the Holy One of Israel, and his Maker, Ask me of things to come concerning my sons, and concerning the work of my hands command ye me."*

The Lord is our Commander in Chief, and He has given us permission to command Him, or in other words, to boldly come unto Him in prayer. Joshua commanded Him in the day of battle against the enemy according to the Word of the Lord: "And the LORD said unto Joshua, Fear them not: for I have delivered them into thine hand; there shall not a man of them stand before thee. . . . Then spake Joshua to the LORD in the day when the LORD delivered up the Amorites before the children of Israel, and he said in the sight of Israel, Sun, stand thou still upon Gibeon; and thou, Moon, in the valley of Ajalon. And the sun stood still, and the moon stayed, until the people had avenged themselves upon their enemies"—Joshua 10:8, 12, 13.

What a contrast this is to our hesitating, timid, and sometimes unbelieving prayers that we are most often accustomed to offering! God's Word is filled with His promises; however, because of our unbelief we many times fail to boldly command the work of His hands. As the Lord Jesus walked this earth He was often putting people in the position to boldly ask of Him. When He entered the city of Jericho, He stood still and asked blind beggars, "What will ye that I shall do unto you?"— Matthew 20:32b.

God has given us this invitation to boldly come to Him, and He has given us His Holy Spirit to intercede for us when we don't know what to pray. "Likewise the Spirit also helpeth our infirmities: for we know not what we should pray for as we ought: but the Spirit itself maketh intercession for us with groanings which cannot be uttered"—Romans 8:26. Consider whether your prayers are bold through the Holy Spirit or weak with unbelief in the flesh. Believe what God has spoken, and with boldness go to Him in prayer, commanding the work of His hands.

# Abounding in the Joy of the Lord

II Chronicles 20:22

*"And when they began to sing and to praise, the LORD set ambushments against the children of Ammon, Moab, and mount Seir, which were come against Judah; and they were smitten."*

Singing and praising the Lord is the glorious key to unlocking the joy of the Lord within us. Our troubles would become as nothing if we would only learn to sing praises to God. Steps were taken in order to get into the place of singing and praising the Lord. King Jehoshaphat made supplication: "And Jehoshaphat stood in the congregation of Judah and Jerusalem, in the house of the LORD, before the new court, And said, O LORD God of our fathers, art not thou God in heaven? And rulest not thou over all the kingdoms of the heathen? And in thine hand is there not power and might, so that none is able to withstand thee?"—II Chronicles 20:5-6. We fail to sing and to praise because, in our independence, we fail to look unto the Lord and call upon His Name to help. Jehoshaphat looked unto the Lord with complete dependency. "O our God, wilt thou not judge them? For we have no might against this great company that cometh against us; neither know we what to do: but our eyes are upon thee"—II Chronicles 20:12. Turn your eyes upon the Lord, make supplication unto Him, open your hearts to worship and to praise Him, and you too will begin to sing. Remember, "the battle is not yours, but God's"—II Chronicles 20:15c, and he "will answer" when we call—Jeremiah 33:3.

How different our troubles would seem to us if we would be God-centered instead of being self-centered! We will abound with joy when we lift up our daily experiences to the Lord and praise Him for those experiences, whether good or bad. It is easier to *sing* our troubles away, than to *reason* them away. Follow the steps that Jehoshaphat and the children of Israel took so that you too can begin to **sing** and to praise the Lord in the midst of your troubles.

## Day 182

# Cannot Be Silent

Psalm 69:30

*"I will praise the name of God with a song, and will magnify him with thanksgiving."*

Sing songs of praise to your Redeemer, Jesus Christ, for with His blood He purchased our pardon, made us whole, and "set [our] feet upon a rock, and established [our] goings. And he hath put a new song in [our] mouth, even praise unto our God"—Psalm 40:2b-3a. The more we think of the power in Jesus' Name, the hope there is in His Name, the answers to prayer we may obtain through His Name, and the inheritance we have as Christians in His Name, the more we will want to sing songs of praise to Him and not be silent. "My lips shall greatly rejoice when I sing unto thee; and my soul, which thou hast redeemed"—Psalm 71:23. Singing praises to God will encourage our hearts, strengthen our resolve to continue in the work of God regardless of struggles, trouble, or opposition, and will affect those who are listening. "This also shall please the LORD better than an ox or bullock that hath horns and hoofs"—Psalm 69:31, meaning, more than great sacrifice.

How better can we magnify the Lord than with thanksgiving? A thankful heart is a rejoicing heart, and a rejoicing heart will sing praises to the Name of God. If we know Jesus Christ through salvation, then our hearts should be full of thanksgiving. It is Jesus Christ that makes the difference in our lives and gives us peace with joy unspeakable and full of glory; therefore magnify Him with thanksgiving. Sing songs of praise to the Name of God and magnify Him with thanksgiving from the time you wake in the morning until you pillow your head at night.

# Inward Cleansing

Matthew 23:26

*"Thou blind Pharisee, cleanse first that which is within the cup and platter, that the outside of them may be clean also."*

The Lord Jesus said, "That except your righteousness shall exceed the righteousness of the scribes and Pharisees, ye shall in no case enter into the kingdom of heaven"—Matthew 5:20. It is not by our good works that we are made clean, for "there is none that doeth good, no, not one"—Romans 3:12b. If we have not received Jesus Christ as our Savior, then we have not been changed from the nature of sin that we were born with, for "who can say, I have made my heart clean, I am pure from my sin?"—Proverbs 20:9. It is only through Jesus Christ that we are made clean and new. "Therefore if any man be in Christ, he is a new creature: old things are passed away; behold, all things are become new"—II Corinthians 5:17.

When our heart has been made clean through salvation in Jesus Christ, then it should be evidenced in our countenance, our attitude, our responses, and our life. It is only by the righteousness of Jesus Christ that we are made clean and righteous from sin. "For he [God] hath made him [Jesus] to be sin for us, who knew no sin; that we might be made the righteousness of God in him"—II Corinthians 5:21. As believers, we need to daily pray, "Create in me a clean heart, O God; and renew a right spirit within me"—Psalm 51:10. When we take care to keep our hearts clean before the Lord, then the nature of Jesus Christ in us will be more noticeable to others. Take care that the inside condition of the heart is first made clean so that the outside may be clean also.

*Day 184*

# Truth—God's Inspired Word

II Timothy 3:16-17

*"All scripture is given by inspiration of God, and is profitable for doctrine, for reproof, for correction, for instruction in righteousness: That the man of God may be perfect, throughly furnished unto all good works."*

It is hard for us to truly comprehend and understand that apart from God there is no love, no righteousness, and no truth. Where science disagrees with the Word of God, then it is wrong, because God is truth, and apart from Him and His Word there is no truth. God's Word is given by inspiration and we are profited by it, because "the words of the LORD are pure words: as silver tried in a furnace of earth, purified seven times"—Psalm 12:6. "Jesus saith . . . I am the truth"—John 14:6; therefore, it is to our profit if we "search the scriptures"—John 5:39a in order to know Jesus Christ, who is the truth. When we know the truth, then we will be less likely to be "carried about with every wind of doctrine, by the sleight of men, and cunning craftiness, whereby they lie in wait to deceive"—Ephesians 4:14b. The more we know the truth of God's Word, the more we will follow sound doctrine and will be open to receive correction and instruction so that we may become more and more like Christ. May we be diligent to walk by the truth of God's Word and not by the philosophy of man.

# A High Mountain Apart

Mark 9:2

*"And after six days Jesus taketh with him Peter, and James, and John, and leadeth them up into an high mountain apart by themselves: and he was transfigured before them."*

In our Christian lives there are times that we are led by the Lord Jesus to "an high mountain" where He gives us a glimpse of His glory and power. Our "mountaintop" experiences often take place when we are alone with Christ and apart from everyone and everything else. Elijah was led to Mount Horeb before the Lord spoke and revealed Himself to Elijah –I Kings 19:8-18. Abraham was on Mount Moriah when the Lord revealed Himself to him –Genesis 22:1-14. The Lord led them to the mount, and it was on the mountain that the Lord revealed Himself and gave instructions.

Our mountaintop experiences are meant to equip us with God's power to live in the routine of everyday life. No one wants to leave the mountain where the Lord has given glimpses into His glory, but it is not on the mountain where we will be greatly used of the Lord; it is in the routine of daily life. It is in heartache, sorrow, and suffering that we are able to reveal God's glory to others.

The Lord uses the mountain experiences to equip us to walk in "the valley of the shadow of death" –Psalm 23:4 where we can be a blessing, a help, and an encouragement to others by exhibiting the great hope we have in Christ. It is in the sorrows and grief of life that we, as Christians, can demonstrate the great character of Christ. Rejoice when the mountaintop experience comes; then allow the experience to strengthen and carry you through the mundane routine of life so that God may be glorified in daily living.

## Day 186

# Make Ready

Luke 22:11-14

*"And ye shall say unto the goodman of the house, The Master saith unto thee, Where is the guest chamber, where I shall eat the Passover with my disciples? And he shall shew you a large upper room furnished: there make ready. And they went, and found as he had said unto them: and they made ready the passover. And when the hour was come, he sat down, and the twelve apostles with him."*

We make ready for company when they are coming to visit, whether it be family or friends. We make ready for holidays, for special events that take place in our lives, for college, for retirement, and for a number of other things. We spend quite a bit of time in preparation for any one of these events, because we want the occasion to go well. As Christians we need to make ready for the coming again of Jesus Christ, our Saviour. The Apostles "made ready the passover" by doing as Jesus instructed them. As Christians, we can make ready for the Saviour's return by doing as He has instructed us. "Watch therefore: for ye know not what hour your Lord doth come. But know this, that if the goodman of the house had known in what watch the thief would come, he would have watched, and would not have suffered his house to be broken up. Therefore be ye also ready: for in such an hour as ye think not the Son of man cometh"— Matthew 24:42-44.

We need to be praying for our family's spiritual welfare and interceding for our brothers and sisters in Christ so that they will stand strong in their faith and be ready for the return of Jesus Christ. When the Apostles got everything ready, the Lord Jesus came as He promised. He is coming again as He promised; therefore, we need to make ready for His coming now, because when He comes there will not be time to get ready.

# Continual Feast

John 6:35

*"And Jesus said unto them, I am the bread of life: he that cometh to me shall never hunger; and he that believeth on me shall never thirst."*

Jesus is the "bread of life" to every Christian, which means He is our sustaining strength to face every new day with its possible struggles and troubles, our joy in every situation of life, and our help to overcome the temptation to sin. Every person that comes to Him can be continually filled with His joy, love, strength, and ability by His Spirit so that the emptiness we sometimes feel can be satisfied. "Blessed are they which do hunger and thirst after righteousness: for they shall be filled"—Matthew 5:6.

As Christians we have a continual spiritual feast, because the Holy Spirit who now lives in us "will guide [us] into all truth: for he shall not speak of himself; but whatsoever he shall hear, that shall he speak: and he will shew [us] things to come."—John 16:13. "For what man knoweth the things of a man, save the spirit of man which is in him? Even so the things of God knoweth no man, but the Spirit of God. Now we have received, not the spirit of the world, but the spirit which is of God; that we might know the things that are freely given to us of God"—I Corinthians 2:11-12. Therefore, it is by daily reading, studying, and meditating on God's Word as well as striving to memorize great portions of the Bible that we can "grow in grace, and in the knowledge of our Lord and Saviour Jesus Christ"—II Peter 3:18a. Just as food that is not eaten cannot strengthen the physical body, the Word of God that is not applied to our hearts cannot strengthen the Christian's life.

When we have Jesus Christ, we do not need alcohol, drugs, or any other worldly substance that many people turn to in their search to fill a void in their life or to escape the hopelessness that they feel. Jesus Christ is the Bread of life and He will satisfy the hungry soul.

*Day 188*

# Be of Good Cheer

Mark 6:50-52

*"For they all saw him, and were troubled. And immediately he talked with them, and saith unto them, Be of good cheer: it is I; be not afraid. And he went up unto them into the ship; and the wind ceased: and they were sore amazed in themselves beyond measure, and wondered. For they considered not the miracle of the loaves: for their heart was hardened."*

How soon we forget what God has done for us! The disciples had just seen the Lord Jesus feed the multitude until they were sufficiently full; however, the disciples were no longer thinking of the recent miracle that Jesus had performed, because the present storm was gripping them with fear.

If we would focus our attention on the Lord and not on our circumstances, then we would be more likely to see the blessings all around us by remembering that He has been working in our lives and performing miracles on our behalf for His glory. The Lord is with us in our "storms," and He will comfort us as He comforted those in the ship when He said, "Be of good cheer: it is I; be not afraid." Though our hearts may be in great sorrow, our lives may be in great danger, or our circumstances may be frightening, we must fight against letting the devil rob us of our joy in the Lord. Our comfort lies in the knowledge that the Lord is with us; therefore, we can choose to be of good cheer.

We can be of good cheer not only because the Lord is with us and He will be our comfort, but He can calm the storm and put an end to it: "And he went up unto them into the ship; and the wind ceased." "He knoweth our frame; he remembereth that we are dust"—Psalm 103:14; therefore, He knows how much we can endure, and any hardship we may experience will never exceed that which He can enable us to handle. Be of good cheer and do not be afraid, for the Lord is there, and He will guide us through every difficulty we may face.

# Cure for an Overwhelmed Heart

Psalm 77:3b

*"I complained, and my spirit was overwhelmed."*

This Psalm is one that King David wrote, and God said of him, "I have found David the son of Jesse, a man after mine own heart, which shall fulfill all my will"—Acts 13:22b. Even so, David's spirit later became overwhelmed. If David's spirit was overwhelmed, then most assuredly our spirit will be overwhelmed at some time or another. David became overwhelmed by complaining. It is human nature to complain, and we tend to complain when we become unthankful and discontented. We become discontented because we long for what we do not have. We think that if we only had _____, then we would be happy and content. We become vain in our imaginations because we think we know better than Almighty God. Neither do we "esteem other better" than ourselves—Philippians 2:3 because our minds are centered upon ourselves and what we wish we had. Longing for what we do not have instead of being thankful and content with what we do have, will always lead us to complain, and complaining causes our spirit to be overwhelmed. We must stop complaining if we want our spirit to be at peace. "In everything give thanks: for this is the will of God in Christ Jesus concerning you"—I Thessalonians 5:18. When we see God as our Benevolent Master in every part of our life, and accept all He allows to occur in our life, we will turn from complaining to rejoicing in Him, which will calm our spirit and give us peace that passes understanding.

**Day 190**

# A Personal Relationship

Matthew 6:9

*"After this manner therefore pray ye: Our Father"*

As Christians, we have a personal relationship with a personal God, and when we talk with Him we may address Him as "***Our*** Father." He is Almighty God, but we may call Him" Father"! He is not a stranger to His children; He is "***Our*** Father"! He is not an acquaintance; He is "***Our*** Father"! Our relationship to Him is even more personal than our relationship to our biological father. He knows each of His children on a personal basis, and we are of such great value to Him that "the very hairs of your [our] head are all numbered" –Matthew 10:30. When we received His Son, Jesus Christ, as our Savior, He opened His arms to us with a loving welcome to His newborn child. He has made Himself available to us at all hours of the day or night, for He "shall neither slumber nor sleep" –Psalm 121:4b. Our relationship with Him is personal, and He desires that we call Him "Our Father."

# A Sure Relationship

Matthew 6:9

*"Our Father which art in heaven"*

We have a sure relationship with a personal God—our Father! His "word is truth" –John 17:17b; therefore, we can be sure that He is in Heaven. Heaven does exist, and our Father is there. The surety of our relationship with Him enables us to "press toward the mark for the prize of the high calling of God in Christ Jesus" –Philippians 3:14. We will encounter difficult obstacles as we live for Christ; however, our Father in Heaven knows "the way that I take: when he hath tried me, I shall come forth as gold" –Job 23:10. There will be times when we feel like giving up, and we will want to "throw in the towel," as the old saying goes, because the way just seems too hard; however, we may be ***sure*** that our Father is in Heaven and He is there for us. We cannot see Him, but we can be ***sure*** He is there, because His Word tells us that He is. Do not despair; we have a sure relationship with our Father who is in Heaven.

**Day 192**

# A Holy Relationship

Matthew 6:9b

*"Our Father which art in heaven, Hallowed be thy name."*

Our Father is holy; His Name is holy; therefore we must hold Him in reverence and regard Him as holy. Throughout the Scriptures He speaks of His holiness and how that holiness requires holiness from His people. This holiness is possible only through His Son, Jesus Christ, at salvation. If we are saved, then we have a holy relationship with the Father.

Because God–Our Father—is holy, our relationship with Him is one of holiness through Jesus Christ. "As he which hath called you is holy, so be ye holy in all manner of conversation; because it is written, Be ye holy; for I am holy" –I Peter 1:15-16. "For if the firstfruit be holy, the lump is also holy: and if the root be holy, so are the branches" –Romans 11:16. "Holy, holy, holy, is the LORD of hosts" –Isaiah 6:3a.

# A Holy Relationship with God in Prayer

Matthew 6:9

*"After this manner therefore pray ye: Our Father which art in heaven, Hallowed be thy name."*

God is holy and "there is none holy as the LORD"—I Samuel 2:2a; therefore we must "humble [ourselves] in the sight of the Lord"—James 4:10a when we pray. As we go to Him in prayer, "let us worship and bow down: let us kneel before the LORD our maker. For he is our God; and we are the people of his pasture, and the sheep of his hand"— Psalm 95:6-7. When we enter into prayer with Him, let us remember that we are coming before *the* King of Heaven and earth; therefore, remember the holiness of our King and revere Him with the respect and holy reverence due unto Him. He told Moses, "Put off thy shoes from thy feet: for the place where thou standest is holy ground"—Acts 7:33. His holiness requires holiness, so take some time to be holy instead of rushing into prayer. ". . . He which hath called you is holy, so be ye holy in all manner of conversation; Because it is written, Be ye holy; for I am holy"—I Peter 1:15-16. Our Father is holy, His name is holy, and our relationship with Him in prayer must be holy.

*Day 194*

# A Dependent Relationship with God in Prayer

Matthew 6:11

*"Give us this day our daily bread."*

As Christians, we have a dependent relationship with God the Father. When we ask for "our daily bread" it teaches us to constantly depend upon Him for our needs. We need daily grace to live honestly and industriously for His glory so that we do not spend our time in idleness—Proverbs 31:27b. We need daily strength to "resist the devil"—James 4:7 and his temptations. We need daily help to "live peaceably with all men"—Romans 12:28, and to "let [our] light so shine before men, that they may see [our] good works, and glorify [our] Father which is in heaven"—Matthew 5:16. When we go to God in prayer for our daily needs it declares our complete dependency upon Him, and is a daily reminder that without God we are helpless. Our hearts may deceive us into thinking we do not need Him to enable us to get out of bed each morning, but as soon as we injure our back, our legs, or another major body part, we are reminded of our need for God's help daily for everything.

Seeking "our daily bread" teaches us to renew the desire of our heart toward the Father as well as our dependency upon Him; therefore, "seek ye first the kingdom of God, and his righteousness"—Matthew 6:33a daily and build this dependent child-and- Father relationship that we have with God. As Christians, we need Him every day; therefore, we must not let one day go by without going to our Father in prayer for "our daily bread."

# A Forgiving Relationship with God in Prayer

Matthew 6:12

*"And forgive us our debts, as we forgive our debtors."*

God's hand of mercy is continually extended toward His children so that He is "ready to forgive"—Psalm 86:5. "If we confess our sins, he is faithful and just to forgive us our sins, and to cleanse us from all unrighteousness"—I John 1:9. This forgiveness from the Father took our scarlet sin and made us clean through the blood of His only Begotten Son, Jesus Christ; and it is also what continues to keep us in a right relationship with Him after we are saved. For "though [our] sins be as scarlet, they shall be as white as snow; though they be red like crimson, they shall be as wool"—Isaiah 1:18. We could not have sweet fellowship with Him in prayer without His forgiveness. "Behold, the LORD's hand is not shortened, that it cannot save; neither his ear heavy, that it cannot hear: But [our] iniquities have separated between [us] and [our] God, and [our] sins have hid his face from [us], that he will not hear"—Isaiah 59:1-2. In order to keep our relationship right with Him and our communication with Him open, we need to confess any sins that are in our hearts.

We must forgive as we hope to be forgiven. "If [we] do not forgive, neither will [our] Father which is in heaven forgive [our] trespasses"—Mark 11:26. If we desire to find mercy with God, then we must show mercy to others. God the Father forgives every time we confess; therefore, He expects us to forgive our Christian brothers and sisters with the same frequency. The Lord Jesus' response to Peter's question, "Lord, how oft shall my brother sin against me, and I forgive him? Till seven times?" was "I say not unto thee, Until seven times: but, Until seventy times seven"—Matthew 18:21-22. "For if [we] forgive men their trespasses, [our] heavenly Father will also forgive [us]: But if [we] forgive not men their trespasses, neither will [our] Father forgive [our] trespasses"—Matthew 6:14-15. Our relationship with God the Father is a forgiving relationship. He forgives us our debts and in like manner we must forgive our debtors if we are to have a right relationship with the Father in prayer.

*Day 196*

# Making Jesus Christ Known

I Chronicles 16:8c, 9c

*"Make known his deeds among the people . . . talk ye of all his wondrous works."*

Make Christ known to the people you live with, live by, work with, and to everyone you come in contact with. "Shew forth his salvation from day to day" –Psalm 96:2b. We need to be like the Apostle Paul and continually tell others how God saved us. Declare joyfully the wonder of God's love and mercy, so that others may be led to receive Him, and likewise adore Him.

Talk adoringly of His magnificence with praise and reverence so that others may be edified and taught to do the same. Exalt the Lord by telling others how He has answered prayer for you, has been a comfort to you, and has loved you so unconditionally. Lift Him up with words of praise, and honor, and glory. We must not let the fear of man silence us from proclaiming the greatness of Almighty God, but rather, we must be bold, and make known His deeds among the people, talking of all His wondrous works.

# Christ Living In Me

Galatians 2:20

*"I am crucified with Christ: nevertheless I live; yet not I, but Christ liveth in me: and the life which I now live in the flesh I live by the faith of the Son of God, who loved me, and gave himself for me."*

Because Christ lives in me, I no longer have to be a servant of sin to unrighteousness. Now "I can do all things through Christ" –Philippians 4:13. Because Christ lives in me, I am able, with His help, to be an extension of the life He lived on earth; and by His Holy Spirit, I am able to "walk not after the flesh, but after the Spirit" –Romans 8:4b. Yielding to Christ enables me to forgive as He forgave, love as He loved, and be kind, gentle, patient, and meek, following His example. Because Christ lives in me, "old things are passed away; behold, all things are become new" –II Corinthians 5:17b.

As Christians we need to pattern our life after the life of Christ. What He did not look upon, neither should we. What He did not do, we must not do. Where He would not go, we must not go. The Lord Jesus "went about doing good" –Acts 10:38b; therefore, so must we. Let's make it our goal to live like Christ, because Christ lives in us. We will be more likely to live like Him when we "live by the faith of the Son of God, who loved [us], and gave Himself for [us].

*Day 198*

# Conforming to Christ

I Corinthians 1:1b

*"Sanctified in Christ Jesus"*

To be "sanctified in Christ" means we are set apart from this world and are being conformed to the likeness of Jesus Christ—growing in holiness as He is holy—I Peter 1:16; growing in purity as He is pure—I John 3:3. It means learning to love others as He loves; learning to be patient toward others as He is patient with us. It is putting off the old man (our sin nature) with his sinful habits, and putting on the new creation in Christ. "In whom also ye are circumcised with the circumcision made without hands, in putting off the body of the sins of the flesh by the circumcision of Christ: Buried with him in baptism, wherein also ye are risen with him through the faith of the operation of God, who hath raised him from the dead"—Colossians 2:11-12.

God does not give us trials, sorrows, and difficulties in order to crush us; rather, they are designed to help us "be conformed to the image of his Son"—Romans 8:29b. When we begin to believe that the Lord is in every circumstance of our life, then we will be less likely to moan and complain, and we will be better able to "rejoice in the Lord alway"—Philippians 4:4a, as well as to "count it all joy when [we] fall into divers temptations"—James 1:2b. We will be able to "glory in [our] infirmities"—II Corinthians 12:9b, and to learn that "in whatsoever state [we are], therewith to be content"—Philippians 4:11b.

Being sanctified in Jesus Christ is an ongoing learning and growing process that one day will be perfected when we depart from this world and enter Heaven. So let us remember, He is still working on each of us so that we will become more conformed to the image of Christ. May we embrace each trial and allow Him to change our old nature to become new creatures in Christ so that we can be more effective tools in His hand to bring others unto Salvation.

# A Happy Christian

Psalm 146:5

*"Happy is he that hath the God of Jacob for his help, whose hope is in the Lord his God."*

When we hope in the Lord we can be sure that we will be happy, for our expectations of God can never be disappointed. Why? Because "not one thing hath failed of all the good things which the Lord your God spake concerning you; all are come to pass unto you, and not one thing hath failed thereof"—Joshua 23:14. We can call upon the Lord for help and be assured that He will help us. He has promised, "It shall come to pass, that before they call, I will answer; and while they are yet speaking, I will hear"—Isaiah 65:24.

When we are unhappy and depressed it is most likely because we are not trusting in the Lord nor placing our hope in Him. Many become discouraged because they are looking for God to work in their time frame; however, [His] thoughts are not your thoughts, neither are your ways [His] ways, saith the Lord"—Isaiah 55:8. To be a truly happy Christian we must strive to "Be still, and know that [He is] God"—Psalm 46:10a, seek His help, and hope in Him.

## *Day 200*

# Complaining Displeases the Lord

Numbers 11:1

*"And when the people complained, it displeased the LORD: and the LORD heard it; and his anger was kindled; and the fire of the LORD burnt among them, and consumed them that were in the uttermost parts of the camp."*

When we complain we are displeasing the Lord and kindling His anger. We have been exhorted, in the Bible, to "be content with such things as ye have" –Hebrews 13:5; unfortunately, however, we sometimes find ourselves discontent, and that is when complaining begins. We "vent" all sorts of grievances concerning our circumstances, because we tend to think "the grass is greener" somewhere else. Discontentment, which is the cause for our complaining spirit, occurs when we lust after worldly things instead of desiring heavenly things –Numbers 11:4-6. We become dissatisfied with the course of our life; therefore, we begin to complain.

When we learn to yield our lives to God and accept every circumstance as His will, then it is more likely that we will say, as did Job, "Naked came I out of my mother's womb, and naked shall I return thither: the LORD gave, and the LORD hath taken away; blessed be the name of the LORD" –Job 1:21. Let us determine, with God's help, not to complain so that we will not displease or anger the Lord.

# I Love the Lord

Psalm 116:1

*"I love the LORD, because he hath heard my voice and my supplications."*

There are many reasons to love the Lord. One would be that the Lord heard our voice and our supplications the day we asked Christ to save us. His love for us opened His ear to our prayers, drew us unto Himself, and forever engraved our names upon the palms of His hands –Isaiah 49:16. If God had never loved us, we would never have loved Him, nor have had any desire to love Him. "We love him, because he first loved us" –I John 4:19. Secondly, we have reason to love the Lord because of all that He has done, and all He continues to do for us. "Blessed be the Lord, who daily loadeth us with benefits, even the God of our salvation" –Psalm 68:19. Every day we receive an abundance of benefits from the Lord! Some particular benefits would be our eyesight and our hearing; we are able to see and hear God's wonderful creation. Then, of course, we have reason to love Him, because of His mercies. "It is of the Lord's mercies that we are not consumed, because his compassions fail not. They are new every morning" –Lamentations 3:22-23a.

We could not exhaust the reasons for which we love the Lord; however, the greatest reason we could have for loving Almighty God is that He loved us when we were not lovely, but rather ugly and undesirable with our sin. He did not have to love us, yet He ***did*** and ***does*** love us. "For scarcely for a righteous man will one die: yet peradventure for a good man some would even dare to die. But God commendeth his love toward us, in that, while we were yet sinners, Christ died for us" –Romans 5:7-8. When we were unworthy, unlovely, and undone, the Lord God Almighty loved us. May it be said of us that we love the Lord.

# In Love With Christ

In love with Christ
The great I Am
In love with He
Who is coming again

In love with Christ
My heart's desire
A yearning, and burning
Unquenchable fire

In love with Christ
My soul does crave
This most High God
Who came to save

In love with Christ
So intense I cannot breathe
Realizing the greater love
He has for me

# So Soon Forgotten

Psalm 106:13a

*"They soon forgat his works"*

How soon we forget what God has done for us! Maybe a certain temptation had plagued us, but God was faithful, and He made "a way to escape" so that we would be able to resist it –I Corinthians 10:13. It may be that some trial had so overwhelmed us that there didn't seem to be any hope of deliverance. However, the Lord did answer when we called; He was with us in the trouble; and He did deliver us –Psalm 91:15. The Lord works wonderful miracles for us, but sadly, it doesn't seem to take us long to forget all He did and continues to do on our behalf.

We need to make a daily practice to take time and reflect on all that God **has** done for us. Once we have reflected, then we need to take time to thank Him and praise Him for His wonderful answers to prayer. We so soon forget, because we do not take the time to remember. If God "will not remember [our] sins" –Isaiah 43:25, then let us not forget all He has done for us.

**Day 203**

# Seeing Clearly

Isaiah 6:1

*"In the year that king Uzziah died I saw also the Lord sitting upon a throne, high and lifted up, and his train filled the temple."*

Many times God chooses to remove something or someone from us, like in the case with the prophet Isaiah, so that we can see the Lord more clearly. It was in the year that King Uzziah died that Isaiah saw the Lord high and lifted up. It is when the obstruction has been removed that we can more clearly see the Lord in His majesty, His glory, and His holiness so that we too can say, "Holy, holy, holy, is the LORD of hosts: the whole earth is full of his glory"—Isaiah 6:3b. Once we have clearly seen the Lord in His holiness, we can better see our lack of holiness. Then, bowing in humility unto Him, we can say like Isaiah, "Woe is me! For I am undone; because I am a man of unclean lips, and I dwell in the midst of a people of unclean lips: for mine eyes have seen the King, the LORD of hosts"—Isaiah 6:5.

Everything about us changes when we truly see the Lord high and lifted up. The opinion we have of ourselves changes; our whole attitude about life changes into an inherent desire to obey God and follow His will. Our response to Him becomes, "Here am I; send me"—Isaiah 6:8b. When we see His worthiness and our unworthiness, we will begin to desire that Christ would continue to live His life through us so that we become an extension of the life He lived on earth. Life no longer centers on ourselves and what we want, but becomes centered on our holy and gracious Lord, and all that He desires of us. Oswald Chambers said, *"He [the Lord] never insists on obedience, but when we do see Him we obey Him instantly. He is easily Lord, and we live in adoration of Him from morning till night."* It is when God removes the obstacles in our life, which have been obstructing a clear view of Him, that we begin to see Him high and lifted up.

# All Day

Psalm 89:16

*"In thy name shall they rejoice all the day: and in thy righteousness shall they be exalted."*

It is a wonderful comfort and strength to the Christian's heart to be able to rejoice all day in the name of Jesus Christ. Our day may be full of troubles, but we can rejoice in the name of Jesus, because He is "the glory of [our] strength"—Psalm 89:17b. "The battle is not [ours], but God's"—II Chronicles 20:15b. Nothing is ever a surprise to the Lord. Even when we receive devastating news, we can rejoice in the name of Jesus, because He never leaves us nor forsakes us. He is already interceding to God the Father, for us. Therefore, "be strong and of a good courage; be not afraid, neither be thou dismayed: for the LORD thy God is with thee whithersoever thou goest"—Joshua 1:9.

Regardless of the circumstances that may fill our day, we can rejoice in the name of Jesus by turning our eyes upon Him. "[Our] help cometh from the LORD, which made heaven and earth. He will not suffer [our] foot to be moved: he that keepeth [us] will not slumber. Behold, he that keepeth Israel shall neither slumber nor sleep. The LORD is thy keeper: the LORD is thy shade upon thy right hand. The sun shall not smite [us] by day, nor the moon by night. The LORD shall preserve [us] from all evil: he shall preserve [our] soul. The LORD shall preserve [our] going out and [our] coming in from this time forth, and even for evermore"—Psalm 121:2-8. In His blessed Name we can rejoice all the day!

**Day 205**

# Rejoicing in God's Will

II Corinthians 6:10a

*"As sorrowful, yet alway rejoicing."*

The will of God may bring sorrow, but it is in the valley of sorrow that we learn to look "unto the hills, from whence cometh [our] help," and realize that "[our] help cometh from the LORD, which made heaven and earth"—Psalm 121:1-2. It is said that the most beautiful alpine flowers blossom and grow in the wild and most rugged mountain passes. The greatest and most noble Psalms, we are told, were the outcome of the profoundest agony of soul. There is going to be sorrow, and it is OK for the tears to flow; however, there is a great lesson many of us miss in the valley of sorrow. It isn't a matter of simply ***enduring*** God's will, or even ***choosing*** God's will, but the greatest lesson we may learn is to ***rejoice*** in God's will, whatever His will may be.

We will be better able to rejoice when we can truthfully say, "God is our refuge and strength, a very present help in trouble. Therefore will not we fear"—Psalm 46:1-2a. It is easier for us to rejoice in the Lord during hard circumstances when we remember that "the Lord of hosts is with us; the God of Jacob is our refuge. Selah"—Psalm 46:7. All things may not be good, but when we put the Lord at the very center of our lives, His Spirit within us will help us to understand that "all things ***work together for good*** to them that love God, to them who are the called according to his purpose"—Romans 8:28b. Keeping our attention upon the Lord through every life situation will help us to be like the Apostle Paul—"as sorrowful, yet alway rejoicing."

# Stumbling Blocks

Ezekiel 14:3

*"Son of man, these men have set up their idols in their heart, and put the stumblingblock of their iniquity before their face: should I be enquired of at all by them?"*

As Christians, we are going to face stumbling blocks. The Lord said through Ezekiel that these stumbling blocks are idols that we have set up in our hearts above God. There are many forms of idolatry that every Christian needs to be aware of so that we do not set up idols in our hearts. Stubbornness is one form of idolatry, as the prophet Samuel said to King Saul, "stubbornness is as iniquity and idolatry"—I Samuel 15:23b. When we become, and continue to be, stubborn, we are setting up an idol in our hearts. Many people make light of a stubborn will, but our Heavenly Father doesn't; and so we need to be careful not to set up stubbornness in our hearts as an idol.

Covetousness is another form of idolatry. By inspiration of the Holy Spirit, the Apostle Paul wrote to the church at Colosse: "Mortify therefore your members which are upon the earth; fornication, uncleanness, inordinate affection, evil concupiscence, and covetousness, which is idolatry"—Colossians 3:5. If covetousness has been set up in our hearts, we must put an end to it. It may be that covetousness lies in the heart unknowingly; therefore, we must be willing to let God search our heart. If covetousness is there, we need to immediately go to work at putting it to death by confessing it as sin and turning from it.

We may be covetous of another person's talent or possessions. Or they may have something that is dear to our heart, but which we don't have. Covetousness is such an abomination to the Lord that He has equaled it to idolatry. "Wherefore, my dearly beloved, flee from idolatry"—I Corinthians 10:14 so that it does not become a stumbling block in our walk with God.

225

**Day 207**

# The Fruit of Our Lips

Hebrews 13:15

*"By him therefore let us offer the sacrifice of praise to God continually, that is, the fruit of our lips giving thanks to his name."*

Praise God morning, noon, and night. Praise Him in sickness and in health. Praise Him when you feel like it and when you don't. Praise Him in sorrow and in joy. Praise Him in **everything**! There is not a time in which we cannot praise the Lord. "Praise him for his mighty acts: praise him according to his excellent greatness. Praise him with the sound of the trumpet: praise him with the psaltery and harp. Praise him with the timbrel and dance: praise him with stringed instruments and organs. Praise him upon the loud cymbals: praise him upon the high sounding cymbals. Let every thing that hath breath praise the Lord. Praise ye the Lord"—Psalm 150:2-6. He is worthy of our praise! Praise will strengthen our resolve to continue in the Christian fight. Praise will defeat Satan's attempts at discouraging us. Praise will turn a frown into a smile. When we praise God, "We [can be] troubled on every side, yet not distressed; we [can be] perplexed, but not in despair; Persecuted, but not forsaken; cast down, but not destroyed"—II Corinthians 4:8-9. Therefore let the fruit of our lips be the sacrifice of praise to God continually! He is worthy of all our praise all the time!

# Do Not Be Afraid

Isaiah 51:12

*"I, even I, am he that comforteth you: who art thou, that thou shouldest be afraid of a man that shall die, and of the son of man which shall be made as grass; and forgettest the LORD thy maker, that hast stretched forth the heavens, and laid the foundations of the earth; and hast feared continually every day because of the fury of the oppressor, as if he were ready to destroy? and where is the fury of the oppressor?"*

Isaiah is telling Israel, **Do Not Be Afraid!** God is telling every Christian, **Do Not Be Afraid**, "for God hath not given us the spirit of fear"—II Timothy 1:7a. When we fear, we are not trusting the Lord. He has told us, "Trust ye in the LORD for ever: for in the LORD JEHOVAH is everlasting strength"—Isaiah 26:4. He will give us the strength to endure difficult and uncertain times that come into our lives, but we must first trust Him and obey. When we give in to fear, we are not obeying, because He has said many times in His Word, Fear not. "Say to them that are of a fearful heart, Be strong, fear not; behold, your God will come with vengeance, even God with a recompence; he will come and save you"—Isaiah 35:4. "Fear thou not; for I am with thee: be not dismayed; for I am thy God: I will strengthen thee; yea, I will help thee; yea, I will uphold thee with the right hand of my righteousness"—Isaiah 41:10.

The weakness of our flesh and the attacks of the Devil upon us are the initiators of fear in us; however, if we turn our attention unto the Lord, remember how He has delivered us in the past, and believe that He will deliver us again, then we can better trust Him and not yield to fear. It was Almighty God who kept Daniel safe in the lion's den, kept the three Hebrew children safe in the fiery furnace, and kept the children of Israel safe from Pharaoh's army. And He can keep us safe during difficulties or dangers we may face; therefore, "Be Not Afraid of sudden fear, neither of the desolation of the wicked, when it cometh. For the LORD shall be thy confidence, and shall keep thy foot from being taken"—Proverbs 3:25-26.

## *Day 209*
# The Key that Opens Prison Doors

Acts 12:10

*"When they were past the first and the second ward, they came unto the iron gate that leadeth unto the city; which opened to them of his own accord: and they went out, and passed on through one street; and forthwith the angel departed from him."*

The Apostle Peter was in prison, bound with heavy chains. There were two soldiers on either side of him, and there were guards at the door of the prison. King Herod was intending to kill him the next day. Humanly speaking everything looked hopeless, and eminent death seemed certain; however, "prayer was made without ceasing of the church unto God for him"—Acts 12:5b. These prayers on Peter's behalf brought an angel of the Lord to the prison. He removed Peter's chains, opened the iron gate which led to the city, and delivered Peter from prison as well as from death.

Many times, our surrounding circumstances may appear hopeless; however, with prayer we too may be delivered from our seemingly hopeless situations. There may not be any earthly help available, but we can always obtain heavenly help through prayer. When we learn to "be careful [anxious worries] for nothing; but in every thing by prayer and supplication with thanksgiving" make our request known to God—Philippians 4:6, then our "iron gates," whatever they may be in our lives, will open to deliver us as they did for Peter. By prayer we can be loosed from any and all strong holds that hinder our usefulness for Christ. Peter's Christian friends were not at the iron gate trying to open it themselves; they were gathered in a house praying, and it was because of their prayers that God sent the angel to deliver Peter from prison. We delight the devil when we fret and worry instead of kneeling to pray, because the devil knows he is powerless when God's people pray. The "iron gates" of our lives will not stay closed when we pray.

# Secrets of the Heart

Psalm 44:21

*"He knoweth the secrets of the heart."*

God knows the innermost thoughts of our heart—the person we truly are. He knows the true motives behind our every action and deed, whether they are being done for His glory or for our own glory. He is able to search our heart and reveal any hidden sin. "He revealeth the deep and secret things: he knoweth what is in the darkness, and the light dwelleth with him" –Daniel 2:22. He knows our deepest desires; and although we may not voice them to anyone, He still knows what they are. We are unable to keep anything from Him, because He knows the secrets of our heart.

God knows the barren woman's deep longing to have a baby. He knows the sorrows of the brokenhearted, and He sees every tear that they shed in private. He knows when bitterness has taken root in the heart. He knows the hardness of an unforgiving heart. He knows when our heart is sincere toward Him. The Lord Jesus said to the Pharisees, "Ye are they which justify yourselves before men; but God knoweth your hearts: for that which is highly esteemed among men is abomination in the sight of God" –Luke 16:15. All that dwells in our heart, whether unknown to others or even to ourselves, is not hidden from God; He knows the secrets of our hearts. We cannot hide anything from Him. Even though the secrets of our heart may grieve Him, His longsuffering with us is beyond our comprehending, and His amazing love embraces all of His children. Thank Him that He knows the secrets of our hearts and still loves us.

## *Day 211*

# The Fullness of Christ

Colossians 1:19

*"For it pleased the Father that in him should all fullness dwell."*

In Jesus Christ dwells all the fullness of God—the fullness of His love, His mercy, His grace, His forgiveness; the fullness of His Holiness, of His purity, His gentleness and goodness; the fullness of His kindness, His peace, and the fullness of His righteousness. And we who are saved by grace through faith in Christ Jesus now have access to this glorious fullness through His Holy Spirit. Therefore, we can draw from this fullness of Christ by His Spirit when circumstances overwhelm us to the point that our joy and peace are beginning to be overpowered by our fears and anxieties so that we can "count it all joy when [we] fall into divers temptations"—James 1:2.

We do not have to try to earn favor with God to gain Heaven, for we could never do that. As Christians we only have favor with God because of His Son, Jesus Christ. Salvation in Jesus Christ clothes us in His righteousness and allows us to go before God the Father in prayer. A fullness of His strength aids our weakness, "for when [we are] weak, then [are we] strong"—II Corinthians 12:10. The fullness of His grace not only gives us what we do not deserve, but makes us "heirs of God and joint-heirs with Christ"—Romans 8:17. His grace is His love in action toward us, which gives to us His "every good gift and every perfect gift"—James 1:17a. Since the fullness of God dwells in Jesus Christ, and His Holy Spirit dwells in every Christian, then we have access to this fullness to help us through any situation or circumstance of life.

# Pleasing Ways

Proverbs 16:7

*"When a man's ways please the LORD, he maketh even his enemies to be at peace with him."*

The Scriptures include many examples of ways we can please the Lord. We please Him when we praise and thank Him. "And Samuel said, Hath the LORD as great delight in burnt offerings and sacrifices, as in obeying the voice of the LORD? Behold, to obey is better than sacrifice, and to hearken than the fat of rams"—I Samuel 15:22. Our obedience pleases the Lord. When we do what He asks us to do, and obey Him when He speaks to us about a particular thing, then we are pleasing Him.

"So then they that are in the flesh cannot please God. But ye are not in the flesh but in the Spirit, if so be that the Spirit of God dwell in you"—Romans 8:8-9. As Christians, we do not please the Lord if we continue to live the same way we did before we were saved. God is pleased when we "walk in the Spirit"—Galatians 5:16a, and demonstrate that "old things are passed away; behold, all things are become new"—II Corinthians 5:17b in our lives.

"Without faith it is impossible to please him: for he that cometh to God must believe that he is, and that he is a rewarder of them that diligently seek him"—Hebrews 11:6. We can please God by simply believing Him and taking Him at His Word—without questioning and doubting.

As Christians we have the Spirit of Christ dwelling in us, and He is the One who will help us to put into practice the various ways that please the Lord. How pleasing are our ways to the Lord? We all need to take time daily to consider how pleasing our ways are to God, and then endeavor to walk in the ways which please Him.

## Day 213

# Magnify the Lord with Praise

Isaiah 25:1

*"O LORD, thou art my God; I will exalt thee, I will praise thy name; for thou hast done wonderful things; thy counsels of old are faithfulness and truth."*

Praising the Lord is another way in which we, as Christians, can get victory over despair, despondency, or depression. Praise magnifies the Lord in our hearts and turns our attentions away from that which has cast a shadow upon our lives. Life's circumstances may seem overwhelming and bleak; however, when we utter praises to our King who reigns forever, our hearts are made glad, because we remember that "our light affliction . . . is but for a moment"—II Corinthians 4:17a. "The LORD reigneth, he is clothed with majesty; the LORD is clothed with strength, wherewith he hath girded himself: the world also is stablished, that it cannot be moved"—Psalm 93:1. The devil is continually seeking to turn our hearts away from praising the Lord, because he knows praise will strengthen us and make us more profitable for the Master's use.

Remember, our God has done wonderful things; therefore, praise Him! He is faithful—praise Him! He is "the way, the truth, and the life"—John 14:6, and worthy of our praise. It may be that your finances are at an all- time low; this is faith's opportunity; therefore, praise Him! He is able "to do exceeding abundantly above all that we ask or think, according to the power that worketh in us"—Ephesians 3:20, and that power is more readily available when we praise the Lord regardless of our circumstances. When we neglect to praise God we are refusing to benefit ourselves, because praise is a great promoter of our spiritual growth. Praise lifts our burdens, renews our hope and restores our faith. Make praising the Lord your daily practice, for He has done wonderful things, and His "counsels of old are faithfulness and truth."

# Continually

Hosea 12:6

*"Therefore turn thou to thy God: keep mercy and judgment, and wait on thy God continually."*

When answers to your prayers are delayed, then turn to God and wait on Him continually. "God is not a man, that he should lie; neither the son of man, that he should repent: hath he said, and shall he not do it? Or hath he spoken, and shall he not make it good?"—Numbers 23:19. When it is unclear which way to go, then turn and wait on God continually; He will guide you; and when the time is right, "thine ears shall hear a word behind thee, saying, This is the way, walk ye in it, when ye turn to the right hand, and when ye turn to the left"—Isaiah 30:21. "For this God is our God for ever and ever: he will be our guide even unto death"—Psalm 48:14. Whatever the circumstance, continually turn to God and wait on Him.

*Day 215*

# God Is with Us

Isaiah 41:10

*"Fear thou not; for I am with thee: be not dismayed; for I am thy God: I will strengthen thee; yea, I will help thee; yea, I will uphold thee with the right hand of my righteousness."*

The prophet Isaiah, through the inspiration of God's Holy Spirit, wrote these words to remind every believer in Jesus Christ that although we may become overwhelmed or distressed, **God is with us.** The situation may look fearful, but "be not dismayed," **God is with us!** He will be our strength to go through any adversity, and is our help in any need. His righteousness will uphold us when we have "made the LORD, which is [our] refuge, even the most High, [our] habitation . . . For he shall give his angels charge over [us], to keep [us] in all [our] ways"—Psalm 91:9, 11. "For this God is our God for ever and ever"—Psalm 48:14a.

The One who sent His Son, Jesus Christ, "to be a propitiation through faith in his blood, to declare his righteousness for the remission of sins that are past, through the forbearance of God"—Romans 3:25 will be with us, will be our help, will be our strength, and will uphold us with His righteousness. God is with us to help us flee temptations, to be strong in our weakness, and to go through every trial uprightly. Whatever the situation, remember, **God is with us.**

# God's Holiness in Me

I Peter 1:16

*"Because it is written, Be ye holy; for I am holy."*

One of the greatest things about being a Christian is not what we do for God, but what we allow Him to do in and through us. Jesus Christ made atonement for our sins when He shed His blood on Calvary's cross, and when we receive Him as our Saviour His Holy Spirit then comes to dwell in us, and it is this power that we now have as Christians to be holy as God is holy. Christ is holy because He is God's Son, and "being in the form of God, thought it not robbery to be equal with God"—Philippians 2:6; therefore the mind of Christ is holy. His thoughts ran along the line of desiring to please the Father, serve others, and deny Himself by His humility and His obedience to the Father. He "made himself of no reputation, and took upon him the form of a servant, and was made in the likeness of men: And being found in fashion as a man, he humbled himself, and became obedient unto death, even the death of the cross"—Philippians 2:7-8. "Let this mind be in you, which was also in Christ Jesus"—Philippians 2:5. In other words, let us have the same attitude, purpose, and humility that Christ had so that we may be holy in mind through the power of the Holy Spirit of Christ working in us.

God's Holy Spirit who dwells in us is able to guide our thoughts, our conversation, our actions and reactions toward holiness if we yield ourselves to Him. "Know ye not, that to whom ye yield yourselves servants to obey, his servants ye are to whom ye obey; whether of sin unto death, or of obedience unto righteousness? . . . [Therefore] yield your members servants to righteousness unto holiness"—Romans 6:16, 19b. When we submit ourselves to God and resist the devil, then the devil will have to leave us, because he does not have power over God. As we continue to submit ourselves to God and resist the devil, God's Holy Spirit continues to enable us to be holy.

"Holiness means unsullied walking with the feet, unsullied talking with the tongue, unsullied thinking with the mind, every detail of the life under the scrutiny of God." –My Utmost for His Highest

**Day 217**

# Sweet Meditations

Psalm 104:34

*"My meditation of him shall be sweet: I will be glad in the LORD."*

I will be glad in the Lord when I spend time meditating upon Him. It will not be my possessions, my circumstances, my financial situation, my family, my friends, or my skills and abilities that will make me glad in the Lord; rather, it will be my meditation of the Lord that will make me glad in Him. My meditations will be sweet when I take time to think that "the Lord hath prepared his throne in the heavens; and his kingdom ruleth over all"—Psalm 103:19. It will make me glad to think about His kingdom ruling over all, because "all power is given unto [Him] in heaven and in earth"—Matthew 28:18; therefore, "we may boldly say, The Lord is my helper, and I will not fear what man shall do unto me"— Hebrews 13:6.

Meditating on the Lord—His greatness, His mercies, His grace, His love—will draw our hearts closer to Him and deepen our love for Him. It's amazing to think that "we love him, because he first loved us"—I John 4:19. Just think, "Herein is love, not that we loved God, but that he loved us, and sent his Son to be the propitiation for our sins"—I John 4:10. We will be glad when we take time to meditate on the glories and greatness of Almighty God.

# Exercise Faith

Luke 17:5-6

*"And the apostles said unto the Lord, Increase our faith. And the Lord said, If ye had faith as a grain of mustard seed, ye might say unto this sycamine tree, Be thou plucked up by the root, and be thou planted in the sea; and it should obey you."*

Like the apostles, many of us Christians ask the Lord to increase our faith. We want to receive miraculous answers to our prayers, and we imagine that we must have a large amount of faith in order for the Lord to send down the answers. However, the Lord Jesus said we can receive amazing answers to prayer if we have "faith as a grain of mustard seed." We do not need large amounts of faith. We just need to exercise the faith that we have been given.

Athletes grow stronger and increase their endurance by consistent exercise. The more they exercise the stronger they become. The principle is the same concerning our faith. Our faith increases when we exercise it. When we exercise the faith that we do have, then God fulfills His promise: "According to your faith be it unto you" –Matthew 9:29b, and our faith is increased and made stronger.

Our problem usually stems from thoughts such as, "I could never pray and receive such miracles as they did." That is exactly what the devil wants us to think, because he knows the Word of God is true, and it makes him tremble to think of God's people praying with faith. Our Lord is gracious and has extended His helping hand to us as He did for the demoniac's father: "And straightway the father of the child cried out, and said with tears, Lord, I believe; help thou mine unbelief. . . . Jesus . . . rebuked the foul spirit, saying unto him, Thou dumb and deaf spirit, I charge thee, come out of him, and enter no more into him" –Mark 9:24-25. If we want to see miraculous answers to prayer, then we must exercise the faith God has given us.

**Day 219**

# The Blessed Life

Psalm 112:1

*"Blessed is the man that feareth the LORD."*

We will be blessed, happy, when we fear the Lord God Almighty. This fear is not the fear that love **casts** out –I John 4:18, but the fear that love **brings in**. We should fear to displease Him; therefore, we need to learn to believe Him. "When a man's ways please the LORD, he maketh even his enemies to be at peace with him" –Proverbs 16:7. We should fear to dishonor Him, "giving no offence in any thing, that the ministry be not blamed: But in all things approving ourselves as the ministers of God" –II Corinthians 6:3-4a. "In a great house there are not only vessels of gold and of silver, but also of wood and of earth; and some to honour, and some to dishonor. If a man therefore purge himself from these, he shall be a vessel unto honour, sanctified, and meet for the master's use, and prepared unto every good work" –II Timothy 2:20-21.

The closer we walk with the Lord and the more we learn of Him, the more we will stand in awe of Him and revere His greatness. It is our reverence of Him that will lead us to fear doing anything that would bring shame to His Name. Blessed is the man that feareth the LORD.

# Conquering Temptation

I Corinthians 10:5

*"But with many of them God was not well pleased: for they were overthrown in the wilderness."*

The Lord Jesus, the very Son of God, was "led up of the Spirit into the wilderness to be tempted of the devil"—Matthew 4:1. Christians today can be certain that they will also experience temptation from the devil. The children of Israel were overthrown in the wilderness because they yielded to the devil's temptations. "Now these things were our examples, to the intent we should not lust after evil things, as they also lusted. Neither be ye idolaters, as were some of them; as it is written, The people sat down to eat and drink, and rose up to play. Neither let us commit fornication, as some of them committed, and fell in one day three and twenty thousand. Neither let us tempt Christ, as some of them also tempted, and were destroyed of serpents. Neither murmur ye, as some of them also murmured, and were destroyed of the destroyer"—I Corinthians 10:6-10.

The Lord Jesus responded to temptation with the Word of God. "When the tempter came to him, he said, If thou be the Son of God, command that these stones be made bread. But he answered and said, It is written, Man shall not live by bread alone, but by every word that proceedeth out of the mouth of God"—Matthew 4:3-4. Jesus Christ quoted Scripture each time the devil tempted Him. Following unsuccessful attempts at tempting Jesus to sin, "the devil leaveth him, and, behold, angels came and ministered unto him"—Matthew 4:11.

We also can battle the devil's temptations and be successful with the help of the Holy Spirit. "There hath no temptation taken you but such as is common to man: but God is faithful, who will not suffer you to be tempted above that ye are able; but will with the temptation also make a way to escape, that ye may be able to bear it"—I Corinthians 10:13. It is the power of God's Spirit in us that enables us to flee temptation and resist the devil. When we yield to the Lord and not to the devil's temptation, then we will please God and glorify Him.

*Day 221*

# Not Our Own

I Corinthians 6:19

*"What? Know ye not that your body is the temple of the Holy Ghost which is in you, which ye have of God, and ye are not your own?"*

As Christians, we belong to God and not to ourselves. "For [we] are bought with a price: therefore glorify God in your body, and in your spirit, which are God's"—I Corinthians 6:20. If we are saved, but do not change our old behavioral habits, and continue to live as we did before we were saved, how can we hope to draw others to Jesus Christ? We need to demonstrate that we have become a new creation in Christ by yielding ourselves to the Lord and His leadership. It is only by allowing His Spirit to control our hearts and lives that we will turn away from the habits of our sinful nature.

When making life decisions, it would be best for us to go to the Lord and seek His will, then put our seal of agreement to it by obediently carrying out His plans. As Christians, we have been given a great privilege and honor, for we have been delivered from the penalty of sin by the redeeming blood of Jesus Christ, and from the power of sin over us; however, we will not truly appropriate that power until we realize that we now belong to God and not to ourselves. He laid down His life for us. Let us yield our lives to Him. He knows what is best for us, and we need to honor and please Him by yielding ourselves to His plan for our lives.

# Time with the Lord

Acts 4:13

*"Now when they saw the boldness of Peter and John, and perceived that they were unlearned and ignorant men, they marveled; and they took knowledge of them, that they had been with Jesus."*

As Christians, when we are interacting with others, we should conduct ourselves so that there is a noticeable difference between us and those who have not received Christ. The Apostles Peter and John were not scholars. In fact, they were called unlearned and ignorant. However, they were bold for Christ and they had spent time with Him.

In order for us to follow their example, we are going to have to spend time with the Lord in Bible reading, Bible study, and prayer. We do not have to be scholars to represent our Saviour. The Bible says that "God hath chosen the weak things of the world to confound the things which are mighty"—I Corinthians 1:27b. When we spend much time with the Lord, others will notice a difference in us. A famous violinist once said that if he missed one day of practice, he noticed. When he missed two days of practice, those closest to him noticed. And when he missed three days of practice, the entire audience noticed. The same principle is true for the Christian: "If any man be in Christ, he is a new creature: old things are passed away; behold, all things are become new"—II Corinthians 5:17; however, the more we neglect spending time with the Lord through prayer and His Word, the less likely we will be to demonstrate Christ likeness to others. Our strength is in Christ, and when we spend time with Him, others will see the change that Christ has made in us. Let us make it a daily priority to spend time with the Lord in the Bible and in prayer. There is no better time than the present to begin spending time with the Lord.

**Day 223**

# With You Always

Matthew 28:20

*"I am with you alway, even unto the end of the world."*

It is comforting to know there is One who is always with us. That One is the Lord Jesus Christ, and He is with us in our joys, in our trials, and in our daily lives. "Hereby know we that we dwell in him, and he in us, because he hath given us of his Spirit"—I John 4:13. He is with us, because He has given us His Spirit to dwell in us. When our hearts are sorrowing, or when Satan greatly tempts us, we have the Holy Spirit to help us. Jesus Christ, our Lord, said, "I will never leave thee, nor forsake thee"—Hebrews 13:5c. The twelve apostles walked side by side with the Lord Jesus; however, when Christ went away into Heaven He gave us His Holy Spirit. His Spirit dwells in each of God's children; therefore, because we have the Spirit in us, we always have Christ with us. He not only ***will not*** leave us, but He ***cannot*** leave us.

Because His Spirit lives in us, we are never separated from our Lord. In trouble He will be our help. In uncertainty He will be our guide. In sorrow He will be our comfort. When we are in need, He will provide. He is our Rock on which we may build a sure foundation so that when the storms of life come we may be secure in Him. Therefore, remember, He is with you always, "even unto the end of the world."

# The Glory of Humility

John 8:50

*"And I seek not mine own glory."*

Our Savior, Jesus Christ, walked in great humility; this verse is just one demonstration of His humility. He did not seek His own glory; nor did He seek to do His own will, but rather only that of His Father in Heaven. He was from the beginning with God: "All things were made by him; and without him was not anything made that was made" –John 1:3. In John 1:1-4, Christ is declared to be the Word and the Creator. In Matthew 1:23, He is "Emmanuel, which being interpreted is, God with us." Hebrews 1:8 declares Him to be equal with God: "But unto the Son he saith, Thy throne, O God, is forever and ever: a sceptre of righteousness is the sceptre of thy kingdom." The Apostle John wrote, "And there are also many other things which Jesus did, the which, if they should be written every one, I suppose that even the world itself could not contain the books that should be written"—John 21:25. The entire Bible is His Word; yet He did not seek His own glory. Such humility ought to inspire our own hearts to abase ourselves and lift up high the name of Jesus Christ, our Lord and Savior.

Whom do you speak most of to others? Much of our conversation is centered upon the pronouns "I" "me" and "mine" when they ought to be centered upon Him, Christ Jesus, the Redeemer of our souls. He knows when a tiny sparrow falls to the ground—Matthew 10:29,31. He knows when the calves are born in the wild. He knows the number of every hair on our heads —Matthew 10:30. He knows our thoughts before we think them. He knows the intents of our hearts —Hebrews 4:12, and He hears every word we speak. Think on His glory, dwell on His humility and seek to imitate your great Savior by humbling yourself before Him. If He chooses, let Him lift you up, but do not seek to lift up yourself. We have the ability to draw souls unto Him if we would simply lift up Christ and the cross of Calvary, and would declare His glory!

# The Picture of Humility

The King of Glory had such an humble birth

For in the manger, wrapped in swaddling clothes,

Lay the Creator of Heaven and earth.

His humility He never laid down.

It followed Him to the cross of Calvary

Where He was whipped, beaten and cruelly crowned.

Oh, Father, such humility the Savior had!

May His humility ever be mine

That I too should make Your heart glad.

# Revering God from the Heart

Deuteronomy 5:29

*"O that there were such an heart in them, that they would fear me, and keep all my commandments always, that it might be well with them, and with their children for ever!"*

Listen to the depth of the Lord's heartfelt cry, "O that there were such an heart in them, that they would fear me, and keep all my commandments always"! His heart desires the same thing for us today – that we would have a heart that would fear Him and keep *all* His commandments. Oh that our hearts would fear to displease Him, fear to disobey Him, fear to be out of fellowship with Him, fear to turn away from Him, fear to walk contrary to His will!

To fear the Lord is to revere Him, which means to show honor and devotion to Him. When we "fear" the Lord, holding Him in highest reverence, we will be more likely to keep His commandments. We will be more apt to be "doers of the word, and not hearers only" –James 1:22. By fearing to displease the Lord we will strive to exercise more faith, for "without faith it is impossible to please him" –Hebrews 11:6a. Fearing to disobey the Lord will turn us toward obedience. "To obey is better than sacrifice, and to hearken than the fat of rams" –I Samuel 15:22b. If we would fear to be out of fellowship with Him, we would be quicker to think on our ways and turn our feet toward His testimonies –Psalm 119:59. Determine today to have a heart that would fear God and keep His commandments so that it might be well with you and your children.

**Day 226**

# Triumphing Over Temptations

Luke 4:1-2

*"And Jesus being full of the Holy Ghost returned from Jordan, and was led by the Spirit into the wilderness, Being forty days tempted of the devil."*

We can be triumphant over temptations by understanding the devious devices of the devil, and by realizing that the closer we get to God, the more we will have to beware of the devil's ploys to tempt us. "And Jesus being full of the Holy Ghost" was "forty days tempted of the devil." *Prosperity Christianity* says that when we follow Jesus Christ and have a close walk with Him, everything will be smooth sailing; however, the Bible truth is completely the opposite. "Then Peter, filled with the Holy Ghost, said unto them, Ye rulers of the people, and elders of Israel, If we this day be examined of the good deed done to the impotent man, by what means he is made whole; Be it known unto you all, and to all the people of Israel, that by the name of Jesus Christ of Nazareth, whom ye crucified, whom God raised from the dead, even by him doth this man stand here before you whole. . . . And they called them, and commanded them not to speak at all nor teach in the name of Jesus. But Peter and John answered and said unto them, Whether it be right in the sight of God to hearken unto you more than unto God, judge ye. For we cannot but speak the things which we have seen and heard"—Acts 4:8-10, 18-20. Peter had previously denied Jesus Christ; John had abandoned Jesus Christ. But both of these apostles realized that, although the devil's temptations are great, through the power of the Holy Spirit, they were able to triumph over temptations.

There are going to be seasons of temptations throughout our Christian life. The devil is never going to completely leave us alone: "And when the devil had ended all the temptation, he departed from him *for a season*"—Luke 4:13. Peter calls the devil our "adversary" and "a roaring lion . . . seeking whom he may devour"—I Peter 5:8. "Submit yourselves therefore to God. Resist the devil, and he will flee from you"—James 4:7. We must realize that we do have an adversary, the devil, and that the more we allow the Holy Spirit to control us, the better able we will be to combat every temptation the devil will bring our way.

# A Roaring Lion

I Peter 5:8

*"Be sober, be vigilant; because your adversary the devil, as a roaring lion, walketh about, seeking whom he may devour."*

We have an adversary, and his name is the Devil. The Bible tells us He is like "a roaring lion" seeking to devour Christians. Like a lion, he stalks his prey, waiting for a time when he can pounce on us and take us down one way or another. He doesn't care by what means he devours us, for he "cometh not, but for to steal, and to kill, and to destroy" the Christian's effectiveness for Christ—John 10:10. Therefore, we must be on guard and be aware of how deadly an enemy he is to us.

"Be sober" means mastering our earthly passions and desires by yielding the control of them to the Holy Spirit. "Every man that striveth for the mastery is temperate [balanced] in all things"—I Corinthians 9:25. The Apostle Paul said, "I therefore so run, not as uncertainly; so fight I, not as one that beateth the air: but I keep under my body, and bring it into subjection: lest that by any means, when I have preached to others, I myself should be a castaway"—I Corinthians 9:26-27. In other words, we must discipline our bodies according to the Word of God, and not allow the desires of our bodies to determine what we do. "Whether therefore ye eat, or drink, or whatsoever ye do, do all to the glory of God"—I Corinthians 10:31.

"Be vigilant" means to be continually watchful for possible dangers. "For there shall arise false Christs, and false prophets, and shall shew great signs and wonders; insomuch that, if it were possible, they shall deceive the very elect"—Matthew 24:24. We must "study to shew [ourselves] approved unto God, a workman that needeth not to be ashamed, rightly dividing the word of truth"—II Timothy 2:15 so that we will know the difference between truth and counterfeit. Satan is very devious; therefore, we must be constantly on guard against his tactics, and pray daily that God the Father will "lead us not into temptation, but deliver us from evil"—Matthew 6:13a.

**Day 228**

# Sacrifices of Praise

Hebrews 13:15

*"By him therefore let us offer the sacrifice of praise to God continually, that is, the fruit of our lips giving thanks to his name."*

The sacrifice of praise mentioned in this verse is referring to a thank offering that is continuous and abundant in every circumstance of our life. It is by Jesus Christ that we can bring our thanksgiving unto God the Father because we have been redeemed through the blood of His Lamb—Jesus Christ—when "by his own blood he entered in once into the holy place, having obtained eternal redemption for us"—Hebrews 9:12b. Therefore, regardless of our circumstances, we can "offer the sacrifice of praise to God continually." We will be able to offer the sacrifice of praise to God continually when we take time to think about the end result of our salvation—Heaven and seeing our Saviour face to face, living with Him forever. When we do this we can better comprehend that our salvation is eternal. Regardless of poverty or wealth, sickness or health, weakness or strength, sorrow or joy, our salvation is eternal and stays with us through all circumstances of life. Therefore, we have reason to continually praise and thank God.

There are times when we do not feel thankful nor full of praise, because our hearts are full of sorrow, anxiety, or trouble of some sort; however, if we remember that our Lord Jesus Christ made the ultimate sacrifice for us when He laid down His life to redeem us for all eternity, then we can get the victory and offer unto God the sacrifice of praise with thanksgiving. Take time each day to meditate on the fullness of what our salvation truly means and we will be able to offer the sacrifice of praise.

# Living Christ's Way

Matthew 11:29

*"Take my yoke upon you, and learn of me; for I am meek and lowly in heart: and ye shall find rest unto your souls."*

Taking the yoke of Jesus Christ is essentially living life Christ's way, which is why He said, "Learn of me." Therefore, in order to find this rest that Jesus spoke of, we need to take a look at His life and the way He lived while here on earth, and then follow His example. As we read the Scriptures, we can see His humility from His birth to the grave. "Who, being in the form of God, thought it not robbery to be equal with God: But made himself of no reputation, and took upon him the form of a servant, and was made in the likeness of men"—Philippians 2:6-7. He is King of kings, Lord of lords, the Creator of all; yet He humbled Himself when He "was made flesh, and dwelt among us"—John 1:14a. He did not seek a reputation of greatness, nor did He seek to be served; rather, He sought to obey the Father in everything and to serve those around Him. His meekness was revealed as He stood before His accusers and did not defend Himself. His meekness was not weakness; it was His inner strength and confidence that kept Him from needing to defend Himself. He knew His purpose was to glorify His Father through obedience so "that the world through him might be saved"—John 3:17b. His life was never about His own will, but the will of the Father.

When God and His Son, Jesus Christ, fill our thoughts and our hearts' desires, then our life becomes about how we may please them. Through discipline, submission, and surrender of our own selfish longings, we can live the Christian life Christ's way. Before a caterpillar becomes a butterfly, it must first go through the metamorphosis process. Within the chrysalis the caterpillar is transforming into a new creature, and after a period of time it emerges, with some struggle, a beautiful butterfly. In like manner, Christians began undergoing a "metamorphosis" process the day we got saved. The Holy Spirit in us can make us to become more and more like Jesus Christ when we are willing to yield to Him and die to ourselves. It is then that we will be better able to live the Christian life Christ's way.

## Day 230

# Self-Consciousness Put to Rest

Matthew 11:28

*"Come unto me . . . and I will give you rest."*

If we are born-again believers in Jesus Christ and thoughts permeate our minds of what people may think of us, then we are in the realm of self-consciousness, because we are more concerned with what people think of us than we are of obeying God. Self-consciousness produces fear of mankind rather than a reverence for God. When we fear being disliked, or ridiculed, or not being accepted by our friends, acquaintances, or even complete strangers, then we are exhibiting self-consciousness, which means we are walking in our flesh and not in the Holy Spirit. The Lord Jesus Christ said, "Come unto me . . . and I will give you rest." When we come to Jesus and abide in Him, then we will have rest from our self-consciousness, and we will begin to learn to walk in His Spirit. This rest that Jesus Christ gives us becomes our pathway to freedom from fear. "For the law of the Spirit of life in Christ Jesus hath made me free from the law of sin and death. . . . That the righteousness of the law might be fulfilled in us, who walk not after the flesh, but after the Spirit . . . For to be carnally minded is death; but to be spiritually minded is life and peace. . . . For ye have not received the spirit of bondage again to fear; but ye have received the Spirit of adoption, whereby we cry, Abba, Father"—Romans 8:2, 4, 6, 15.

The Holy Spirit, who lives in us, becomes our Guide, and when we follow His leading, then the sweet rest that Jesus Christ spoke of in Matthew 11:28 can fill our lives. By coming to Christ and receiving His rest we will be able to conquer that fear which says, "I can't," when the Holy Spirit leads us to do something we would not naturally think to do. That rest will give us holy boldness to obey the Spirit's leading and will fill our hearts with joy, because the Holy Spirit is not being quenched. If the fear of rejection by people becomes the center of our thoughts, then those fears will keep us from following the Holy Spirit's leading in our lives. Let us resist the devil, who has kept us in bondage long enough, and go to Jesus where we will find peace and rest.

# Sing a New Song

Psalm 96:1

*"O sing unto the LORD a new song: sing unto the LORD, all the earth."*

Sing unto the Lord the new song of Salvation! Jesus Christ went to the cross where He paid the penalty for our sin once and forever, and it was on that cross that He declared, "It is finished"—John 19:30b. Therefore, "sing unto the LORD, bless his name; shew forth his salvation from day to day"—Psalm 96:2. We need to tell others about eternal life and how they also can have that "lively hope by the resurrection of Jesus Christ from the dead, to an inheritance incorruptible, and undefiled, and that fadeth not away, reserved in heaven for [them]"—I Peter 1:3c-4.

As one who has been redeemed by the blood of the Lamb, Jesus Christ, we have so much to sing about; therefore, let us sing and "give unto the LORD the glory due unto his name"—Psalm 96:8a so that others may marvel at our joy, and so we might have the blessing of leading them to know Jesus as their personal Lord and Savior. When we are depressed, discouraged, or defeated by life and every circumstance it may throw at us, singing to the Lord will do more good than hours of counseling. May we wake in the morning with a song in our heart, then sing throughout the day, and go to bed singing of the glories of salvation. "O sing unto the LORD a new song!

**Day 232**

# Sufficient Grace

II Corinthians 12:9

*"And he said unto me, My grace is sufficient for thee: for my strength is made perfect in weakness. Most gladly therefore will I rather glory in my infirmities, that the power of Christ may rest upon me."*

"My grace is sufficient for thee" means that God's influence upon our heart is enough. His influence of joy, gratitude, humility, and other characterictics of Christ upon our hearts are enough for us to get through trials of any sort. It is when we "seek the LORD and his strength"—I Chronicles 16:11a in the midst of difficult trials that we discover the availability and sufficiency of His grace. Joy is not in the trials, but in the Lord; and when we are under the influence of His joy, then we can say as Paul did, "most gladly therefore will I rather glory in my infirmities, that the power of Christ may rest upon me."

When we learn to be thankful in our trials, and humble ourselves before the Lord during the trials, we will discover that His grace overshadows the difficulty and makes it bearable, which is why His grace is sufficient for us. Our focus can then be centered upon Him and not on ourselves or our infirmities. Without trials we would never know how sufficient His grace can be, nor how we can glory in His power over us. If you are going through a trial, then remember, His grace is sufficient for you.

# Been with Jesus

Acts 4:13

*"Now when they saw the boldness of Peter and John, and perceived that they were unlearned and ignorant men, they marveled; and they took knowledge of them, that they had been with Jesus."*

The fear of man will not consume us when we have been with Jesus. Our weaknesses will not overcome us when we have been with Jesus. When we have been with Jesus we will be more inclined to attempt the impossible; "for with God all things are possible" –Mark 10:27. Our understanding and our knowledge are enlarged when we spend time with Jesus. We begin to understand how dependent upon Him we are, and the truth of His Word in John 15:5, "I [Jesus] am the vine, ye are the branches: He that abideth in me, and I in him, the same bringeth forth much fruit: for without me ye can do nothing." The more we get to know Him, the more we will want to know Him.

Others will notice when we have been with Jesus, especially those closest to us. Our old nature of the flesh will be tempered by the graces of the Holy Spirit when we have been with Jesus. Instead of hateful words, we will speak with love and kindness. Instead of acting selfishly and pridefully, we will exhibit more meekness and humility by thinking of the needs of others and how better we may serve them. We must spend time with Jesus for it to be said of us that "they took knowledge of them, that they had been with Jesus."

## Day 234
# Trust Brings Blessing

Psalm 84:12

*"O LORD of hosts, blessed is the man that trusteth in thee."*

We are blessed, happy, when we trust in the Lord. Trusting in the Lord soothes our anxieties, because believing God produces a peaceful calmness within us. God has admonished us to "be careful [anxious] for nothing"—Philippians 4:6a, instructing us that, "in every thing by prayer and supplication with thanksgiving let [our] requests be made known unto God"—Philippians 4:6b. When we do, "the peace of God, which passeth all understanding, shall keep [our] hearts and minds through Christ Jesus"—Philippians 4:7. The more we read, memorize, and meditate on God's Word, the less anxious we will be, and the greater our trust in the Lord will grow, because "faith cometh by hearing, and hearing by the word of God"—Romans 10:17. How can we trust in someone whom we do not know, or do not know very well? It is when we spend more time in the Word of God and alone with Him in prayer that the Holy Spirit, who lives in us, is able to strengthen and increase our trust in the Lord.

God also admonishes us from His Word, saying, "prove me now herewith, saith the LORD of hosts, if I will not open you the windows of heaven, and pour you out a blessing, that there shall not be room enough to receive it"—Malachi 3:10b. We prove Him by obeying Him and trusting the promises He has given us. He promised us that if we bring our tithes to His house, which is the church, He would pour out a blessing to us and would "rebuke the devourer for [our] sakes"—Malachi 3:11a. He promised us that "when a man's ways please the LORD, he maketh even his enemies to be at peace with him"—Proverbs 16:7. Throughout Scripture we can read of God's promises and the conditions required for those promises to be fulfilled. Trusting the Lord precedes the promised blessing. Many times we fail to trust the Lord because we have not taken the time to know Him and what He has promised us. When we try and prove His promises we will come to know they are true. The closer we grow in our relationship with the Lord, the more we will grow to trust Him, and trusting the Lord brings us blessings.

# God's Way Versus Man's Way

Psalm 37:1,3,7,8

*"Fret not thyself... Trust in the LORD, and do good... Rest in the LORD, and wait patiently for him: fret not thyself because of him who prospereth in his way... fret not thyself in any wise to do evil."*

Fretting means we are at a distance in our relationship with the Lord. It is not His desire for us to worry or to become anxious. He wants us to "be careful [anxious] for nothing; but in every thing by prayer and supplication with thanksgiving let [our] requests be made known unto [Him]"—Philippians 4:6. It sounds so easy to say, "Rest in the Lord, trust in Him"; however, when the children get sick, finances get low, or any number of circumstances occur to turn our world upside down, we may be tempted to doubt this resting and trusting. Trusting and resting in the Lord do not depend on our external circumstances, but on our relationship with Him. When our relationship with the Lord is close and consistent, then the Spirit of God in us will lead us to His rest and help us to trust in Him. Anxiety begins when we doubt God's Word, when we desire to have our own way in a matter, and we do not want to yield our will to the will of the Father. In our pride and arrogance we imagine that we know better than our Omniscient [all- knowing] and Almighty God.

If we would realize that peace comes from resting and trusting in the Lord, then we would better understand that we must seek the "God that made the world and all things therein, seeing that he is Lord of heaven and earth, dwelleth not in temples made with hands; Neither is worshipped with men's hands, as though he needed any thing, seeing he giveth to all life, and breath, and all things; And hath made of one blood all nations of men for to dwell on all the face of the earth, and hath determined the times before appointed, and the bounds of their habitation; That they should seek the Lord, if haply they might feel after him, and find him, though he be not far from every one of us: For in him we live, and move, and have our being"—Acts 17:24-28a. Therefore, we need to build a close, loving, and strong relationship with the Lord through prayer and the reading of His Word so that we will not fret; but rather, we will trust and rest in the Lord God Almighty.

# Day 236
# Our Help—Adequate and Complete

Isaiah 31:1

*"Woe to them that go down to Egypt for help; and stay [rely] on horses, and trust in chariots, because they are many; and in horsemen, because they are very strong; but they look not unto the Holy One of Israel, neither seek the Lord!"*

It is our natural tendency, when in trouble, perplexed, or generally needing help, to look to that which we can tangibly see and understand instead of relying on the Lord. Therefore, it is easy to turn to some form of the world for our help, whether it is our government, our community, or our friends and family. We sometimes fail to realize that God our Father and His Son, Jesus Christ, are the One who created the world and everything in it. It is they "who alone doeth great wonders . . . that by wisdom made the heavens . . . that stretched out the earth above the waters . . . that made great lights . . . the sun to rule by day . . . the moon and stars to rule by night . . . that smote Egypt in their firstborn . . . And brought out Israel from among them . . . which divided the Red sea into parts . . . And made Israel to pass through the midst of it . . . But overthrew Pharaoh and his host in the Red sea . . . which led his people through the wilderness . . . which smote great kings . . . And gave their land for an heritage . . . Even an heritage unto Israel his servant . . . Who remembered us in our low estate . . . And hath redeemed us from our enemies . . . Who giveth food to all flesh: for his mercy endureth forever" –Psalm 136:4-17,21-25. "This God is our God for ever and ever: he will be our guide even unto death" –Psalm 48:14.

We will not find complete and fulfilling help by turning to anyone or anything other than the Lord of lords and King of kings. Only He is able to meet our needs completely and adequately. Our troubles may be self inflicted, but God's mercies endure forever; therefore, He will make a way for us out of our troubles better than anyone else. Let us not "go down to Egypt for help." Instead, let us look unto our true source of help –Almighty God.

# Living Hope

Psalm 71:5

*"For thou art my hope, O Lord God: thou art my trust from my youth."*

The Lord is our Hope for the present, because only He is "a very present help in trouble"—Psalm 46:1b. He is our Help for the present. Whatever trouble we may be experiencing, He is our true source of help. "He will be our guide even unto death"—Psalm 48:14b. "Yea, though [we] walk through the valley of the shadow of death, [we] will fear no evil: for thou art with [us]; thy rod and thy staff they comfort [us]"—Psalm 23:4. Whatever our situation may be in life we can hope in the Lord. He is called "Wonderful, Counsellor, The mighty God, The everlasting Father, The Prince of Peace"—Isaiah 9:6b. His Word is truth: "For the word of the Lord is right; and all his works are done in truth"—Psalm 33:4. Better yet, He is the truth! "Jesus saith unto him, I am the way, the truth, and the life: no man cometh unto the Father, but by me"—John 14:6. Therefore, we can say with the Psalmist, "Thou art my hope, O Lord God."

We cannot boast of tomorrow, according to Proverbs 27:1, for we "know not what shall be on the morrow"—James 4:14a; however, we can hope in the Lord God for whatever our tomorrows will hold, because He is the hope of our future. "I know the thoughts that I think toward you, saith the Lord, thoughts of peace, and not of evil, to give you an expected end"—Jeremiah 29:11. As Christians, whatever we may be going through today, we have the wonderful hope of Heaven and eternity with Jesus Christ, who can comfort us in sorrow and give us hope for tomorrow. May we take courage and gain strength by remembering that our hope is in the Lord God Almighty.

**Day 238**

# The Christian's Goal

I Peter 1:15-16

*"But as he which hath called you is holy, so be ye holy in all manner of conversation; Because it is written, Be ye holy; for I am holy."*

As Christians, our goal should be holiness, not happiness, although by seeking holiness we will ultimately be happy. It is the holiness of our Lord and Saviour, Jesus Christ, that every Christian ought to desire—holiness in how we conduct ourselves, holiness in what we think, and holiness in "all manner of conversation." We can be holy because we have the Holy Spirit of Christ living in us, and He is able to manifest holiness in and through us when we yield ourselves to Him. "Know ye not, that to whom ye yield yourselves servants to obey, his servants ye are to whom ye obey; whether of sin unto death, or of obedience unto righteousness?"—Romans 6:16. Yielding ourselves to the Holy Spirit and following as He leads us will put us on the path of holiness; therefore, "as ye have yielded your members servants to uncleanness and to iniquity unto iniquity; even so now yield your members servants to righteousness unto holiness"—Romans 6:19b. Obeying the Holy Spirit can lead to holiness in our lives.

Being saved does not give us the liberty to do whatever we want; it gives us the privilege of being holy as our Saviour, Jesus Christ, is holy. Salvation comes from receiving Christ; His holiness comes through daily surrendering ourselves to the Holy Spirit who dwells in us. Therefore, we need to ask ourselves some questions in order to "make [our] calling and election sure"—II Peter 1:10b. Do I believe the Scripture says that I need to be holy as the Lord is holy? Do I believe the Holy Spirit of God has come to live in me and that He can make me holy? Am I surrendering myself to Him and allowing Him to have His own way in me? Holiness can only come by God through the power of His Holy Spirit living in us. Today and every day it should be our desire and goal to be holy as Christ Jesus is holy.

# Working on Our Behalf

Psalm 71:14

*"But I will hope continually, and will yet praise thee more and more."*

We can hope continually because our blessed Heavenly Father is working on our behalf to guide us, to provide for us, to help us, and when necessary, to correct us so that we will continue in His ways. Jesus Christ, our Saviour, "ever liveth to make intercession for [us]"—Hebrews 7:25c. The Lord sits "upon a throne, high and lifted up"—Isaiah 6:1b. "Thine, O LORD, is the greatness, and the power, and the glory, and the victory, and the majesty: for all that is in the heaven and in the earth is thine; thine is the kingdom, O LORD, and thou are exalted as head above all"—I Chronicles 29:11. He has all power, all glory, all victory, and all majesty; therefore, the Lord God Almighty is in control, and He reigns supreme and sovereign over all; therefore, may we not lose hope, for He is working on our behalf.

The mercies of the Lord "are new every morning"—Lamentations 3:23a; therefore, let us praise Him for being so abundantly merciful toward us. He is eternal, and He is love; therefore, His love to us never fails. At times, human love is unstable, but God's love endures forever. He extends His amazing grace to us, and He is ready to forgive us when we come to Him and confess our sin. Our friends and our families may fail us, but God will never fail us. Because He remains the same and never changes, we can hope continually in Him, and praise Him that He is working on our behalf.

*Day 240*

# Being Full

Acts 6:5,8

*"And the saying pleased the whole multitude: and they chose Stephen, a man full of faith and of the Holy Ghost, and Philip, and Prochorus, and Nicanor, and Timon, and Parmenas, and Nicolas a proselyte of Antioch . . . And Stephen, full of faith and power, did great wonders and miracles among the people."*

Stephen was full of faith and power because he was full of loving devotion to the Lord Jesus Christ. His heart was full of Christ; therefore, he was filled with wisdom so that "they were not able to resist the wisdom and the spirit by which he spake"—Acts 6:10. It changed his countenance so that "all that sat in the council, looking stedfastly on him, saw his face as it had been the face of an angel"—Acts 6:15. Stephen's faith gave him boldness to expound the Scriptures, as we can read in Acts 7. It turned his eyes heavenward when "they gnashed on him with their teeth"—Acts 7:54, and he "saw the glory of God, and Jesus standing on the right hand of God"—Acts 7:55.

Stephen's life was not about what he desired or wanted for himself; rather, he centered his life on promoting Jesus Christ and lifting Him up to the people. The life of Stephen is a challenge for us today to be so filled with love and devotion to Jesus Christ that we mirror the character and life of Christ. We will become an extension of the life of Christ when we grow into a fullness of love for Him, and daily nurture that love so it continually builds.

# Edifying and Gracious Communication

Ephesians 4:29

*"Let no corrupt communication proceed out of your mouth, but that which is good to the use of edifying, that it may minister grace unto the hearers."*

The old adage, "If you can't say something nice, then don't say anything at all," applies to this portion of Scripture. As Christians, we should not let any slander, gossip, angry outburst, lie, off-color joke, or unkind words become part of our conversation. When we do, we grieve the Holy Spirit. The Apostle Paul, inspired by the Holy Spirit, wrote to the Ephesian Christians, saying, "And grieve not the Holy Spirit of God, whereby ye are sealed unto the day of redemption"—Ephesians 4:30. He further wrote, "Let all bitterness, and wrath, and anger, and clamour, and evil speaking, be put away from you, with all malice: And be ye kind one to another, tenderhearted, forgiving one another, even as God for Christ's sake hath forgiven you"—Ephesians 4:31-32. We must "put off concerning the former conversation the old man, which is corrupt according to the deceitful lusts; and be renewed in the spirit of [our] mind"—Ephesians 4:22-23. When we harbor bitterness, wrath, and anger in our hearts toward others, at some point, our communication is going to reveal it. In our own power, we cannot turn from these natural tendencies of our flesh. However, our communication will be more edifying when we fill our hearts and minds with His Word, ask the Lord to help us, and yield our old nature to His Spirit, who lives in us.

We are God's ambassadors for Christ, and we need to be careful to represent Him effectively with gracious, kind and loving communication to believers and non-believers. Our conversations will be more edifying and less corrupt when we walk in humility and "all lowliness and meekness, with longsuffering, forbearing one another in love; endeavoring to keep the unity of the Spirit in the bond of peace"—Ephesians 4:2-3.

## Day 242

# But Prayer

Acts 12:5

*"Peter therefore was kept in prison: but prayer was made without ceasing of the church unto God for him."*

Peter was in prison, and it seemed that the Jews were triumphant. King Herod was in supreme power, and death appeared imminent for the Apostle. ***But prayer!*** It was in answer to prayer being made without ceasing that opened the prison doors, removed the chains that shackled Peter, kept the guards in a deep sleep, and set Peter free. Prayer is our power to receive the incredible and to accomplish the impossible. All that is impossible with man *is* possible with God, and it is prayer that opens the way for Him to work on our behalf in such a mighty way. Believing God in prayer for the impossible not only brings incredible answers from God, but causes the Word of God to continue on in greater victory, and abundantly glorifies Him.

This supernatural weapon is ours, but do we really know how powerful it is? Are we using it with a faith that commands as well as asks? "Jesus said unto him, If thou canst believe, all things are possible to him that believeth" –Mark 9:23. If we do not believe, we will not ask with authority and confidence that He is able to perform such impossible feats. The Lord God Almighty does not want *us* to be great; He wants us to dare to prove ***His*** greatness. We do that by prayer –***but prayer***.

# Overpowering the Enemy

Luke 10:19

*"Behold, I give unto you power . . . over all the power of the enemy."*

Matthew 13:39

*"The enemy . . . is the devil . . ."*

As Christians, we have an enemy who "walketh about, seeking whom he may devour"—I Peter 5:8c, and his name is the Devil. He also is called Satan—Luke 10:18, our adversary—I Peter 5:8, the wicked one—Matthew 13:19. He is subtle, devious, cunning, deceptive; and he can be "transformed into an angel of light"—II Corinthians 11:14b. However, through the Spirit of Christ, we have been given power over him, "because greater is he that is in you, than he that is in the world"—I John 4:4b. We have power over him when we resist him "stedfast in the faith"—I Peter 5:9a. "Submit yourselves therefore to God. Resist the devil, and he will flee from you"—James 4:7.

This power that we have been given over our enemy comes when we "humble [ourselves] in the sight of the Lord"—James 4:10a, and realize that apart from Christ we are powerless. We cannot try hard enough or work hard enough in order to overpower the Devil, because in our flesh—in our own strength—we are unable and helpless. The power has already been given to us in the Person of the Holy Spirit. It is by walking in the Spirit that we are able to utilize this power over our enemy; however, when we stubbornly seek our own will and way, then we are weakened and our enemy is able to exercise his power over us. The power to overcome the enemy lives inside every believer; therefore, may we live in victory today and overpower the enemy who is seeking to devour our Christian testimony.

**Day 244**

# A New Life

Galatians 2:20-21

*"I am crucified with Christ: nevertheless I live; yet not I , but Christ liveth in me: and the life which I now live in the flesh I live by the faith of the Son of God, who loved me, and gave himself for me. I do not frustrate the grace of God: for if righteousness come by the law, then Christ is dead in vain."*

Jesus Christ gave Himself for us, and when we received Him as our Saviour His Spirit came to live in us. Jesus Christ, our High Priest, declares to the Father that we have been washed in His blood; therefore, we have access to the Father in prayer because we have been accepted in His beloved Son. "I am crucified with Christ" means that it was our sin that nailed Jesus to the cross; "he was wounded for our transgressions, he was bruised for our iniquities: the chastisement of our peace was upon him; and with his stripes we are healed"—Isaiah 53:5.

As a bride takes on the last name of her groom, so at salvation we take on the name of Jesus Christ and become known by His Name, Christian. "Knowing this, that our old man is crucified with him, that the body of sin might be destroyed, that henceforth we should not serve sin"—Romans 6:6. "Therefore if any man be in Christ, he is a new creature: old things are passed away; behold, all things are become new"—II Corinthians 5:17. We have been set free from the penalty of sin and will be set free from the power of sin over us for "greater is he that is in you, than he that is in the world"—I John 4:4b. As Christians, our life can now become the hands, the feet, the heart, the mouth of Jesus Christ through His Spirit who lives in us. It is simply a process of drawing closer to the Lord in order to increase our faith in Him and our walk for Him. We "do not frustrate the grace of God" by continuing to live as we lived before Jesus Christ saved us. To do that would be to love ourselves more than we love Christ, to want our will more than His, to have little regard for the great love we have been shown, and to ignore the power of His Holy Spirit who dwells in us. Therefore, we must daily remember the grace that saved us, look unto Jesus, yield ourselves to His Spirit, and allow Him to live His life through us.

# Wait upon God

Psalm 62:5

*"My soul, wait thou only upon God; for my expectation is from him."*

One of the hardest things for us to do is to wait. Most of us are so impatient that we do not wait upon God, so we foolishly walk ahead of Him instead of waiting for His plan to unfold. The prophet Elijah went to the brook Cherith in obedience to the word of the Lord, "and it came to pass after a while, that the brook dried up, because there had been no rain in the land" –I Kings 17:7. Elijah watched the brook dwindle week after week, but with unwavering faith he remained beside the brook, waiting upon God to tell him where to go next, for his expectation was from God. Would we have paced up and down beside the dwindling stream, exhausting ourselves with planning and scheming what our next move should be? Would we have ceased our songs of praise long before the stream dried up, and with red, puffy eyes from weeping, would we have loudly moaned and complained? Would we have devised some plan and asked God's blessing on it, and then moved on without waiting upon God to reveal His plan?

Elijah waited upon God; therefore, he received God's next direction, "Arise, get thee to Zarephath, which belongeth to Zidon, and dwell there: behold, I have commanded a widow woman there to sustain thee" –I Kings 17:9. If we would wait for the unfolding of God's plan for us, we would never need to retrace our steps with tears of shame and remorse. God has a plan, and He wants to direct us according to His perfect timing. Therefore, let us wait only upon Him, for our expectation is from Him.

**Day 246**

# Getting Nearer to God Is Good

Psalm 73:28

*"But it is good for me to draw near to God."*

Like the psalmist, we often find ourselves immersed in afflictions because we have not sought the nearness of Almighty God. When we are at a distance from God we become "envious at the foolish" –Psalm 73:3, and become afraid that we will offend them –Psalm 73:15. When we draw near to God then we escape such dilemmas; and by continuing to draw closer to Him we will be kept from reoccurrences of these same afflictions. The greater our closeness to God, the less we are attracted or distracted by the world.

It is perilous for us not to grow close to God, "For, lo, they that are far from thee shall perish . . ." –Psalm 73:27. When we draw close to God, our hearts are happier and more restful, because the nearer we grow to God, the more of Himself He reveals to us. When we draw near to God, our understanding becomes enlightened, our minds become filled with Him, our will is more surrendered to His will, and our love deepens toward Him as well as toward others around us. This close communion with God brings us joy, so that our soul pants after God "as the hart panteth after the water brooks" –Psalm 42:1.

Drawing near to God is never a single act, but a continual drawing, a continual coming, a continual getting closer for as long as we live on this earth. It is a continual realization of our dependency on Him, a continual building of our confidence through Him, and a continual deepening of our trust in Him. We need to make it a daily encounter because it is good for us to draw near to God.

*Nothing between my soul and my Savior, Naught of this world's delusive dream; I have renounced all sinful pleasure; Jesus is mine, there's nothing between –C.A. Tindley*

# Seek the Lord

Psalm 34:10

*"They that seek the Lord shall not want [lack] any good thing."*

The Lord Jesus said, "Seek, and ye shall find" – Matthew 7:7. If we seek the Lord we will find Him faithful to keep His promises. We will be able to say as did Joshua, "Not one thing hath failed of all the good things which the Lord your God spake concerning you; all are come to pass unto you, and not one thing hath failed thereof" –Joshua 23:14.

If we seek the Lord, we will find Him merciful and will be able to say with assurance, as did the prophet Jeremiah, "It is of the Lord's mercies that we are not consumed, because his compassions fail not" – Lamentations 3:22. If we seek the Lord we will find His grace sufficient, as did the Apostle Paul when he wrote, "And he said unto me, My grace is sufficient for thee: for my strength is made perfect in weakness" –II Corinthians 12:9. If we seek the Lord we will find "a friend that sticketh closer than a brother" –Proverbs 18:24b. If we seek the Lord we will find that "every good gift and every perfect gift is from above, and cometh down from the Father of lights, with whom is no variableness, neither shadow of turning" –James 1:17.

Seek the Lord and you will find a refuge, a hiding place, a shelter in the time of storm, and peace that will pass all your understanding. The Lord is good; in Him we can find everything we will ever need; therefore, let's choose to seek the Lord and we will not lack any good thing. "Ye shall seek me, and find me, when ye shall search for me with all your heart" –Jeremiah 29:13.

**Day 248**

# Rejoicing and Praising the Lord

Luke 19:37-38

*". . . the whole multitude of the disciples began to rejoice and praise God with a loud voice for all the mighty works that they had seen; Saying, Blessed be the King that cometh in the name of the Lord: peace in heaven, and glory in the highest."*

Christian, are you rejoicing and praising God with a loud voice? Are you remembering the day of your salvation and the mighty work of redemption that Christ, by His grace, worked in you? If so, open wide your mouth and shout your praises to your King! Proclaim His name to all those around you that they too may know the glorious power of salvation. "The heavens declare the glory of God; and the firmament sheweth his handiwork" –Psalm 19:1; therefore, shouldn't you also declare the glory of Christ which dwells within you – the power of His resurrection, the eternal home in Heaven He is preparing for you, the access He made for you to God the Father? His glories are without limit. If you remain silent, "the stones would immediately cry out" – Luke 19:40. Do you exhibit His handiwork of grace, of forgiveness, of patience, of mercies toward you by extending them to your brother or sister in Christ or to your neighbor or to your enemy? Stand up and proclaim His glories, His power, and His might! He is worthy of honor and praise! Cease from being silent and begin today to "rejoice and praise God with a loud voice."

Oh, glorious King
And Most High God,
You have given me everything
As in Thy steps I trod.

From the fullness of my heart
I must exclaim
That truly the heavens
Declare the glories of Your Name.

The green of the hills
The blue of the skies
The glory of your handiwork
I do see with my eyes.

# Offer unto God Thanksgiving

Psalm 50:14

*"Offer unto God thanksgiving"*

All of us would benefit tremendously if we would thank the Lord and cease our complaining. If we are saved, let's thank Him for His mercies that have kept us from Hell. Thank Him for His grace that has assured us of Heaven! Thank Him for His love that suffers long with us and never fails. Thank Him for daily loading us with benefits so numerous we could never list them all. Thank Him for "divers temptations; knowing this, that the trying of your faith worketh patience" –James 1:2b-3. Offering thanksgiving to God will make the downcast joyful and trials more bearable. It was when the Psalmist complained that his spirit was overwhelmed –Psalm 77:3. It is when we are unthankful that we complain, and complaining overwhelms our spirit. Thank God that we have a Savior who understands our afflictions, our heartaches, and our difficulties! "Surely he hath borne our griefs, and carried our sorrows" – Isaiah 53:4. Become a thankful person and make it a daily habit to offer thanksgiving to God.

## Day 250

# Come Up in the Morning

Exodus 34:2

*"And be ready in the morning, and come up in the morning unto mount Sinai, and present thyself there to me in the top of the mount."*

The person whose day begins with God in prayer will be better able, with His strength, to withstand the pressures and stresses of daily life. The morning is fresh and new, still and silent, and our bodies are rested from a night of sleep. First thing in the morning our flesh has not yet been weakened by physical work, or hours of attempting to resist the devil's temptations. Our day is better lived when we meet with God in the morning. Our life is more at rest after having spent sweet fellowship with our Lord in the morning. We are better able to face our "giants" during the day when we have been renewed and refreshed by God through prayer alone with Him in the morning.

Our Lord Jesus taught us by example to come into the Father's presence and pray in the morning: "And in the morning, rising up a great while before day, he went out, and departed into a solitary place, and there prayed" –Mark 1:35. In the morning our heart's ear is more attentive, because the clamor of the world's voices has not yet fully entered in. In the stillness of the early morning hour there is limited or no activity to distract us from attending to what God, the Father, wants us to learn when we read His Word and talk to Him in prayer. Therefore, "be ready in the morning, and come up in the morning" to meet with God in prayer and Bible reading. Let us say, like the psalmist, "My voice shalt thou hear in the morning, O LORD; in the morning will I direct my prayer unto thee, and will look up" –Psalm 5:3.

# Leaning on Christ as Our Beloved

Song of Solomon 8:5

*"Who is this that cometh up from the wilderness, leaning upon her beloved?"*

As believers, we have the blessing and privilege to lean upon our Beloved, Jesus Christ, in all areas of our life. He is our Security, our Protector, our Advocate, and our dearest Love. When we lean upon Him, He will shield us from the attacks Satan will hurl against us; He will speak encouragingly to us during our lowest points of life; and He will sustain us. "He shall never suffer the righteous to be moved" –Psalm 55:22.

As a soldier would depend upon another on the battlefield, we may lean upon our Beloved on the battlefield of life. As a child leans upon a parent for safety and security, we may lean upon our Beloved. He will keep us safe and secure, not only in this life, but in the life to come, for nothing and no one is able to pluck us out of His hand –John 10:28. As a husband is the protector of his wife, so is our Beloved to us. He will protect us from the enemy; He will fight for us. We may lean upon our Beloved in any and all of life's circumstances. "I am my beloved's, and my beloved is mine" –Song of Solomon 6:3a. May we all learn to lean upon Jesus Christ, the Beloved.

*Day 252*

# Strength for the Day

Deuteronomy 33:25b

*"As thy days, so shall thy strength be"*

God promised to give us strength each day for whatever our particular need may be. He will graciously and continually support us through our trials and troubles. "The eternal God is thy refuge, and underneath are the everlasting arms"—Deuteronomy 33:27. "He shall cover thee with his feathers, and under his wings shalt thou trust: his truth shall be thy shield and buckler"—Psalm 91:4.

Whatever it is that we have to do, He will give us strength to do it. Whatever burdens we bear He will give us the strength to carry them, or He will carry them for us. "They that wait upon the LORD shall renew their strength; they shall mount up with wings as eagles; they shall run, and not be weary; and they shall walk, and not faint"—Isaiah 40:31. When we go forth in God's strength we will not faint, or fall. When we look to the Lord, He will give us the strength we need to go forward, for "as thy days, so shall thy strength be."

# Confident Expectations

Psalm 42:11a

*"Why art thou cast down, O my soul? and why art thou disquieted within me? Hope thou in God."*

King David, also known as the sweet Psalmist of Israel, became discouraged and despondent. He revealed his human side in this verse, but he also gave the solution to discouragement and despondency, which was to ***hope in God!*** Hope is simply having confident expectations in someone or something. David is in essence saying, *Confidently expect God to see you through any and all troubles.*

The Lord Jesus said, "lo, I am with you always, even unto the end of the world"—Matthew 28:20b. It is natural for our human nature to experience times of discouragement or even depression. When we are feeling alone—perhaps because friends have forsaken us, loved ones have gone on before us or rejected us, or for any number of reasons—this is a good time to confidently acknowledge that Jesus Christ *is* with us. "And David said to Solomon his son, Be strong and of good courage . . . for the LORD God, even my God, ***will be with thee***; he will not fail thee, nor forsake thee"—I Chronicles 28:20.

When the devil and his demons seem to be getting you down with their accusations, remember to shout the victory in Jesus Christ, for "he is risen, as he said"—Matthew 28:6; "[He] will come again"—John 14:3b. "All power is given unto [Jesus] in heaven and in earth"—Matthew 28:18. Continue to confidently expect Him to have the victory! Turn away from every fear and doubt, and hope in God!

## Day 254

# Prisoner of the Lord

Ephesians 4:1a

*". . . The prisoner of the Lord . . ."*

The Apostle Paul is in prison. Look at how he responded to his situation. He did not write to the Ephesians that he was a prisoner of Caesar, nor did he claim to be a victim of the Sanhedrin. No, he wrote that he was a "prisoner of the Lord." He did not sulk, complain, or cast blame; he saw only the hand of God in it all. Many Christians may seem to flourish in abundant activity for the Lord, and may even endure suffering in their active service; however, when laid aside from Christian activities and forced into close confinement and inactivity, they sometimes break down. The confinement may be a literal prison like Paul was in, or it may be the confinement of a sick bed. But whatever the confinement might be, may we, like Paul, see the hand of the Lord in it, "For it is God which worketh in you both to will and to do of his good pleasure"—Philippians 2:13. The Lord has a plan to deepen our walk with Him, to refine us more into the likeness of His Son, Jesus Christ, and to use us in a greater way to bring Him glory. Sometimes that can only be done by being set aside in some type of confinement. Therefore, "consider him that endured such contradiction of sinners against himself, lest ye be wearied and faint in your minds"—Hebrews 12:3.

Think of the many Christians who have lived after the Apostle Paul did and experienced their own confinement. John Bunyan was in the Bedford jail for 12 long years, but from that prison he wrote The Pilgrim's Progress, a book that reportedly is the second most read book next to the Bible. Susanna Spurgeon was an invalid and never left her bed for 16 years, but it was from that bedside that she organized the largest Christian bookstore of that day. The Lord mightily used these and others whom He put into a season of confinement. Perhaps He is preparing many of us to be used in some way that could never happen without just such a season in our own life. Therefore, we must continue to keep our eyes on Him and remember that He has a greater plan for us than we can see right now.

# God Hears Prayer

Psalm 6:9

*"The LORD hath heard my supplication; the LORD will receive my prayer."*

When the Lord tarries in answering prayer, or when His answer is no, we can be sure that He has heard and received prayer because the Bible says He has, and His "word is truth"—John 17:17b. The devil wants us to believe that God doesn't care and that He doesn't hear us, because the devil doesn't like it when we pray. He knows that prayer is our most powerful weapon against him; therefore, if he can keep us out of our prayer closet and turn our hearts away from praying, then he will have accomplished his goal. As believers, we need to remember that the devil is a liar, and "there is no truth in him. When he speaketh a lie, he speaketh of his own: for he is a liar, and the father of it"—John 8:44b. The Bible says, "The LORD is far from the wicked: but he heareth the prayer of the righteous"—Proverbs 15:29. "I cried by reason of mine affliction unto the LORD, and he heard me"—Jonah 2:2a. "And the LORD said unto him, I have heard thy prayer and thy supplication, that thou hast made before me"—I Kings 9:3a. "I cried unto the LORD with my voice, and he heard me out of his holy hill. Selah"—Psalm 3:4. "This poor man cried, and the LORD heard him, and saved him out of all his troubles"—Psalm 34:6.

The Lord ***does*** hear prayer! "His ear [is not] heavy, that it cannot hear"—Isaiah 59:1b. It may be that sin in our life has hindered our prayers and made it necessary for the Lord to temporarily hide His face from us, "that he will not hear"—Isaiah 59:2b. However, we may be sure that God ***does*** hear prayer! Therefore, let's pray and then pray some more until we begin to "pray without ceasing"—I Thessalonians 5:17, because God does hear and receive prayer.

*Day 256*

# Take Heed to Walk in the Ways of the Lord

II Kings 10:31

*"But Jehu took no heed to walk in the law of the LORD God of Israel with all his heart: for he departed not from the sins of Jeroboam, which made Israel to sin."*

Jehu performed a mighty act for the Lord when he slew the worshippers of Baal [Satan], burned their images of Baal, destroyed the statue of Baal, and destroyed the house of Baal; however, he did not take heed to walk in the law of the Lord with *all* his heart. He zealously destroyed the false religion, but in the true religion–the law of the LORD God of Israel–he did not act with the same zealousness to please God, for he took no heed to walk with the Lord with all his heart.

God desires that we walk with Him with our entire heart devoted to Him. When we walk with the Lord halfheartedly, we do not receive His fullest blessings; yet, no service for God will go unnoticed, because His mercies endure forever. We must take heed to serve the Lord with all of our heart, so that we will be "doers of the word, and not hearers only" –James 1:22. May we take heed to wholeheartedly follow the Lord God Almighty, and abstain from anything and everything that would keep us from walking with the Lord with all our heart.

# The Greatness and Glory of God's Creation

Psalm 33:6

*"By the word of the Lord were the heavens made; and all the host of them by the breath of his mouth."*

Herein lies the greatness and the glory of our Lord God Almighty: He ***spoke*** and the heavens were made; He ***breathed*** all the host of them into existence. The magnitude of this incredible glory is beyond the realm of our finite minds to fully comprehend. As a result, many people do not believe the extraordinary, yet simple, truth about creation. "In the beginning God created the heaven and the earth. And the earth was without form, and void; and darkness was upon the face of the deep. . . . And God ***said***, Let there be a firmament in the midst of the waters, and let it divide the waters from the waters. . . . And God called the firmament Heaven" –Genesis 1:1-2a,6,8. "And God said, Let there be lights in the firmament of the heaven to divide the day from the night . . . And let them be for lights in the firmament of the heaven to give light upon the earth: and it was so. And God made two great lights . . . he made the stars also" –Genesis 1:14-16. The heavens were made by the words of His mouth, "And all the host of them by the ***breath*** of His mouth." The heavens being created by His spoken word is glorious, but the host of them being created by His breath is exceedingly glorious! The multitude of galaxies and all the complexity of their existence were created by the ***breath*** of His mouth. Astrologers have been fascinated by the mysteries, the  magnitude, and the beauty of the heavens –all of which were created by the very word and breath of Almighty God. "The heavens declare the glory of God; and the firmament sheweth his handywork" –Psalm 19:1. "The heavens declare his righteousness, and all the people see his glory" –Psalm 97:6.

277

*Day 258*

# The Joy of the Lord Is Your Strength

Nehemiah 8:10c

*"The joy of the Lord is your strength."*

The joy of the Lord is salvation—that restored fellowship between God and man when Jesus Christ shed His blood on the cross of Calvary. The resurrection of Jesus Christ from the grave as He conquered death and hell, for all eternity, is the joy of the Lord. The Lord Jesus, "who for the joy that was set before him endured the cross, despising the shame, and is set down at the right hand of the throne of God" –Hebrews 12:2b.

This joy of the Lord is our strength to forgive, because He has forgiven. It is our strength to love and not hate, because He so loved us that He laid down His life for us –John 10:17-18. His joy is our strength to obey, because He "became obedient unto death, even the death of the cross" –Philippians 2:8b so that lost souls could be saved. The joy of the Lord is our strength in the darkest trial, because His trial was darker still when He went to the pits of hell for us and prevailed. The joy of the Lord is our strength to submit ourselves unto Him who submitted Himself unto the will of the Father by leaving Heaven's throne and coming to earth with the purpose of dying so that men may live.

There is no anguish so deep that the joy of the Lord does not go deeper still, to strengthen our hearts and minds, in Christ Jesus. We should not allow circumstances to dictate to us our joy. If we have received Christ as our Savior, we can rejoice that our names are written down in Heaven, and let the joy of the Lord be our strength.

# God's Pure Word

Proverbs 30:5

*"Every word of God is pure."*

EVERY Word of God is pure! There aren't any contaminates in the Word of God. As pure water is good for the body, the pure Word of God is good for the heart and soul. As the pureness of a mountain stream delights the parched tongue, so the pure Word of God delights the soul of the Christian. His words give refreshment in an impure world. They are nourishing strength of righteousness for a sinful heart. They are a guide upon the path of life. They are perfection in an imperfect world. They are "health to thy navel, and marrow to thy bones" –Proverbs 3:8. The pure Word of God is like a breath of fresh air, strengthening and delighting the soul. The wonder of it all is that *every* Word of God is pure, not just some words, but *every* word! God is pure; therefore, His Word is pure, and is for our benefit, our help, our sustenance, and our growth. The Word of God should not be taken lightly, but held in highest esteem and handled with the greatest of care, for "the words of the LORD are pure words: as silver tried in a furnace of earth, purified seven times" –Psalm 12:6.

## *Day 260*

# Continual Hope

Psalm 71:14

*"But I will hope continually, and will yet praise thee more and more."*

As believers, we can hope continually in the Lord, because in Him we have a confident expectation that everything He promises to do, **He will do**. Moses said to Joshua, "The LORD, he it is that doth go before thee; he will be with thee, he will not fail thee, neither forsake thee: fear not, neither be dismayed" –Deuteronomy 31:8. Then at the end of Joshua's life, he triumphantly said, "Behold, this day I am going the way of all the earth: and ye know in all your hearts and in all your souls, that not one thing hath failed of all the good things which the Lord your God spake concerning you; all are come to pass unto you, and not one thing hath failed thereof" –Joshua 23:14.

If our circumstances seem impossible, may we remind ourselves that God never fails. "Know therefore that the LORD thy God, he is God, the faithful God, which keepeth covenant and mercy with them that love him and keep his commandments to a thousand generations" –Deuteronomy 7:9. What He has promised, be assured He **will** do. We may claim His promises, stand upon them, and they will encourage us to hope continually in the Lord.

When we hope in the Lord, our expectations in Him will be fulfilled; our hearts will overflow with praise; our confidence to hope again will increase; and we will have cause to praise Him more and more. If our hope is placed in anything or anyone else, we will be left with failed expectations; therefore, let us hope continually in the Lord. His promises never fail!

# From the Lord

I Kings 12:24b

*"Thus saith the Lord, Ye shall not go up, nor fight against your brethren the children of Israel: return every man to his house; for this thing is from me."*

The hard circumstances, the joyful days, the trials, and everything that occurs in our lives are from the Lord. He has a purpose and a plan for everything that He allows to take place, and the sooner we begin to see His hand in everything, the better we will be able to experience His rest and His peace. All that concerns us, concerns Him also, because anything "that toucheth you toucheth the apple of his eye" –Zechariah 2:8b. "When thou passest through the waters, I will be with thee; and through the rivers, they shall not overflow thee: when thou walkest through the fire, thou shalt not be burned; neither shall the flame kindle upon thee" –Isaiah 43:2. He may allow difficult times to occur in our lives, but He is with us in them and goes with us through them. Like Job, there may be some part of our character that needs to be better molded into the likeness of Christ; therefore, difficulty is allowed to come, but only for our good and for God's glory so that we may be more greatly used by Him in His service.

These various trials and temptations are for our education to teach us that our weakness needs His might, our safety lies in letting Him fight for us, and that our very existence depends upon Him for everything. Therefore, when our finances are low and it seems impossible to make ends meet, remember, He desires that we learn and apply His promise to "supply all [our] need according to his riches in glory by Christ Jesus" – Philippians 4:19. When a trusted friend or close family member betrays or forsakes us, it is then we can learn that "when my father and my mother forsake me, then the Lord will take me up" –Psalm 27:10. May we begin to hear Him say, "This thing is from me," that we may begin to learn all He desires for us to learn so that we may become more like Christ. The sting of our circumstances will begin to subside when we begin to see Him in everything.

*Day 262*

# None Other

Exodus 15:11

*"Who is like unto thee, O LORD, among the gods? who is like thee, glorious in holiness, fearful in praises, doing wonders?"*

God is glorious in holiness!  God is so holy, because He does not have the presence of sin, the ability to sin, or the thought of sin.  He is completely and absolutely without sin, and there is no one who compares to Him, because He is perfect.  Our finite minds cannot fully comprehend the magnitude of God's holiness, because whereas we are sinful, He is holy, and His holiness exceeds our comprehension.  Just as we cannot describe His power, we cannot describe His holiness.  However, the more we consider and meditate upon His holiness, the more we will be in awe of His love and grace toward us who are so unholy.

God is fearful (awe-inspiring) in praises!  When we begin to truly comprehend His great holiness, our hearts can't help but overflow with reverence for Him, and we desire to declare our praises to Him.  The Israelites sang this song to honor God, exalt Him, praise Him, and celebrate Him. He alone is worthy to be magnified.  If we have been saved, then we too should exalt and magnify Him in songs of praise, "singing and making melody in [our] heart to the Lord"—Ephesians 5:19.  We should "give unto the LORD the glory due unto his name . . . [and] worship the LORD in the beauty of holiness"—I Chronicles 16:29.  We are weak, sinful, and prone to yield to temptation; but God's grace is our strength.  Let us take time every day to consider His holiness and worship Him with praise.

## Seasons

Ecclesiastes 3:1

"To every thing there is a season, and a time to every purpose under the heaven."

There is a season in our lives when all is going well and we are having what is most commonly referred to as a *mountaintop* experience. During this season, our faces are glowing with delighted smiles and we sing joyfully and exuberantly. Our countenance is contagious to all those around us and we are able to infect them with the joy we are feeling. Our step is light and carefree, and during this season there isn't a cloud to darken our day. God is near and we feel secure in the strength of His hand so that we confidently say, "The Lord is my helper, and I will not fear what man shall do unto me"—Hebrews 13:6. There is another season where the shadows appear so big that they seem to hide the shining sun. This season is commonly known as *the valley*. We are no longer lighthearted, and our light steps have turned into laborious ones. There is no longer a confident sense of God's presence, and insecurity has engulfed us. We may begin to lament, like Job, saying, "Let the day perish wherein I was born"—Job 3:3a.

Whether we are on the *mountaintop* or in *the valley*, we can be certain that many are His "thoughts which are to usward . . . they are more than can be numbered"—Psalm 40:5b. "The LORD God is [our] strength, and he will make [our] feet like hinds' feet, and he will make [us] to walk upon [our] high places"—Habakkuk 3:19. The Lord is on the mountain as well as in the valley, and wherever we are, He is there. If we are in *the valley*, we must not believe the devil's lies that God has abandoned us, and that He no longer loves us. That is simply impossible, and we must not believe it; for "the LORD hath appeared of old unto me, saying, Yea, I have loved thee with an everlasting love: therefore with loving kindness have I drawn thee"—Jeremiah 31:3. If we are on the *mountaintop* we must not become self-reliant, but rather, remain dependent upon the Lord Jesus Christ. Remember, whatever season we may be walking in, God is there and He has a purpose for that season in our lives, so remain ever close to Him.

**Day 264**

# Full Service

II Chronicles 31:21

*"And in every work that he began in the service of the house of God, and in the law, and in the commandments, to seek his God, he did it with all his heart, and prospered."*

Has every service that you began in the house of God been done with all your heart? Has the intent of your service been to seek and to glorify God? Many times service begins in the house of God with selfish motives, which is the reason there is so little follow- through, so little impact, and so little interest in the serving. We must consider our motives behind our service. Are we doing the service for God's glory or for man's approval? To know our motives we must consider whether we are following God or following a religious routine that we have learned. Many acts of service in the name of the Lord have been done so that we will be accepted with people. Do you know why you believe what you believe, or do you blindly follow what someone tells you without searching the Scriptures to see if it is true or not? The Apostle Paul said, "These [Berean Christians] were more noble than those in Thessalonica, in that they received the word with all readiness of mind, and searched the scriptures daily, whether those things were so"—Acts 17:11. If we only follow after the rules of man, at some point we may become disillusioned, bitter, and possibly even turn from the things of God; however, when we are following God out of a pure heart we will seek to do service for Him with devotion and for His glory. Whatever the service, whether it be singing, teaching, greeting, helping, or even cleaning, be sure to do so with all your heart for God's glory and honor.

# Enter Not into Temptation

Luke 22:46

*"Why sleep ye? Rise and pray, lest ye enter into temptation."*

There is a temptation to deny our Lord; and if the Apostle Peter entered into that temptation, then so might we. There is a temptation to forsake the Lord; and if the men who were closest to Jesus Christ all forsook Him, then we must understand that we are susceptible to the same temptation. There is a temptation to disobey God. If Abraham, who "was called the Friend of God" –James 2:23, disobeyed Him, then we are just as susceptible to be disobedient. There are many temptations that we could face; however, our safeguard against temptation is prayer; but we must first rise up out of our slumber.

This question and exhortation that the Lord Jesus posed to His disciples in the Garden of Gethsemane, just before His capture and crucifixion, is the same question and exhortation He is posing to His disciples today: "Why sleep ye? Rise and pray, lest ye enter into temptation." "The spirit indeed is willing, but the flesh is weak" – Matthew 26:41b; therefore, we need to daily enter into our prayer closets and pray so that we will not enter into temptation.

*Day 266*

# Pride Brings Shame

Proverbs 11:2a

*"When pride cometh, then cometh shame"*

Anger that ignites our tempers into contentious behavior has its root in pride, for "only by pride cometh contention" –Proverbs 13:10. Whenever we explode into an angry outburst, it is pride that lights the fuse, and by pride we are brought to shame: "for anger resteth in the bosom of fools" –Ecclesiastes 7:9b. Pride not only produces anger, but it can also produce vanity, self-conceit, and critical or judgmental thinking. When we become absorbed with ourselves, it is easy to develop a haughty spirit. Pride can puff us up and we imagine ourselves to be more than we really are. Such an air of arrogance can certainly lead to our demise, because "pride goeth before destruction, and an haughty spirit before a fall" –Proverbs 16:18. King Belshazzar, like his father, King Nebuchadnezzar, lifted himself up in pride "against the Lord of heaven"; therefore, the kingdom of King Belshazzar was "divided, and given to the Medes and Persians" –Daniel 5:23-28. Pride took Lucifer, the archangel of Heaven, and made him the devil –Isaiah 14:12. Pride, in whatever form it comes, will always bring shame.

# Making a Joyful Noise

Psalm 100:1

*"Make a joyful noise unto the Lord, all ye lands."*

This exhortation is for every child of God. We have been redeemed by the blood of the Holy Lamb, Jesus Christ; therefore, as children of God, we must lift up our voices and make a joyful noise unto Him "in psalms and hymns and spiritual songs, singing and making melody in your heart to the Lord" –Ephesians 5:19. Singing to the Lord in the midst of sorrow will bring a healing balm. Singing in the midst of hard trials, as Paul and Silas did in Acts 16:25-34, can be instrumental in releasing the prisoner, leading the lost to Christ, and bringing glory to God. All of God's people have reason to sing for joy. "Jesus Christ [is] the same yesterday, and to day, and for ever" –Hebrews 13:8; therefore, let's make a joyful noise unto Him. "He hath said, I will never leave thee, nor forsake thee" –Hebrews 13:5. Make a joyful noise unto Him. The Lord understands the heartaches and sorrows of His people, because He was "a man of sorrows, and acquainted with grief" –Isaiah 53:3. Make a joyful noise unto Him.

When we remember that He is the God who will fight for us, the God who owns "the cattle upon a thousand hills" –Psalm 50:10, the God who will supply all our needs, the God who is mighty to save, to help and to deliver; then will we make a joyful noise unto Him. Our hearts will sing songs of joyful praise when our hearts are filled with Christ and our minds are focused upon Him.

*Day 268*

# Multiplying Grace and Peace

II Peter 1:2

*"Grace and peace be multiplied unto you through the knowledge of God, and of Jesus our Lord."*

At the moment we trusted Christ as our Savior, we encountered grace–God's unmerited favor–and peace. As glorious as that encounter was, it was only the beginning. As Christians, this grace and peace can be multiplied in our lives "through the knowledge of God, and of Jesus our Lord." If we desire that God's grace and peace be multiplied in our lives, then we must seek to know more of Him and His Son, Jesus Christ.

We must get to know the personality, the characteristics, and the mind and heart of our Lord. We may be sure that the grace and peace that we received at salvation will not grow in us unless we deepen our knowledge of God the Father and His Son, Jesus Christ. However, if we "grow in grace, and in the knowledge of our Lord and Saviour Jesus Christ" –II Peter 3:17, then we may be certain that His abundant grace and peace will increase in us as we daily learn more about Him.

We have been given a beautiful handbook, the Bible, which tells us about our Heavenly Father and His Son. It tells us of Their precious promises, Their unceasing love, Their almighty power; it also reveals how They desire for us to live our lives as "ambassadors for Christ" –II Corinthians 5:20a. Grace and peace cannot be multiplied in our lives if we do not regard and regularly read the Bible–God's written Word to mankind. Determine today to increase your knowledge of God and His Son, Jesus Christ, so that grace and peace may be multiplied unto you.

# To Whom Are You Yielding?

Romans 6:16

*"Know ye not, that to whom ye yield yourselves servants to obey, his servants ye are to whom ye obey; whether of sin unto death, or of obedience unto righteousness?"*

I am alive in Christ, and although I still live in a body of flesh, I have power, through Christ, to no longer be a servant to my sinful flesh. I no longer need to yield my members to the desires of the flesh. Rather, through the power of Christ's resurrection, I now have power over my flesh and am able, by His Spirit, to yield myself unto Christ instead. I yield myself unto the Lord when I reckon myself to be dead to sin, "but alive unto God through Jesus Christ our Lord. As Christians, we are told, "Let not sin therefore reign in your mortal body, that ye should obey it in the lusts thereof. Neither yield ye your members as instruments of unrighteousness unto sin: but yield yourselves unto God, as those that are alive from the dead, and your members as instruments of righteousness unto God. For sin shall not have dominion over you: for ye are not under the law, but under grace"—Romans 6:11b-14.

Daily I must yield my mind to His so that my thoughts will be pure and Christ-like. I must yield my heart to His so that the desires of my heart will be in accordance with His and not that of my flesh. I must yield my tongue to Him so that my words will be pleasing in His ears. I must yield my feet to Him so that they only walk where He leads. I must yield my hands to Him so that they only serve as He directs. I must yield my ears to Him so that they are tuned to hear His still small voice. I must also yield my will to His so that He has complete control in all I do with my life. To whom are you yielding? Seek daily to resist the devil and to yield yourself to the Lord.

***Day 270***

# Christ Living in Me

Philippians 1:21

*"For me to live is Christ."*

Contemplate the following questions to see if they are applicable in your life as a child of God. Am I living in such a way that I am striving to imitate Christ's character, Christ's gracious way of speaking, as well as Christ's humility in thought and action on a daily basis? Am I seeking to apply to my life the appeal in Romans 13:14, "But put ye on the Lord Jesus Christ, and make not provision for the flesh, to fulfill the lusts thereof"? To be able to say with Paul "For me to live is Christ" involves much more than salvation and a form of religion. It is getting to know the Lord Jesus Christ better and in the same way Mary of Bethany did as she "sat at Jesus' feet, and heard his word"—Luke 10:39.

The closer we grow in our relationship with Jesus Christ by spending time with Him in prayer and in the Bible, the more we will become like Him. It will help us better imitate His character. He must become everything to us, our confidence, our strength, our all in all as we live the Christian life. Is your life centered on Jesus Christ, realizing that without Him, life would be bleak and frightful? May you strive to be able to say with the Apostle Paul, "for me to live is Christ" so that you may experience the joy of the Lord in all circumstances of life.

# God's Word Endures Forever

I Peter 1:25a

*"The word of the Lord endureth for ever."*

"In the beginning was the Word, and the Word was with God, and the Word was God" –John 1:1. Jesus Christ is the Word, and He is "the same yesterday, and to day, and for ever" –Hebrews 13:8; *the Word of the Lord endures forever.* Many have tried changing God's Word to make it more to their liking, but His eternal Word endures forever. Because He never changes, neither does His Word. The words He spoke to the prophets, to the apostles, and to others remain the same today. The meaning and application of God's Word have not changed, and never will change, *because the Word of the Lord endureth for ever.*

Because the Word of the Lord endures forever, we have a sure foundation on which we can build our Christian lives. God's Word is not going to fade, deteriorate, or falter. It is, and was, and always will be God's sure word of promise. If we have been saved, by faith, through Christ, then we have been "born again, not of corruptible seed, but of incorruptible, by the word of God, which liveth and abideth for ever" –I Peter 1:23. Rejoice, dear Christian, because *the Word of the Lord endureth for ever.*

## *Day 272*

# All Things Common

Acts 4:32

*"And the multitude of them that believed were of one heart and of one soul: neither said any of them that ought [any] of the things which he possessed was his own; but they had all things common."*

They had all things common, because the riches of this world were no longer their desire. Their affections were "on things above, not on things on the earth"—Colossians 3:2. Property and possessions did not have a hold on them; they were simply stewards for the Lord and gave as it had been given unto them. When we hold too tightly to our possessions we can become miserly, believing that it all belongs to us and that parting with our possessions would be too difficult. However, once we are "of one heart and of one soul" in Christ, then we will be willing to share what we have with others, knowing that "he which soweth sparingly shall reap also sparingly; and he which soweth bountifully shall reap also bountifully. Every man according as he purposeth in his heart, so let him give; not grudgingly, or of necessity: for God loveth a cheerful giver"—II Corinthians 9:6-7. They did not covet one another's property, because being one in Christ, they realized that all they possessed came from God; therefore, it was His to divide among them as He saw fit, and they were willing to give according to the need.

They "were of one heart and of one soul" because "they were all filled with the Holy Ghost"—Acts 4:31b; therefore, they were led by the Holy Spirit of God and not by their own desires. When we surrender the control of our lives to the Spirit of Christ Who lives within us, then we too can cease to hold so tightly to our possessions and can become cheerful givers.

# No Place Like Home

Deuteronomy 33:27

*"The eternal God is thy refuge."*

The word refuge may be defined as a *dwelling place* or *home*. This verse is saying that the eternal God is our home, our dwelling place. Regardless of the size or grandeur of the structure, home is the dearest place to our hearts. Such sayings as *All hearts come home at Christmas* and *There's no place like home* are not just quaint sayings, but expressions of the deep feelings our hearts have for *home*. Dearer than any earthly structure we call home, though, is our eternal God in whom "we live, and move, and have our being"—Acts 17:28a.

Home is where we feel safe, and where we can shut out the world and feel secure. So it is with our eternal God, for when we are with Him, we "fear no evil"—Psalm 23:4b, because "he is our help and our shield"—Psalm 33:20b. He is our abiding refuge, a shelter and a retreat. Home is a place of rest. It is where we can unwind and relax after a hard day's work. We can also find rest in God from life's conflicts. When we go to Him with our troubles we find the rest the Lord Jesus Christ promised in Matthew 11:28 and our souls are put at ease. Home is also where we feel more comfortable and at ease and should not fear being misunderstood or rejected by our family members. So it is with our eternal God. We can open up to Him and share with Him our deepest longings and heart's desires, our hurts and our sorrows, without fear of reprisal because He cares for us—I Peter 5:8. Home is also a place of our truest and purest happiness. Just the thought of home can make our hearts glad. And so it is that our hearts find their deepest delight in our eternal God. We find that "the joy of the Lord is [our] strength"—Nehemiah 8:10. Home is a place where we also find our greatest peace and comfort. And so it is true that when we abide with our eternal God we possess His blessed peace and comfort, "and the peace of God, which passeth all understanding, shall keep [our] hearts and minds through Christ Jesus"—Philippians 4:7. There is no place like home, and what a joy to have our eternal God as our refuge—our *home*. Happy are those who have the eternal God for their refuge.

*Day 274*

# Greatly Praise the Lord

Psalm 109:30

*"I will greatly praise the LORD with my mouth; yea, I will praise Him among the multitude."*

The Lord who is high and lifted up; the Lord who is mighty to save; the Lord who is touched with the feeling of our infirmities; the Lord who never leaves nor forsakes any of His children; the Lord who never sleeps nor slumbers; the Lord who created the heavens and the earth; the Lord who fashioned every living soul in their mother's womb; the Lord who is on the wings of the morning, in the depths of the sea, and who went to hell for us; this is the Lord we should greatly praise. He is worthy of all our praise, honor, and adoration. We can never praise the Lord enough. Take time to consider all that the Lord has done, and then praise Him for His wonderful works among the children of men. Do not let a day go by in which you do not praise the Lord! "He ever liveth to make intercession" for us –Hebrews 7:25; therefore, praise Him! He laid down His life that we can experience life everlasting; therefore, praise Him! His love for us surpasses any other love we may know; therefore, praise Him! He is ready to forgive us; therefore, praise Him! Determine today to greatly praise the Lord.

# Conversation That Pleases Christ

Philippians 1:27

*"Only let your conversation be as it becometh the gospel of Christ."*

"Conversation" includes much more than verbal communication; it also includes the whole of our Christian character and conduct before a lost and dying world. Christ's character was that of love, humility, truth, and holiness, just to name a few. Letting our conversation "be as it becometh the gospel of Christ" is then, first, to love. "By this shall all men know that ye are my disciples, if ye have love one to another" –John 13:35.

Jesus Christ was also full of humility: "Who, being in the form of God, thought it not robbery to be equal with God: But made himself of no reputation, and took upon him the form of a servant, and was made in the likeness of men: and being found in fashion as a man, he humbled himself, and became obedient unto death, even the death of the cross"—Philippians 2:6-8. Therefore, we are exhorted by the Apostle Peter to be "clothed with humility"—I Peter 5:5. So, secondly, letting our conversation "be as it becometh the gospel of Christ" also means to conduct ourselves in a spirit of humility.

Jesus said, "I am . . . the truth"—John 14:6. We, then, as His disciples, are to speak and live the truth to all men. Walk truly by the Word set before you, and your conversation—your manner of life –shall be that which "becometh the gospel of Christ."

The Gospel of Christ is also Holy, for our Savior, Jesus Christ, was as "a lamb without blemish and without spot"—I Peter 1:19. Through the Apostle Peter we are instructed to be holy as He is holy—I Peter 1:15, so that our actions and reactions will be holy; our speech will be holy; our thoughts will be holy; our entire life's conduct will be holy. May we strive daily to seek to let our conversation be as it becometh the Gospel of Christ, so that we would please our Father in Heaven and glorify our Savior, Jesus Christ.

*"Those who profess the Gospel of Christ should live as becomes those who believe Gospel truths, submit to Gospel laws, and depend upon Gospel promises." --Matthew Henry*

## Day 276

# Being Led in the Lord's Righteousness

Psalm 5:8

*"Lead me, O Lord, in thy righteousness"*

Unless our righteousness be in Jesus Christ, our Lord and Savior, we have no righteousness. Therefore, we need to be led by the Lord in *His* righteousness. "Lead me, O Lord," as a father leads his child, as a blind man is guided by his friend. We are safe when we are led by the Lord in *His* righteousness, because He *is* righteousness. It must never be our righteousness that leads us, because that is imperfect. "We are his people, and the sheep of his pasture"—Psalm 100:3c; therefore, we should let Him be our righteous Guide. He will not lead us astray, but every path He chooses for us will be the right path. He is the good Shepherd, "and he calleth his own sheep by name, and leadeth them out. And when he putteth forth his own sheep, he goeth before them, and the sheep follow him: for they know his voice" –John 10:3b-4. The path upon which He leads us will not be without difficulty; but, by His leading, any pitfalls can be safely traversed, and He will masterfully direct us through any trouble. If the path in our situation seems uncertain, then this is the time to echo the psalmist's plea, "Lead me, O Lord, in thy righteousness."

# The Trial of Our Faith

I Peter 1:7

*"That the trial of your faith, being much more precious than of gold that perisheth, though it be tried with fire, might be found unto praise and honour and glory at the appearing of Jesus Christ."*

Our Heavenly Father will test our faith in order to remove our imperfections so that the image of His Son may be more clearly seen in us. The trial of our faith may be tried with fire; however, we can be encouraged when we read that the Son of God walks through the fire with His children –Daniel 3:24-25. When we are experiencing overwhelming heartache or battling against "the fiery darts of the wicked" –Ephesians 6:16b, let us remember, we "are kept by the power of God through faith" –I Peter 1:5a. His love for us will not allow us "to be tempted above that ye are able; but will with the temptation also make a way to escape, that ye may be able to bear it" –I Corinthians 10:13b. We may "walk through the valley of the shadow of death" –Psalm 23:4a, but our Lord is there with us to help and to comfort us. We may weep and the fiery trials may seem almost to overwhelm us, but if we look to Him, who is there with us in the trials and testings, we will be able to endure and persevere for His praise and honor and glory.

*Day 278*

# Continual Praise

Psalm 71:6c

*"My praise shall be continually of thee."*

My praise will be of God. I will praise Him for His goodness, His lovingkindness, His unending mercies, His unfailing compassions, His eternal love, His beautiful creation, His wonders all around me, and His watchful care over me. I will praise Him for "every good and every perfect gift" –James 1:17, as well as for trials and sorrows of life, for "when he hath tried me, I shall come forth as gold" –Job 23:10b. "Although the fig tree shall not blossom, neither shall fruit be in the vines; the labour of the olive shall fail, and the fields shall yield no meat [food]; the flock shall be cut off from the fold, and there shall be no herd in the stalls: Yet I will rejoice in the LORD, I will joy in the God of my salvation" –Habakkuk 3:17-18. I will praise Him for salvation, which is the joy and hope of my life. I will praise Him regardless of my circumstances, because He "is my strength, and he will make my feet like hinds' feet, and he will make me to walk upon mine high places" –Habakkuk 3:19.

Not only should I praise God, but I should praise Him continually. When I awake in the morning I should praise Him for keeping me through the night. Throughout the day I should praise Him for His help, His strength, and His amazing grace. In the evening I should praise Him; and as I pillow my head I should praise Him for giving me another day of life. In the night seasons, if I were to awake, I should praise Him that He is there. Although I can never praise Him enough, God is worthy of all praise, and I should continually praise Him.

# Seeking Fellowship with the Lord

Mark 16:1-2

*"And when the Sabbath was past, Mary Magdalene, and Mary the mother of James, and Salome, had bought sweet spices, that they might come and anoint him. And very early in the morning the first day of the week, they came unto the sepulchre at the rising of the sun."*

We can learn from these women how to have fellowship with the Lord Jesus Christ. First, they sought Him very early in the morning–at the rising of the sun. The Lord will not deny fellowship to those whose hearts are hungering and thirsting to meet with Him. Secondly, they sought the Lord with boldness. If we are to have fellowship with our Lord, then we also must boldly seek Him, regardless of what obstacles seem to obstruct our way.

Next we see their earnestness as "Mary stood without [outside] at the sepulchre weeping" –John 20:11a. We will find fellowship with the Lord Jesus when we seek Him earnestly with tears. Tears often are an expression of the heart's deep desire to know the presence of the Lord in close fellowship, and they move the Savior's heart to make Himself known to us. "Jesus saith unto her, Mary" –John 20:16a. Finally we see that Mary sought only the Lord. Looking into the sepulchre, she saw two angels sitting where the Lord Jesus had lain, and even after they had spoken to her she turned away from them to continue her search for the Lord –John 20:12-14. If Christ is to be our first and greatest love, we must remove from our heart all that would rival that love. Then we can experience the comfort of His presence in sweet fellowship with Him.

Let us learn from these women to have the same intensity of love toward our Lord, and seek Him with hearts of love as they did. May our hearts be so full of Christ that we will not be satisfied with anything less than fellowship with Him.

*Day 280*

# Fainting for Want of Faith

Psalm 27:13

*"I had fainted, unless I had believed to see the goodness of the Lord in the land of the living."*

It is because of a lack of faith that Christians are fainting, giving up, and losing heart. They waver in their faith and therefore become "like a wave of the sea driven with the wind and tossed" –James 1:6b. Except they *see*, like the Apostle Thomas, they will not believe –John 20:24-25; however, the Lord Jesus said, "Blessed are they that have not seen, and yet have believed" –John 20:29b.

King David testified that he would have fainted unless he had believed to see the goodness of the Lord in the land of the living. He believed the Lord to be his light, his salvation, and his strength in the midst of his wicked enemies –Psalm 27:1-2; therefore, he ***did not*** give up. He strengthened his faith by prayer and worship. With joy, he sang "praises unto the Lord" –Psalm 27:4-6, which kept Him from fainting, because he put his faith in God and His Son, Jesus Christ. It was in the house of the Lord and in the sanctuary of their communion that he sought their help.

Our faith will fail and we will begin to faint when we allow the enemy to overwhelm our hearts and minds and keep us from prayer and from the house of the Lord. Personal fellowship with God draws us closer to Him, strengthens our hearts, and weakens the enemy's attacks. We will not faint if we, like David, believe to see the goodness of the Lord in the land of the living.

# Doing the Will of the Father

John 4:34

*"Jesus saith unto them, My meat is to do the will of him that sent me, and to finish his work."*

Our Lord and Savior, Jesus Christ, left us an example that we may do the will of the Father with diligence, with delight, and with pleasure. His "meat" that He derived strength from, was doing the will of the Father. His body was weary with His journey, but doing the will of the Father brought a nourishment to His soul that gave strength to His body unlike any natural food possibly could give. Diligently pursuing the will of the Father, and experiencing the power of His Spirit working through us, will bring delight and pleasure to our soul so that we may enthusiastically carry out the work of the Lord.

Our "meat" –our nourishment – as a child of God is to do His will. Our meat is not in how well known we may be as a Christian, or in how great a blessing God may make us to others, or in any self-recognition, but our meat should be simply to do His will so that His will would be done "in earth, as it is in heaven" –Matthew 6:10. Weariness is not a license for us to slacken our performance of His will; rather, it is our opportunity to demonstrate that "when I am weak, then am I strong" –II Corinthians 12:10b. When we desire to pursue the will of God above all else, and delight in His will, then we will be able to say with the Lord Jesus, "My meat is to do the will of him that sent me, and to finish his work."

## Day 282

# The Name of Jesus

Luke 1:31

*"And, behold, thou shalt conceive in thy womb, and bring forth a son, and shalt call his name JESUS."*

Have you ever taken time to meditate on the Name of Jesus? No other name has been more widely known, whether loved or hated. Isaiah declared that "his name shall be called Wonderful, Counsellor, The mighty God, The everlasting Father, The Prince of Peace" –Isaiah 9:6. Jeremiah wrote, "he shall be called, THE LORD OUR RIGHTEOUSNESS" – Jeremiah 23:6. In the book of Matthew the Bible says, "they shall call his name Emmanuel, which being interpreted is, God with us" –Matthew 1:23. There is so much in His Name!

In His Name the lame walk, the blind see, and the sick are healed. "Be it known unto you all, and to all the people of Israel, that by the *name* of Jesus Christ of Nazareth . . . even by him doth this man stand here before you whole" –Acts 4:10. Only in His Name is there salvation. "Neither is there salvation in any other: for there is none other *name* under heaven given among men, whereby we must be saved" –Acts 4:12. His Name is full of power, so much so, the devils tremble and fear Him. The Name of Jesus is Wonderful, is Mighty, is Everlasting, is Righteous, and far surpasses any human description. Think on His Name and glorify the King of kings and Lord of lords.

The Name of Jesus is a solid rock on which to stand

His Name brings peace to a sin- torn land

No other Name ever sounded so sweet

In His Name we are sealed and made complete

# Promoting the Name of the Lord

Psalm 145:1

*"I will bless thy name for ever and ever."*

In the Bible we read that the Name of the Lord Jesus is "Wonderful, Counsellor, The mighty God . . ." –Isaiah 9:6. His Name causes the demons to tremble, and the saints to gain the ear of their Heavenly Father. His Name is "above every name" –Philippians 2:9. One day every knee will bow to Him and every tongue will confess that He is Lord. It is this Name the Psalmist has declared to bless for ever and ever. To bless the Name of Jesus is to reverently praise Him and to celebrate His perfections, for He is worthy of all praise! No one but Him created the world. No one but Him walked on water. No one but Him defeated the devil and rose victoriously over death, hell and the grave. No one but Him forgives and pardons sins. No one but Him laid down His life to redeem sinful souls. The list of His glories is endless; therefore, it is our duty and great privilege to bless His Name continually.

Be thankful for His mercies, His grace and His love. Bless His Name in the act of adoration and proclaim His greatness unto others. He has done such great things for us; He daily loads us with benefits— Psalm 68:19. Bless His Name continually! All that we have in our possession is from Him; "Every good gift and every perfect gift is from above, and cometh down from the Father of lights, with whom is no variableness, neither shadow of turning" –James 1:17. Bless His Name for ever! Even in our most severe trials He is working for our good: "all things work together for good to them that love God, to them who are the called according to his purpose" –Romans 8:28. Bless His Name for ever and ever! If you are a child of this glorious King, may you begin, if you haven't already, to take time and meditate on His greatness, bless His Name, then, make Him known to all the people.

*Our Lord and our King*
*Regal in Royal Majesty,*
*Unto Thee we will sing*
*Of salvation so full and free*

## *Day 284*

# Shadow of the Almighty

Psalm 91:1

*"Abide under the shadow of the Almighty."*

It is when you make the secret place your habitation and a continual resort that you come under the canopy of His protection. The shadow of the Almighty will shield you from the fiercest storms, bringing you through undamaged. Under His shadow, all are safe from the enemy's attacks. "The Lord is my light and my salvation; whom shall I fear? The Lord is the strength of my life; of whom shall I be afraid? When the wicked, even mine enemies and my foes, came upon me to eat up my flesh, they stumbled and fell. Though an host should encamp against me, my heart shall not fear: though war should rise against me, in this will I be confident. One thing have I desired of the Lord, that will I seek after; that I may dwell in the house of the Lord all the days of my life, to behold the beauty of the Lord, and to enquire in his temple. For in the time of trouble he shall hide me in his pavilion: in the secret of his tabernacle shall he hide me; he shall set me up upon a rock. And now shall mine head be lifted up above mine enemies round about me: therefore will I offer in his tabernacle sacrifices of joy; I will sing, yea, I will sing praises unto the Lord"—Psalm 27:1-6.

Under the shadow of the Almighty there is strength to stand, and the faint-hearted will garner courage to be bold. Are you abiding under the shadow of the Almighty? Resort to your secret place of the Most High today and begin to abide under the Almighty shadow.

# A Glad Heart

Psalm 100:2

*"Serve the LORD with gladness: come before his presence with singing."*

When we serve the Lord with gladness we will not be murmuring or complaining, two things we must guard against. The Psalmist said, "I complained, and my spirit was overwhelmed. Selah" –Psalm 77:3. The children of Israel in the wilderness "murmured in their tents, and hearkened not unto the voice of the LORD. Therefore he lifted up his hand against them, to overthrow them in the wilderness" –Psalm 106:25-26. We must also guard against unbelief. "They believed not his word, but murmured" –Psalm 106:24b-25a. In order to serve the Lord with gladness we must not give any liberty to doubting God's love for us, and His faithfulness to us in everything. We must also guard against forgetting all that God has done for us. The children of Israel "forgat God their saviour, which had done great things in Egypt; Wondrous works in the land of Ham, and terrible [awesome] things by the Red sea –Psalm 106:21-22. It is by remembering God's love for us, His faithfulness to us, and His mercies and grace toward us that will enable us to serve the Lord with gladness.

## Day 286

# It Is Time

Hosea 10:12

*"Sow to yourselves in righteousness, reap in mercy; break up your fallow ground: for **it is time to seek the Lord**, till he come and rain righteousness upon you."*

It is time to "seek ye first the kingdom of God, and his righteousness"—Matthew 6:33a. It is time to "seek the LORD and his strength, [and] seek his face continually"—I Chronicles 16:11. It is time to seek the Lord "by prayer and supplications, with fasting"—Daniel 9:3b. It is time to enter into our prayer closets, become still before Him, and let Him speak to us from His Word of truth—the Bible. Today, the general thought of many Christians seems to be that the busier they are for the Lord, the more godly they think they are. It is true that we need to serve Him, but we must first seek Him in prayer and His Word.

Mary of Bethany "sat at Jesus' feet, and heard his word"—Luke 10:39b. Jesus told her sister, Martha, "One thing is needful: and Mary hath chosen that good part"—Luke 10:42a. It is sometimes a hard thing to get still before the Lord and be silent. Our minds begin to think of so many things we *think* we need to be doing. In order to accomplish the Lord's work, we need His strength, His wisdom, His knowledge; and we acquire that by being with Him in prayer and the Word. By seeking to *know* Him we will begin to understand the great love He has for us and the world. It is this love that we need to have in our Christian life so that we may demonstrate His love to others and be effective witnesses for Christ. We need to also learn more of His righteousness, mercy, and grace so that we may become imitators of Jesus Christ. We learn all of this by seeking Him. May we prioritize our day so that we **make** the time to seek the Lord and learn of Him in order to be "a vessel unto honour, sanctified, and meet for the master's use, and prepared unto every good work"—II Timothy 2:21. It isn't what we can do for the Lord as a Christian that is most important; rather, it is what He can do through us as His children when we seek Him. It is time to seek the Lord.

# A Voice for the Lord

Luke 19:37-38

*"And when he was come nigh, even now at the descent of the mount of Olives, the whole multitude of* **the disciples began to rejoice and praise God with a loud voice** *for all the mighty works that they had seen; saying, Blessed be the King that cometh in the name of the Lord: peace in heaven, and glory in the highest."*

As Christians, are we rejoicing and praising God with a loud voice like the disciples did? When we realize how God saved us from our sin and eternal damnation, then we will begin to rejoice and praise God. "All we like sheep have gone astray; we have turned every one to his own way; and the LORD hath laid on him the iniquity of us all"—Isaiah 53:6. God the Father put all our wretched sinfulness on His Son—His only Begotten Son—at Calvary so that we may experience redemption and a relationship with the Father and His Son. Jesus Christ bore our sin on the cross and became temporarily separated from fellowship with the Father in order to restore fellowship between sinful man and a holy God. That is a mighty work for which we, as believers, can rejoice and praise God with a loud voice. We would be more constantly rejoicing and praising God if we would daily read the account of Calvary and meditate on it, envisioning the Saviour agonizing for each breath, His visage marred beyond human recognition, and his awful pain as He cried out, "My God, my God, why hast thou forsaken me?"—Mark 15:34b.

Think of the great blessing of grace that God worked in each of us who have called on the name of Jesus for salvation. We received unmerited favor, and for that mighty work we can rejoice and praise God. Consider God's unconditional love that He shows to each of His children. In spite of our failures, our periods of unbelief and fear, our selfish hearts, and our sin in general, He never stops loving us. When we remember His great work of unconditional love toward us, we will begin to rejoice and praise God with a loud voice. May we become like the disciples—Christians who rejoice and praise God with a loud voice and give Him the glory due unto His name.

## Day 288

# Sanctify the Lord

Isaiah 8:13

"Sanctify the LORD of hosts himself; and let him be your fear, and let him be your dread."

Set the Lord apart from all other gods, for He alone is the true God. "Know therefore this day, and consider it in thine heart, that the LORD he is God in heaven above, and upon the earth beneath: there is none else" –Deuteronomy 4:39. We must think rightly of the greatness and glory of God in order to see the power of our enemies restrained. God is with us in all of life's ups and downs, and He will be a sanctuary for all who will trust in Him. God Almighty is a righteous God, and He is holy; therefore, our believing fear [reverence] of the Lord God Almighty can protect us from the disquieting fear of man.

It is foolish to put someone or something else in the place of God. But when we set Almighty God apart and make Him our hope and our fear [reverence], then we will know sweet rest within His sanctuary. In times of trouble, let us not fear, because fear can put us on a crooked course that leads us away from the security of the Lord's sanctuary. Set apart the Lord of hosts, think rightly of His glory, and He will be a blessed sanctuary.

# Confident and Happy

Psalm 146:5

*"Happy is he that hath the God of Jacob for his help, whose hope is in the Lord his God."*

When our hope is in the Lord, then we can confidently expect that He will help us when we are in trouble, and that He will provide for our every need. It is this confidence that brings us happiness, because our hope is in the One who owns "the cattle upon a thousand hills"—Psalm 50:10b, who paves the streets of Heaven with "pure gold, as it were transparent glass"—Revelation 21:21b, who is "great in power"—Nahum 1:3b, and who "so loved the world, that he gave his only begotten Son, that whosoever believeth in him should not perish, but have everlasting life. For God sent not his Son into the world to condemn the world; but that the world through him might be saved"—John 3:16-17.

Whatever trouble we may presently face we can remember that we have the God of Jacob for our help, and He is "a very present help in trouble"—Psalm 46:1b. When we have the God of Jacob for our help, then happy are we, even in the midst of troubles.

**Day 290**

# Identifying the Christian

Matthew 7:20

*"Wherefore by their fruits ye shall know them."*

It is said that in the early years of our nation, a specific type of tree was planted on the street with its corresponding name so that the farmer, who usually was illiterate, would be able to find the street he was looking for. Therefore, maple trees were planted on Maple Street, oak trees were planted on Oak Street, and cherry trees were planted on Cherry Street.

The popular song of the 1970's, ***They Will Know We are Christians by Our Love***, was saying what the Lord Jesus Christ said to His disciples: "A new commandment I give unto you, That ye love one another; as I have loved you, that ye also love one another. By this shall all men know that ye are my disciples, if ye have love one to another"—John 13:34-35. Everyone will know we are followers of Christ if we love one another as Christ has loved us. As a particular tree identified the name of a street, demonstrating the love of Christ identifies us as Christians: "wherefore by their fruits ye shall know them." The first fruit of the Spirit is love—Galatians 5:22, and by love we will make Christ known to others.

# Rise Up and Come Away

Song of Solomon 2:10-12

*"My beloved spake, and said unto me, Rise up, my love, my fair one, and come away. For, lo, the winter is past, the rain is over and gone; the flowers appear on the earth; the time of the singing of birds is come . . . "*

The dormancy of winter has given way to the new life of spring. On the day of our salvation, "living water" began to flow within us. Christ, as the Vine, now fills us, the branches, with all that is needed to sustain our Christian life. Where unrighteousness reigned, we now have been made the righteousness of God in Christ. Where death possessed us, now life – eternal life— is our claim. Where our flesh controlled us, now the Spirit has opportunity "to breathe His power upon us" so that we may produce the fruit of the Spirit listed in Galatians 5:22-23.

As Christians, we have received new life. Now, let's allow that new life to blossom into the fullness of Christ. Do not remain dormant, but allow the life of Christ to flow through you, that you may become like Christ who is "the rose of Sharon, and the lily of the valleys"—Song of Solomon 2:1.

Hear His voice as He calls to you, then rise up and come away. Come away from the old habits that bound you. Come away from the lusts of the flesh. Come away from the pride of life. Come away from the death of sin and rise up to the life of righteousness. Rise up to humility. Rise up to forgiveness. Rise up to the fullness of Christ's character. Let the seed of Christ in you grow so that you will not remain as "babe in Christ"—I Corinthians 3:1. Instead, "as newborn babes, desire the sincere milk of the word, that ye may grow thereby" –I Peter 2:2.

Rise up, O Christian, and come away with your beloved Bridegroom. Do not lie dormant, but blossom into the beauty of the Rose and the Lily.

*Day 292*

# Behaving Wisely in a Perfect Way

Psalm 101:2

*"I will behave myself wisely in a perfect way. O when wilt thou come unto me?"*

***I will behave myself wisely in a perfect way!*** A perfect way would be a sanctified way, which means yielding our obedience unto God Almighty. Our bodies of sinful flesh will never be perfect, but Christ living in us is perfect; and through Him we may behave wisely in a perfect way. We are able, as the Apostle Paul stated, to "do all things through Christ" –Philippians 4:13. This includes behaving ourselves wisely in a perfect way. The more aware we are of our sinfulness and shortcomings, the more likely we will be to behave in a perfect way. Being aware of our imperfections will spur us on to "press toward the mark for the prize of the high calling of God in Christ Jesus –Philippians 3:14.

Some ways to accomplish walking in a perfect way would be to remove the "cloak" of pride and "be clothed with humility"--I Peter 5:5; "let each esteem other better than themselves" – Philippians 2:3; and seek to serve instead of desiring to be served. By not thinking more highly of ourselves than we ought to think, we will be that much closer to walking like Christ in graciousness and humility, which leads to the perfect way of walking as a Christian.

# The Everlasting Mercies of the Lord

Psalm 100:5

*"For the LORD is good; his mercy is everlasting; and his truth endureth to all generations."*

The mercies of the Lord are everlasting; His compassions "are new every morning" –Lamentations 3:23. As each new day dawns, we are given a fresh supply from the treasury of His abundant mercies. We never have to worry about yesterday's mercies carrying over to today, or for today's mercies being enough for tomorrow, because each new day receives new mercies. We are going to battle the temptations of sin during our lifetime on earth; however, the mercy of the Lord is everlasting. At times, when by the weakness of our flesh, we yield to temptation, the Lord is merciful to forgive. David, the king, desired to fall upon the mercies of the Lord rather than fall into the hands of man –II Samuel 24:14. The children of Israel were delivered many times. It was because of the great mercies of the Lord that they were not utterly consumed by their enemies –Nehemiah 9:29-31. The Lord has entered into a covenant with His people; He will never alter His declaration that His mercy is everlasting.

His mercy is everlasting; therefore, we are able even today to plead the mercy of the Lord. Though we may seek after selfish gain, neglect our great God and Savior, or be indifferent toward Him, when we humble ourselves in His sight and confess our sins, He will be merciful to us, because His mercy is everlasting.

## Day 294

# Savoring that of God or that of Man?

Mark 8:31-33

*"And he began to teach them, that the Son of man must suffer many things, and be rejected of the elders, and of the chief priests, and scribes, and be killed, and after three days rise again. And he spake that saying openly. And Peter took him, and began to rebuke him. But when he had turned about and looked on his disciples, he rebuked Peter, saying, Get thee behind me, Satan: for thou savourest not the things that be of God, but the things that be of men."*

Christ's crucifixion was of God, but that is hard for the human mind to grasp because the flesh looks only at the superficial level of love. It doesn't see the necessity of such a sacrifice to save the people. But God's love goes far beyond the comprehension of man's finite mind.

Full surrender and obedience to God the Father yields unspeakable joy; and only until a Christian has come to the place of full surrender can he know such joy. To the carnal person it is foolishness, but to the spiritual person it is glorious! The heart of man doesn't want to believe he is so deplorable that he would need such a sacrifice as Christ's crucifixion. But the Bible says, "The heart is deceitful above all things, and desperately wicked: who can know it?" –Jeremiah 17:9. Almighty God answered this question in Jeremiah 17:10, "I the Lord search the heart, I try the reins, even to give every man according to his ways, and according to the fruit of his doings." The deceitfulness of the human heart is one of the reasons the child of God must spend time daily with the Lord of lords.

Many times, we fail to recognize God's will in a situation because we are looking at things from a human perspective. We may be quick to form a wrong opinion, as Peter did, and not consider that God has a higher purpose than what <u>we</u> can see. To consider what is God's will we must saturate our heart and mind with the Word of God and with much communion with Him in prayer.

# Becoming Fishers of Men

Mark 1:17

*"And Jesus said unto them, Come ye after me, and I will make you to become fishers of men."*

Christ's reason for coming to earth was "to seek and to save that which was lost" –Luke 19:10. It is not the natural tendency of the human heart to be "fishers of men"; however, when we follow after Christ and spend much time with Him in prayer and His Word, He enables us "to become fishers of men." We will become more like Christ when we spend more time with Him.

The fellowship between God and man was severed in the Garden of Eden when Adam and Eve disobeyed God and ate of the forbidden fruit –Genesis 3. The Lord Jesus Christ so loved the souls of men that He gave His life to renew that fellowship between God and man. As we spend time with the Lord, He will put in our heart a desire to see souls saved. We will love those around us enough to tell them of the wonderful salvation that is available in Jesus Christ. His desire for souls to be saved will become our desire; His love for mankind will become our love for them; and as a result, we will be obedient to His Spirit's leading to be a witness for Him so that those around us might come to know Him. Dear readers, if you are a child of God, today hear His voice as He says, "Come ye after me, and I will make you to become fishers of men." Let us begin each new day with the intentional purpose to be "fishers of men" and bring them to Christ.

## Day 296

# Seeking the Honor of God

John 5:44

*"How can ye believe, which receive honour one of another, and seek not the honour that cometh from God only?"*

The only honor worth receiving is the honor that comes from God. Many people do good deeds, not expecting anything in return. But if they do these things merely to receive recognition or honor from others, they may feel emptiness in their hearts, or they may be puffed up with pride. The same can be true of believers. What is our motive behind the things we do in the name of Christianity? If our motive is merely to receive the applause from people, then it cannot be God's honor that we are seeking. May we not be like the Pharisees, who knew the Scriptures, but they did not know the Lord of the Scriptures or His power. Their form of religion undervalued God, because they admired and overvalued themselves.

Do we pray with pride and to justify ourselves, like the Pharisee who "stood and prayed thus with himself, God, I thank thee, that I am not as other men are . . . I fast twice in the week, I give tithes of all that I possess" –Luke 18:11-12? The Lord Jesus Christ said, "When thou prayest, thou shalt not be as the hypocrites are: for they love to pray standing in the synagogues and in the corners of the streets, that they may be seen of men. . . . But thou, when thou prayest, enter into thy closet, and when thou hast shut thy door, pray to thy Father which is in secret; and thy Father which seeth in secret shall reward thee openly" – Matthew 6:5-6.

Let us examine our heart to determine what our answer would be to the Lord Jesus' question. Are we seeking honor from one another, or are we seeking the honor that comes from God?

# Everlasting God

Psalm 90:2

*"Before the mountains were brought forth, or ever thou hadst formed the earth and the world, even from everlasting to everlasting, thou art God."*

When "the earth was without form, and void" –Genesis 1:2a, there was God! He is "Alpha and Omega, the beginning and the ending, saith the Lord, which is, and which was, and which is to come, the Almighty" –Revelation 1:8. "O Lord God of Israel, which dwellest between the cherubims, thou art the God, even thou alone, of all the kingdoms of the earth; thou hast made heaven and earth" –II Kings 19:15. He is God, and the magnitude of His person is beyond our human ability to describe. "Before the mountains were brought forth," there was God! Before the heavens and the earth were formed, there was God! Before any of us were born, there was God!

He created us; therefore, He knows us and understands us. He is God and He will help us. He is God and He will answer when we call. He is God and He will strengthen us. He is God and He will enable us to carry out any task He gives us. He is God and He will meet our every need. "He that planted the ear, shall he not hear? He that formed the eye, shall he not see?" –Psalm 94:9. He does hear us; therefore, may we not neglect to talk with Him. He does see us; therefore, let us "abstain from all appearance of evil" –I Thessalonians 5:22. He is God from everlasting to everlasting.

*Day 298*

# Committing Ourselves to the Lord

Proverbs 16:3

"Commit thy works unto the LORD, and thy thoughts shall be established."

Bring to the Lord the cares of your life —whether they are your daily labors, your life's daily routine, or your heart's innermost struggles —and place them in the hands of God. Do not take them up again, to worry and fret; but leave every detail and care of your life with the Lord. Yield all control to Him to safely direct your steps through each day. Allow Him to be your Guide, and relinquish your will to His. Put yourself under His benevolent leadership, and your mind will be free from fear and worry. "God himself is with us for our captain" —II Chronicles 13:12a; therefore, put yourself into His perfect care and follow Him.

When we commit ourselves unto the Lord, we will not "fret" over the "detours" of daily life or moan over the "bumps in the road." Instead, our confidence will be in Him, and not in any temporal circumstance. Committing the works of our life to the Lord frees our mind of uncertainty and doubt, because we have placed ourselves in the hands of Him who speaks to the storm, "Peace, be still" —Mark 4:39. "God is not a man, that he should lie; neither the son of man, that he should repent: hath he said, and shall he not do it? Or hath he spoken, and shall he not make it good?" —Numbers 23:19. "Every word of God is pure: he is a shield unto them that put their trust in him" —Proverbs 30:5. Therefore, as children of God, let us heed and obey His Word by committing our works unto Him so that our thoughts will be established.

# Dancing in the Air

I sat and watched the birds
As they seemingly danced through the sky
Flitting here and flitting there
It was pure joy watching them pass by

They were colored yellow, blue and red
While others were speckled grey
A veritable rainbow
Which brightened up the day

It was God's own air show
Dazzling the eye
As the variety of His birds
Were dancing through the sky

The lesson then I learned
Do not worry or despair
Simply rest in Christ
And speak to Him in prayer

Everything about this day
He knows and has prepared
Therefore be reminded
Of His birds dancing in the air

# Delight to Do God's Will

Psalm 40:8a

*"I delight to do thy will, O my God."*

Only the Lord Jesus could do the will of God completely. He not only did the Father's will, but He found delight in it. His desire, "before the foundation of the world" –I Peter 1:20, was to do the will of His Father. His entire submission to the Father's will, which was the essence of His obedience, was His victory over temptation on earth. The devotion of His heart to the Father brought Him delight in doing the Father's will. Even when in Gethsemane, shortly before His crucifixion, He set aside His own will, praying, "O my Father, if this cup may not pass away from me, except I drink it, thy will be done" –Matthew 26:42.

In our human bodies, we can never fulfill the Lord's will to the uttermost; however, our Lord's obedience, which is our righteousness, is every bit able to keep us from falling prey to temptation. When we, like Christ, have a devoted heart to the Father, and not merely an outward expression of devotion, we will also find delight in God's will for our lives. The delight will be in pleasing Him, obeying Him, bringing glory to Him, and bringing many souls with us into His Kingdom.

Christ was fully surrendered to the Father, and His example should be our goal for daily Christian living. A fully surrendered heart will desire the Father's will above our own comforts and pleasures. It will also deepen our understanding of His great love for us–why He, Who is all Holiness, would desire to fellowship with us, who are so sinful. May we be faithful to spend time with the Father and His Son, in prayer and in meditation of the Word, in order that our hearts may grow in deep devotion toward God, and we may find delight in doing His will.

# The Word of the Lord

Psalm 33:4

*"For the word of the Lord is right . . ."*

The Lord Jesus Christ said in answer to the Devil's temptation, "It is written, That man shall not live by bread alone, but by every word of God" –Luke 4:4. And as our text declares, "the word of the Lord is right." Because the Word of the Lord is right, it will guide us to do right. How often, then, are you opening the pages of God's Word, that you may read what He has said is right?

The more we read the Bible, the less we will be swayed with "every wind of doctrine" –Ephesians 4:14. When we delve into the depths of the Word of God, He will begin to make known to us His glorious wonders and truths, which are an essential part of Himself. When we look into the heavens, we will not simply see clouds floating by, but we shall see them as "the dust of his feet" –Nahum 1:3b, and our hearts will be warmed, remembering that He is near. A rainbow will not just dazzle our eyes, but will remind us of God's promise to never again flood the earth –Genesis 9:12-16. God's Word is like a mirror, revealing what we are and what we are not. It tells us what we are doing right and what we are doing wrong. It is the "yard stick" for every Christian to know right from wrong, to know God's way from man's way. Over 400 times in the Bible we will read the words, "thus saith the Lord" which is a sure indicator that the Word of the Lord *is* right!

**Day 301**

# Come to Christ for Rest

Matthew 11:28

*"Come unto me . . . and I will give you rest."*

Christ will give you rest from fear, from anxiety, from worry, from heartache, and from the cares of this life. He is "a man of sorrows, and acquainted with grief" –Isaiah 53:3, and is "touched with the feeling of our infirmities" –Hebrews 4:15. He experienced weariness, the pain of betrayal, the sorrow of abandonment and the rejection of family and friends.

Who better to go to and find solace, comfort and ultimately rest from every heartache and sorrow of life? All the resorts in this world cannot satisfy and completely rest your body and soul like Christ can. He is a refuge in a sin-sick world. Flee to Him who is able to give you "living water" –John 4:10. In His presence your soul will be refreshed, your spirit will be renewed, and your joy will be "unspeakable and full of glory" –I Peter 1:8b. Allow the Living Water to flow through you, till the strength from His rest fills you once more. The labors are strenuous in the fields, but the rest that Christ gives refreshes the soul. Do not tarry any longer, but come unto Him today. Lay your burdens down at His feet and He will give you rest.

# Soul-Joyful

Psalm 35:9

*"And my soul shall be joyful in the LORD: it shall rejoice in his salvation."*

Joy that is felt in our soul doesn't come from knowing ***about*** the Lord; it comes from ***knowing*** Him. When we begin to ***know*** the Lord, our soul becomes joyful in Him, and we experience "joy unspeakable and full of glory"—I Peter 1:8b. Studying the Bible and memorizing Scripture is necessary to grow in our knowledge of the Lord, but it is at His feet, in the stillness of His presence, without any distractions—that we begin to ***know*** Him—that He is God. He sweetly reveals Himself to us at those times, teaching us His power, His mercies, His love, His grace, His strength, His greatness that is "past finding out; yea, and wonders without number"—Job 9:10. Take some unhurried time today and every day to be still in the presence of the Lord. Do not allow the busyness of serving cause you to neglect that good part that the Lord Jesus told Martha would not be taken from her sister, Mary. Fill your soul with joy by spending time alone with God, listening to Him speak to you from His Word. Talk to Him and unburden your heart to Him. If we seek Him, we will find Him. It is He that fills us with joy.

## Day 303

# Fruit of Suffering

Hebrews 5:8-9

*"Though he were a Son, yet learned he obedience by the things which he suffered; And being made perfect, he became the author of eternal salvation unto all them that obey him."*

We never desire suffering, and suffering is never pleasant; however, times of suffering can produce in us lessons we would not otherwise learn. It is through "the fellowship of his [Jesus'] sufferings"—Philippians 3:10b that we may grow to know Him. Jesus Christ was the Son of God in human flesh, "yet learned he obedience by the things which he suffered." Suffering can lead us to learn obedience to God the Father so that we desire His will above our own will. The greatest desire we can have as a child of God is to want His will for our life. It takes faith in our great God to be able to go through the school of discipline that suffering produces, and be able to say as the Lord Jesus, "the cup which my Father hath given me, shall I not drink it?"—John 18:11b Great faith isn't exhibited so much by **doing** something as it is by **going through** some form of suffering. Suffering enables us to sympathize and help others, for we are only able to comfort others "by the comfort wherewith we ourselves are comforted of God. We could never have a sympathizing God without a suffering Saviour. We receive great comfort in talking with someone of a kindred spirit who has gone through similar afflictions.

"We have this treasure in earthen vessels, that the excellency of the power may be of God, and not of us. Always bearing about in the body the dying of the Lord Jesus, that the life also of Jesus might be made manifest in our body. . . . For our light affliction, which is but for a moment, worketh for us a far more exceeding and eternal weight of glory"—II Corinthians 4:7,10, 15, 17. The present suffering which you may be experiencing, if surrendered to Christ, is the best tool in the Father's hand to enable you to be more like Christ. Therefore, do not rebel against the trial and suffering the Lord allows to come into your life. Instead, put your trust in Him so that you will not lose the eternal fruit it produces.

# Thankfulness

I Chronicles 16:8a

*"Give thanks unto the LORD."*

We live in a society today where people are unthankful. Instead of being thankful for what we have, many complain about what they do not have. The greed of our hearts and the lust of our flesh are never satisfied; therefore, we become unthankful. As Christians –saved by grace through faith in Christ –we need to give thanks unto the Lord. Thank Him for so loving mankind "that he gave his only begotten Son, that whosoever believeth in him should not perish, but have everlasting life" –John 3:16. Thank Him for salvation. Thank Him for His love. Thank Him that He "is no respecter of persons" –Acts 10:34b: "whosoever shall call upon the name of the Lord shall be saved" –Romans 10:13. Thank Him that the young and old, the poor and rich, the beautiful and the ugly, the Jew and the Gentile, the "whosoevers" may come unto Him, and He "will in no wise cast them out" –John 6:37b. Thank the Lord Jesus Christ that He understands our heartaches and troubles, having been Himself "a man of sorrows, and acquainted with grief" –Isaiah 53:3b. Thank Him that He is able to comfort us and does comfort us.

Begin every day by giving thanks unto the Lord. If we would take the time to consider all the goodness of the Lord, and all that He has done, and all He continues to do for us, we would be more thankful. Let's thank Him in the morning, in the afternoon, in the evening, and as we lay down to sleep. May we not be negligent to give thanks unto the Lord.

## Day 305

# The Christian's Source of Power

John 8:1-2

*"Jesus went unto the mount of Olives. And early in the morning he came again into the temple, and all the people came unto him; and he sat down, and taught them."*

One of the places where the Lord Jesus spent time in prayer with the Father was the Mount of Olives. The Lord Jesus met with the Father before He went to the temple to teach, because it was in prayer that the Father strengthened Him, instructed Him, and empowered Him to go and do His work. If we are going to teach God's Word, advise someone according to God's Word, or do some service for the Lord, then we must first meet with the Father in prayer so that we may receive His instruction, His strength, and His power. He also went to "a mountain apart to pray"—Matthew 14:23b. This indicates that when we spend time with our Heavenly Father, we need to have a specific place that will be free from distractions and interruptions. God will be better able to speak or work through us when we follow the example of Jesus Christ and first spend time with the Father in prayer.

*"I had been invited to speak a few words on the Revival in the Khassia Hills . . . I had travelled by night from Allahabad to Ludhiana, and reached there early in the morning. I was introduced to Mr. Hyde . . . and his first word was, "Come with me to the prayer room." I told him that I had travelled all night, and that I was tired, and had to speak at four o'clock, but I went with him. Hyde went down on his face before the Lord. I knelt down and a strange feeling crept over me. Several prayed, and then Hyde began, and I remember very little more. I knew that I was in the presence of God Himself, and had no desire to leave the place. We had entered the room at eight o'clock in the morning. Meals had been forgotten, and my tired feeling had gone, and the Revival account and message that I was to deliver, and concerning which I had been very anxious, had gone out of my mind, until about three-thirty. . . ." I know the Lord spoke that night. I realized the power of prayer."*—Account of Reverend J. Pengwern Jones from Praying Hyde: A Challenge to Prayer.

# Take Heed

"Psalm 81:11b

*"But my people would not hearken to my voice."*

As a Christian, are you listening to and obeying that still small voice of God's Holy Spirit when He speaks to you? Are you paying attention when He pricks your heart concerning something in your life that is contrary to His righteousness, whether a great or small matter? Our hearts gradually harden each time we do not obey the voice of the Lord. "Take heed, brethren, lest there be in any of you an evil heart of unbelief, in departing from the living God. But exhort one another daily, while it is called To day; lest any of you be hardened through the deceitfulness of sin. For we are made partakers of Christ, if we hold the beginning of our confidence stedfast unto the end; While it is said, To day if ye will hear his voice, harden not your hearts, as in the provocation"—Hebrews 3:12-15.

The Lord is continuing to say to His children today, "Give ear, O my people, to my law: incline your ears to the words of my mouth"— Psalm 78:1. We need to listen when He speaks, and pay close attention when He pricks our heart to hearken to His voice. Take time today to consider whether or not you are listening to the voice of God, and then take heed to obey what He says.

**Day 307**

# Living for the Lord Jesus Christ

II Corinthians 5:15

*"And that he died for all, that they which live should not henceforth live unto themselves, but unto him which died for them, and rose again."*

The Lord Jesus Christ "laid down his life for us" –I John 3:16. "For when we were yet without strength, in due time Christ died for the ungodly. . . . But God commendeth his love toward us, in that, while we were yet sinners, Christ died for us. Much more then, being now justified by his blood, we shall be saved from wrath through him" –Romans 5:6, 8 - 9. Therefore, we should not live to satisfy our own desires, to indulge in our own lusts, or to demand to have our own way if we have been saved by grace through faith in Jesus Christ. As Christians we should strive to please Him, obey Him, submit to His will for our lives and not grieve His Spirit. Remember, "he hath borne our griefs, and carried our sorrows . . . he was wounded for our transgressions, he was bruised for our iniquities: the chastisement of our peace was upon him; and with his stripes we are healed" –Isaiah 53:4-5. We will be more likely to live for Him when we remember all that He did for us.

We will become better acquainted with our Lord when we daily read His Word and spend seasons of prayer with Him. The better we know Him the more we will desire to live less for ourselves and more for Him. He will become our focus, and we will want to live in a way that will please Him. Today, make it your goal to live for Him who died for you.

# Applying Knowledge

Colossians 3:16a

*"Let the word of Christ dwell in you richly in all wisdom."*

Wisdom is the application of knowledge in our life; therefore, knowledge without proper application is folly. We can read the Bible every day, memorize verses, whole passages, or even entire books of the Bible; however, if we do not apply God's Word to our life we will lack wisdom. We do need to read our Bibles every day and memorize Scripture; however, we need God's Word to live in us in **all** wisdom. We may know to "love [our] neighbor as [ourselves]"—Matthew 22:39b, but are we actually loving them as we love ourselves? We have read that we are to "Love [our] enemies, do good to them which hate [us], Bless them that curse [us], and pray for them which despitefully use [us]"—Luke 6:27, but how many of us are actually **doing** that? We memorize verses like, "Be kindly affectioned one to another with brotherly love; in honour preferring one another"—Romans 12:10, but are we applying this teaching to our daily encounters with the people in our lives?

In order for the Word of God to live in us in all wisdom we must make life application with what we learn from God's Word. If we are going to "let the word of Christ dwell in [us] richly," we must saturate our hearts and minds with God's Word by memorization and daily reading. Then we must be "doers of the word, and not hearers only"—James 1:22a. By making application of what we know to do according to God's Word, then the Word of Jesus Christ will dwell in us with all wisdom.

**Day 309**

# The Truth

Psalm 33:4

*"All his works are done in truth."*

Jesus said of Himself, "I am the way, the truth, and the life" –John 14:6. "All his works are done in truth" because He is truth!   If you have trusted Christ as your Savior, the Holy Spirit dwells within you.  You can rest assured that He will reveal to you the truths of God's Word because the Lord Jesus said, "When he, the Spirit of truth, is come, he will guide you into all truth:  for he shall not speak of himself; but whatsoever he shall hear, that shall he speak:  and he will shew you things to come. He shall glorify me:  for he shall receive of mine, and shall shew it unto you"—John 16:13-14.

If you are taught anything that is contrary to what the Bible says, you may be certain it is **not** the truth.  The Lord Jesus Christ not only said that He is "the truth," but He also said to the unbelieving, "Ye are of your father the devil, and the lusts of your father ye will do.  He . . . abode not in the truth, because there is no truth in him.  When he speaketh a lie, he speaketh of his own:  for he is a liar, and the father of it" –John 8:44.  We will learn the truths of God and be able to discern between His works of truth and the Devil's works of deceit when we daily read and study the Bible.  Begin today to read the Word of God and learn His truths, for truly "all His works are done in truth."

# Needful

Luke 10:42

*"But one thing is needful: and Mary hath chosen that good part, which shall not be taken away from her."*

Being with the Lord Jesus is the ***one thing*** we need above serving, above helping, above ALL ELSE. It is being with Him that will give us rest when we are weary, strength when we are weak, help when we are troubled, and joy regardless of our situation. The one thing that is needful is Jesus Christ! Only He can soften our tempers, calm our anxieties, quench our thirsty souls for righteousness, and give us victory over death and hell.

It is needful to humble ourselves before Him when we spend time with Him in prayer and the study of His Word. We would benefit greatly if we would follow Mary's example and position ourselves at His feet –Luke 10:39. "Before honour is humility" –Proverbs 18:12b, and we ***need*** to humble ourselves "in the sight of the Lord" –James 4:10.

We, like Martha, may be "cumbered about much serving," but the Lord Jesus said, "Martha, Martha, thou art careful [anxious, fretful] and troubled about many things: But one thing is needful: and Mary hath chosen that good part, which shall not be taken away from her" – Luke 10:41-42. We ***need*** to serve, but we must guard against becoming "cumbered" with the serving. Our service for Christ becomes cumbered when we neglect our prayer closets and our study chambers. We may have the richest, most luxurious place to meet with the Lord or we may have only a beggar's shelter; but if our time with the Lord is neglected we will certainly become fretful and troubled in our service for Christ. We ***need*** to spend time with our Lord, because He said it was the one thing that is needful; therefore, may we not neglect prayer or Bible study.

## *Day 311*

# Count It All Joy

James 1:2

*"My brethren, count it all joy when ye fall into divers temptations."*

When the events of your day do not go as planned, count it all joy. When stranded along the side of the road with a flat tire, count it all joy. When the children test your patience to the very limit, count it all joy. When friends hurt you, count it all joy. When there is not much food in the pantry and even less money in the bank, count it all joy. Out of a loving heart, our Heavenly Father sends diversified trials to test and strengthen our faith in Him. For "when he hath tried me, I shall come forth as gold" –Job 23:10. Count it all joy, "knowing that tribulation worketh patience; and patience, experience; and experience, hope: and hope maketh not ashamed; because the love of God is shed abroad in our hearts by the Holy Ghost which is given unto us" –Romans 5:3b-5. The Lord is orchestrating the days of our lives, and He has only our good in mind; therefore, whatever comes our way, may we count it all joy.

# Godly Transformation

Romans 12:2

*"And be not conformed to this world: but be ye transformed by the renewing of your mind."*

Child of God, do not be conformed to this world by behaving according to its socially accepted standards and conventions: "For all that is in the world . . . is not of the Father" –I John 2:16. Although we live in this world, and we come in close proximity to unsaved people, we should be spectrums apart in our desires and manner of life. This can take place only as we are "transformed" by the renewing of our minds. This renewal begins at our conversion, for "if any man be in Christ, he is a new creature: old things are passed away; behold, all things are become new" –II Corinthians 5:17. It will continue to progress as we die to sin and live to righteousness. Our greatest enemy to the renewing of our mind is conformity to this world. We need to be careful not to make plans as though our happiness is dependent upon the things of the world; rather, we must set our "affection on things above, not on things on the earth" –Colossians 3:2.

We are able to continue the renewing of our mind by not thinking more highly of ourselves than we ought to think, by performing the ministry that Christ has given to us without coveting some other office of ministry, by loving one another with sincerity, by hating evil and clinging to all that is good, by putting one another before ourselves, by being "fervent in spirit; serving the Lord; rejoicing in hope; patient in tribulation; continuing instant in prayer" –Romans 12:11b-12. "Ye are the temple of the living God . . . Wherefore come out from among them, and be ye separate, saith the Lord" –II Corinthians 6:16b-17b. When we separate ourselves unto godliness we will not conform to the world, but will experience a blessed transformation that will continue by this renewing of our mind.

**Day 313**

# He Shall Bring It to Pass

Psalm 37:5

*"Commit thy way unto the LORD; trust also in him; and he shall bring it to pass."*

After we pray for some particular situation in our lives or in the lives of loved ones, it is not our duty to then try and help God. Instead, we must trust in Him and wait patiently. When Sarah remained barren for many years, she and Abraham contrived to help God out by giving Sarah's handmaid to Abraham for a wife. A son was born, but it was not the son that God had promised to give Abraham and Sarah –Genesis 16-22.

As Christians, we should pray believing, and then wait expectantly in the spirit of praise for God to answer. Too often, however, we do not pray with faith nor do we continue fervently in prayer until we, like Jacob or like Hannah, receive the Word of blessing from God that He will bring it to pass. We give up too soon and become baffled as to why we are not helped. Often, our desired end does not come to pass, because we do not commit our way unto the Lord, or trust in Him to bring it to pass. It isn't a question of whether God is able to bring it to pass, because His Word clearly says that He **shall** bring it to pass. There are some conditions that we must meet, however, before He will bring it to pass. First, we must commit our way unto Him; second, we must trust Him. When we relinquish our control and exercise faith, then His Word will be fulfilled and *"he shall bring it to pass."* He will never be slack in carrying out His promises, but we must always meet His conditions. Therefore, let us commit our way unto the Lord; trust also in Him; and He shall bring it to pass.

334

# Sing unto the Lord

Psalm 95:1

*"O come, let us sing unto the Lord."*

Singing unto the Lord brings joy to the heart and courage to the soul even in the severest trials. Singing chases away despondency and glorifies the Lord. Singing during life's lowest points testifies of Christ's power within and the devil's inability to conquer. We will sing when our hearts are full of Christ and our eyes are looking unto Him. When we rejoice to be counted worthy to suffer shame for His name, then we will sing unto the Lord. The joy of the Lord demonstrated in songs of praise, during times of severe trials, greatly enables the power of the Holy Spirit, dwelling within us, to greatly affect others for Christ. "And at midnight Paul and Silas prayed, and sang praises unto God: and the prisoners heard them. And suddenly there was a great earthquake, so that the foundations of the prison were shaken: and immediately all the doors were opened, and every one's bands were loosed. And the keeper of the prison . . . called for a light, and sprang in, and came trembling, and fell down before Paul and Silas, and brought them out, and said, Sirs, what must I do to be saved? And they said, Believe on the Lord Jesus Christ, and thou shalt be saved, and thy house" –Acts 16:25-31.

If we would sing unto the Lord, we would have more power to win souls for Christ. We should strive to follow Paul and Silas's example and sing, regardless of our circumstances. Is your child sick or severely ill? Sing unto the Lord, praising Him, "That in heaven their angels do always behold the face of my Father which is in heaven" –Matthew 18:10b. Are your finances at an all time low? Sing unto the Lord, remembering that He owns "the cattle upon a thousand hills" –Psalm 50:10, and He will not withhold any good thing from His children. Have you been betrayed by a close, trusted friend? Sing unto the Lord, rejoicing that Christ "is a friend that sticketh closer than a brother" –Proverbs 18:24. Has the foundation and security of your home been ripped apart by divorce? Sing unto the Lord, for there is "a city which hath foundations, whose builder and maker is God" –Hebrews 11:10. O come, let us sing unto the Lord, for, in Him, we have much to sing about.

*Day 315*

# The Lord Is Worthy

Psalm 78:38-39

*"But he, being full of compassion, forgave their iniquity, and destroyed them not: yea, many a time turned he his anger away, and did not stir up all his wrath. For he remembered that they were but flesh; a wind that passeth away, and cometh not again."*

The Lord God our Father is such a gracious and loving Father! He is compassionate and forgiving. He remembers that we are sinful flesh and that we came from plain old dirt. Our flesh is corruptible and unrighteous, and the only good we have is Christ in us. Yet, His great love for us turned the abundance of His anger away from us.

It may be that there are difficult people right now in your life, and you are finding it difficult to love them. Remembering that "God commendeth [shows] his love toward us, in that, while we were yet sinners, Christ died for us"—Romans 5:8 will help us to better love those that are difficult to love. Maybe you have been terribly hurt by someone and the thought of forgiving them is out of the question. Remember the words of our Lord Jesus as He was hanging on the cross, "Father, forgive them; for they know not what they do"—Luke 23:34a. "For if ye forgive men their trespasses, your heavenly Father will also forgive you: But if ye forgive not men their trespasses, neither will your Father forgive your trespasses"—Matthew 6:14-15.

Let us rejoice in the fact that God our Father and Jesus Christ His Son remember the insignificant substance with which we are made; yet, He is full of compassion and forgiveness toward us. The Lord is worthy of our praise! He is also worthy of our obedience to His Word so that we may become imitators of Him who loved us and forgave us.

# Being Influenced

Ephesians 5:17-18

*"Wherefore be ye not unwise, but understanding what the will of the Lord is. And be not drunk with wine, wherein is excess; but be filled with the Spirit."*

The will of the Lord is that Christians be filled with the Holy Spirit. Being filled with the Spirit simply means that we are to be under His influence by yielding ourselves to Him. Everyone is under an influence of some kind. The Ephesians were possibly under the influence of alcohol, because in this verse the Apostle Paul urged them not to be "drunk with wine, wherein is excess." Some are influenced by their culture, by friends, by circumstances, by the world, and even by that which is evil. If we are filled with the Spirit, then we are less susceptible to coming under any other influence.

When we come under the Spirit's influence, then we will pray and be a witness with boldness as they did in the book of Acts when "they lifted up their voice to God with one accord, and said, Lord, thou art God, which hast made heaven, and earth, and the sea, and all that in them is: . . . And now, Lord, behold their threatenings: and grant unto thy servants, that with all boldness they may speak thy word . . . and they spake the word of God with boldness"—Acts 4:24, 29, 31. It was by the Holy Spirit that the apostles spoke the Word of Christ with boldness. It was by the Holy Spirit that the people prayed so dynamically. We cannot bear spiritual fruit if we are not filled with the Spirit. And it is by yielding ourselves to the Spirit's control and letting Him influence our actions, reactions, decision making, and general living that we become full of Him. It is by dying to self and surrendering to the will of the Father that the Holy Spirit, living in every Christian, can empower us. May we understand that being filled with the Holy Spirit is the will of God for every believer in Christ, and may we wisely yield ourselves unto Him.

**Day 317**

# Conquering Our Weak Flesh

Matthew 26:41

*"Watch and pray, that ye enter not into temptation: the spirit indeed is willing, but the flesh is weak."*

How weak the human flesh is! The Apostle Peter was sincere when he said to the Lord Jesus, "Though I should die with thee, yet will I not deny thee"—Matthew 26:35a. However, he did deny the Lord—three times: "And when he [Peter] was gone out into the porch, another maid saw him, and said unto them that were there, This fellow was also with Jesus of Nazareth. And again he denied with an oath, I do not know the man. And after a while came unto him they that stood by, and said to Peter, Surely thou also art one of them; for thy speech bewrayeth thee. Then began he to curse and to swear, saying, I know not the man. And immediately the cock crew. And Peter remembered the word of Jesus, which said unto him, Before the cock crow, thou shalt deny me thrice. And he went out, and wept bitterly"—Matthew 26:71-75. Peter's spirit was indeed willing, but his flesh was weak, because he did not watch and pray as the Lord Jesus Christ had instructed.

Our flesh is not any stronger than the Apostle Peter's. If we are going to stand with courage for the cause of Jesus Christ, then we must watch and pray. We will all be tempted by the devil. The flesh of every Christian is weak; therefore, it is by "praying always with all prayer and supplication in the Spirit, and watching thereunto with all perseverance and supplication for all saints"—Ephesians 6:18 that we can overcome the weakness of our flesh in times of temptation. The spirit indeed is willing, but the flesh is weak, so be diligent to watch and pray.

# Learning

Philippians 4:11

*"Not that I speak in respect of want: **for I have learned**, in whatsoever state I am, therewith to be content."*

Contentment is not something we obtain suddenly; it is learned. Our path to contentment contains a number of lessons that we must learn in order to achieve contentment with whatever life brings us. We must learn to "stand fast in the Lord"—Philippians 4:1b, so "that we henceforth be no more children, tossed to and fro, and carried about with every wind of doctrine, by the sleight of men, and cunning craftiness, whereby they lie in wait to deceive"—Ephesians 4:14. Studying the Word of God, reading the Word of God, and spending time with God in prayer will make our belief in God that much more steady and secure so that we will see God in every part of our life with a conscious awareness that He knows our circumstances.

Other lessons that we must learn on this path to contentment is to "be glad in the LORD, and rejoice . . . and shout for joy"—Psalm 32:11. When we learn to rejoice in the Lord regardless of sickness, health, poverty, wealth, or whatever situation we face, then we will learn to be content in any circumstance of life. We also need to learn to be thankful in order to learn to be content. Un-thankfulness yields discontentment; therefore, "in every thing give thanks"—I Thessalonians 5:18a. The path to contentment isn't always an easy path, but the lessons we learn will bring contentment.

**Day 319**

# Rejoice Before God

Psalm 68:3

*"But let the righteous be glad; let them rejoice before God: yea, let them exceedingly rejoice."*

If anyone should be glad, it is the children of God–those who have been redeemed by the blood of the Lamb and have been cleansed from all unrighteousness – those who are wearing the righteousness of Jesus Christ and through Jesus Christ have been given access to the Father in Heaven! If you have trusted Christ as your Savior, then rejoice and be glad that Heaven will one day be your home. Heaven, where our Lord Jesus lives, where we shall ever be with Him! There will be no more tears in Heaven, no more sickness, no more pain, and no more sin. In Heaven we will praise the King of kings forever. So why not begin now to turn that frown into a smile and be glad and rejoice that your name is written down in Glory!

Are you discouraged today? Have the cares of this life become overwhelming to you? "Rejoice in the Lord, O ye righteous: for praise is comely for the upright" –Psalm 33:1. We cannot go where He cannot come. REJOICE! "Whither shall I go from thy spirit? Or whither shall I flee from thy presence? If I ascend up into heaven, thou art there: if I make my bed in hell, behold, thou art there. If I take the wings of the morning, and dwell in the uttermost parts of the sea; even there shall thy hand lead me, and thy right hand shall hold me. If I say, Surely the darkness shall cover me; even the night shall be light about me. Yea, the darkness hideth not from thee; but the night shineth as the day: the darkness and the light are both alike to thee. For thou hast possessed my reins: thou hast covered me in my mother's womb" –Psalm 139:7-13.

He lives with you. Wherever you are, He is there; therefore, be glad and rejoice! Do not sorrow as those who have no hope –I Thessalonians 4:13. Instead, turn your eyes upon Jesus and begin to rejoice. We have hope in Christ Jesus, and in Him our hearts are made glad, so let's begin today and rejoice with exceeding great joy!

# Your Countenance

Proverbs 15:13

*"A merry heart maketh a cheerful countenance."*

What is your countenance like today? According to Proverbs 15:13 the condition of your heart will determine your countenance. If you are grumbling and complaining, then your countenance is definitely not cheerful. Wearing a frown does not exhibit a merry heart; and of all people who should be merry in heart, it is God's people – those who have been washed in the blood of the Lamb and redeemed, saved and on their way to Heaven.

Cling to your hope of Heaven when the going gets rough, and look unto your Redeemer during sore trials and temptations. Let your heart be merry, giving you a cheerful countenance. Declare with the Psalmist, "I will be glad and rejoice in thee: I will sing praise to thy name, O thou most High" –Psalm 9:2. Singing in times of dire circumstances will rejoice the heart, please God, and demonstrate God's power! Rejoice in the Lord and your heart will be merry; sing unto the Lord and your countenance will be cheerful; look unto the Lord and you will have cause to sing and be merry. There is nothing too hard for the Lord, for "with God all things are possible" –Matthew 19:26. Therefore, do not be discouraged by your storm, but turn your eyes upon the Lord and your heart shall be merry, radiating a cheerful countenance.

*Day 321*

# Is His Salvation Showing in Your Life?

Psalm 96:2b

*"Shew forth his salvation from day to day."*

If we have been redeemed by the blood of the Lamb and know that Heaven is our eternal home, let us walk in newness of life. We ought to show our friends and family, co-workers and strangers the joy of salvation. "We are more than conquerors through him that loved us . . . neither death, nor life, nor angels, nor principalities, nor powers, nor things present, nor things to come, nor height, nor depth, nor any other creature, shall be able to separate us from the love of God, which is in Christ Jesus our Lord" –Romans 8:37-38. Therefore, we should not live as though we have no hope; instead, we need to keep this blessed hope uppermost in our heart and mind so that we might influence others to put their faith in Christ.

We can show the salvation of the Lord by loving our neighbors, our Christian brothers and sisters, and our enemies–regardless of whether or not our love is returned: "For if ye love them which love you, what thank have ye? For sinners also love those that love them" –Luke 6:32. Therefore, show forth His salvation, "and walk in love, as Christ also hath loved us, and hath given himself for us an offering and a sacrifice to God for a sweet smelling savour" –Ephesians 5:2. Also show the salvation of the Lord by being "ready always to give an answer to every man that asketh you a reason of the hope that is in you with meekness and fear" –I Peter 3:15b.

Too many Christians are living in fear and anxiety because of all that is happening in the world instead of living victoriously in Christ. The psalmist challenged us to daily show the salvation of the Lord; therefore, we ought to show those around us there is joy in sorrow when we have Christ; there is peace in turmoil when we have Christ; there is hope in despair when we have Christ; there is courage in danger when we have Christ; there is life eternal when we have Christ. If you have been saved by faith in Jesus Christ, then today, show forth the salvation of the Lord.

# It is by Dying that We Live

John 12:24

*"Verily, verily, I say unto you, Except a corn of wheat fall into the ground and die, it abideth alone: but if it die, it bringeth forth much fruit."*

A grain of wheat has to die in order to fulfill its purpose and bring forth more wheat. The Lord Jesus Christ had to die in order to give us eternal life: "For as in Adam all die, even so in Christ shall all be made alive" –I Corinthians 15:22. As Christians, we need to die to ourselves so that the Holy Spirit will produce His fruit more abundantly in us.

If we will die to hate, then the love of God will grow in us. If we will die to despair, then we will grow more in the joy of the Lord. If we will die to fear, then we will experience abundant peace. If we will die to impatience, then we will become more patient. If we will die to being gruff and surly, we will become more gentle. If we will die to meanness, then goodness will flow from us. If we will die to unbelief, then we will exercise faith. If we will die to pride, then we will live in humility. If we will die to self- indulgence, then we would be more temperate in all areas of our life. "And they that are Christ's have crucified the flesh with the affections and lusts" –Galatians 5:24; therefore, if we die to self, the Spirit will bring forth much fruit in us, and we will become more like our Savior.

## Day 323

# JEHOVAH

Psalm 83:18

*"That men may know that thou, whose name alone is JEHOVAH, art the most high over all the earth."*

JEHOVAH, being spelled in all capital letters, signifies the all-inclusiveness of Almighty God. He **alone** is JEHOVAH! Only He is Jehovah-jireh –The Lord will provide –Genesis 22:14. He supplied the ram on Mount Moriah for Abraham. He supplied the food in the wilderness for the children of Israel. He supplied the strength for David to slay a bear and a lion while he was tending the sheep. The Apostle Paul said, "My God shall supply all your need according to his riches in glory by Christ Jesus" –Philippians 4:19.

Only He is Jehovah-nissi –The Lord is my banner, which represents His covenant to fight for His children so that they will ultimately prevail against their enemies –Exodus 17:15. We do not need to fear our enemies, "for the Lord your God he shall fight for you" –Deuteronomy 3:22b. He will be victorious over every foe! Only He is Jehovah-shalom –the Lord is peace –Judges 6:24. He is the peace that passes all understanding in the midst of persecution, trouble and unrest.

Only He is Jehovah-shamma –the Lord is there –Ezekiel 48:35. "Whither shall I go from thy spirit? Or whither shall I flee from thy presence? If I ascend up into heaven, thou art there: if I make my bed in hell, behold, thou art there. If I take the wings of the morning, and dwell in the uttermost parts of the sea; even there shall thy hand lead me, and thy right hand shall hold me" –Psalm 139:7-10. His Name alone is JEHOVAH! Rejoice in His provision, His banner, His peace, and His presence; then glorify Him whose name alone is JEHOVAH.

# Revive Us Again

Psalm 85:6

*"Wilt thou not revive us again: that thy people may rejoice in thee?"*

Revival is needed when a church is near "death." Christianity today is on the brink of death. Many churches lack vibrancy of life, because they are not walking and living in the power of God's Holy Spirit. Some have followed after other gods–gods of vanity and pride, gods of worldliness, gods of self; and they must be revived to have no other gods before God Almighty. There must be a surrendering of self-will to God's will. "He must increase," but we "must decrease" –John 3:30.

Revival comes by prayer. "If my people, which are called by my name, shall humble themselves, and pray, and seek my face, and turn from their wicked ways; then will I hear from heaven and will forgive their sin, and will heal their land" –II Chronicles 7:14. The prayer of humility, the prayer of earnestness, and the prayer of repentance will gain the ear of our Lord.

## Day 325

# Everlasting Ways of God

Habbakuk 3:6c

*"His ways are everlasting."*

The foundational strength of a Christian is in God the Father and His Son, Jesus Christ, who are "from everlasting to everlasting" –Psalm 90:2c. In a world that is ever changing, we can have great confidence in our everlasting Almighty God. God's ways are everlasting; therefore, what He has done before, He will do again. When we are in need of His mercy, He will be merciful again and again, because "his mercy is everlasting" –Psalm 100:5b. Everything about God is everlasting. His righteousness is everlasting, His truth is everlasting, His Kingdom is everlasting, His covenant is everlasting, *He* is everlasting, and, therefore, all His ways are everlasting.

The high rate of divorce in the world today has made the foundation of many homes unstable. However, "the foundation of God standeth sure, having this seal, The Lord knoweth them that are his" –II Timothy 2:19. This assurance is the joy and strength of the Christian.

If "your world" has been shattered by divorce, or some other devastating trial, then look unto Jesus; He is "the same yesterday, and to day, and for ever" –Hebrews 13:8. He never changes! Because His ways are everlasting, so is His love, and He loves us with an everlasting love. The variables of our life may change from year to year, but the ways of God never change; they are everlasting!

There is a strong confidence in God's unchanging ways

He is a sure foundation

that anchors all our days

Never changing, always the same

A sure foundation

anchored in Jesus' Name

346

# Heavenly Rest

Hebrews 4:3,10

*"For we which have believed do enter into rest, as he said, As I have sworn in my wrath, if they shall enter into my rest: although the works were finished from the foundation of the world. . . . For he that is entered into his rest, he also hath ceased from his own works, as God did from his."*

We can enter God's rest when we come unto Him, surrender ourselves to Him, and allow Him to work His righteousness, His goodness, His ability, His character in and through us. His rest includes that of grace: "For by grace are ye saved through faith; and that not of yourselves: it is the gift of God"—Ephesians 2:8. His rest also includes that of comfort, for Jesus said, "Come unto me, all ye that labour and are heavy laden, and I will give you rest"—Matthew 11:28. His rest further includes that of holiness: "To the end he may stablish your hearts unblameable in holiness before God, even our Father, at the coming of our Lord Jesus Christ with all his saints"—I Thessalonians 3:13. Then it is a final rest, in that glorious land called Heaven, where the people of God will enjoy the end of their faith, for we will see our Saviour face to face.

It is human nature to worry, to fear, and to doubt, but these things never give us rest; however, in Christ we can be free from these tendencies by resting in Him and His Word. When we doubt our salvation we are not resting in His grace, because we are not trusting in His Word. When we fear death, we are not resting in His everlasting arms of security, because our relationship with Him has not grown deeper and deeper. God does not want us to worry or fear. ***He is*** able to save lost sinners, comfort hearts, and care for His children. It is in Christ that we can have this heavenly rest, for "we which have believed do enter into rest."

# God's Resting Place

In the stillness of the morning hour
Before the rising of the sun
I am given renewed power
To accomplish all that must get done

For in my secret place with God Most High
I am reminded --be still and know
The Lord Jehovah is at my side
And always with me He will go

Oh for grace to put to flight
Every anxious thought and care
That throughout the day just might
Overwhelm and cause me to despair

There in the secret place my heart with joy sings
Of sweet fellowship with God, Most High
While Secure beneath His outspread wings
Closer drawn to Him am I

When anxious thoughts attempt to take control
It is then I must return unto my rest
And let the Word of God consume my soul
While leaning confident upon His breast

Come unto me and rest the Lord does call
My yoke is easy and My burden light
Cast upon Him every care, cast it all
Always He is there, in the day and through the night

# Learning Obedience by Suffering

Hebrews 5:8

*"Though he were a Son, yet learned he obedience by the things which he suffered."*

The Lord Jesus, God's only begotten Son, learned obedience through the things which He suffered. Therefore, as a child of God, we should not be surprised when seasons of suffering come into our lives; nor should we murmur and complain that it is unjust. If the Captain of our salvation, who was "without blemish and without spot" –I Peter 1:19, had to learn obedience through suffering, then we who are sinful and who are far from being perfect, should expect to suffer so that we also would learn obedience. Should the head be crowned with thorns while the other members of the body are gently cradled upon the laps of ease? Our Captain was made perfect through suffering and He "became the author of eternal salvation unto all them that obey him" –Hebrews 5:9.

The apostles rejoiced "that they were counted worthy to suffer shame for his name" –Acts 5:41b; therefore, we learn that suffering is honorable for a Christian, because in suffering patiently, we are made more like Christ. We may also take comfort that Christ is with us in our suffering. Because He suffered He is able to sympathize with us and understand our heartache and difficulty. Therefore, let the thought of Jesus strengthen you in times of suffering, and find support in His tender sympathy. "For our light affliction, which is but for a moment, worketh for us a far more exceeding and eternal weight of glory" –II Corinthians 4:17, knowing that "If we suffer, we shall also reign with him" –II Timothy 2:12a. If we are to learn obedience and be more closely conformed to the person of Christ, then we must expect to suffer, and consider the suffering, when it comes, an honorable thing which will produce in us the glory of Christ.

**Day 328**

# The Potter and the Clay

Romans 9:20

*"Nay but, O man, who art thou that repliest against God? Shall the thing formed say to him that formed it, Why hast thou made me thus?"*

Do we question God's making of us? Are we so presumptuous as to reproach our Creator for making us the way He did? If we had a greater understanding of Him as Supreme and Almighty; if we had a vision, as Isaiah did, and would see God "high and lifted up" –Isaiah 6:1, then we would never question why He made us the way He did. It is our pride that opens our mouth to covetously complain that He did not make us with this or that desired talent or ability which we see in someone else. If we would walk in humility, then we would not dare question why God made us the way we are, or attempt to blame Him for the weaknesses of our flesh. In humility we would be able to say, "But now, O LORD, thou art our father; we are the clay, and thou our potter; and we all are the work of thy hand" –Isaiah 64:8.

It isn't our place to question why we were not created differently. We may not have as winsome a personality with the ability to handle any situation with ease and style, as someone else may have. We may not have as naturally a gentle and tender disposition as that of another brother or sister. We may not have as much physical beauty as someone else. However, as children of the King, we have "the Spirit of the living God" and "our sufficiency is of God" –II Corinthians 3:3,5. Regardless of what our weaknesses may be, we are able to "do all things through Christ" –Philippians 4:13: "For in him we live, and move, and have our being" –Acts 17:28a. "As every man hath received the gift, even so minister the same one to another, as good stewards of the manifold grace of God" –I Peter 4:10. "Shall the thing formed say to him that formed it, Why hast thou made me thus?" when we have the grace of God, the strength of Christ, and the power of His Spirit to become the vessel that He created us to be?

# Every Day Thanksgiving Day

I Thessalonians 5:18

*"In every thing give thanks: for this is the will of God in Christ Jesus concerning you."*

When you are tempted to complain, be thankful! Being thankful in everything is the will of God for every one of His children; therefore, begin to thank God in every situation. You are going to face difficult circumstances in life, and the seasons of your life will perhaps bring about unwanted change, but instead of complaining, begin to thank God. Take time to remember all that He has done, all that He has brought you through, and make every day a Thanksgiving Day!

We rob ourselves of joy and the peace of God when we are not thankful. Let's thank Him in the morning that He has given us another day to serve Him. Thank Him in the afternoon that He is with us and has never left us. Thank Him in the evening that He "giveth his beloved sleep" –Psalm 127:2c. We would not lack for thanksgiving if we would "pray without ceasing" –I Thessalonians 5:17. When we are thankful in everything, we will not "quench" the Spirit –I Thessalonians 5:19. Let's make it a practice to be thankful in everything.

**Day 330**

# The Lord Is with Us

Psalm 46:11

*"The Lord of hosts is with us; the God of Jacob is our refuge."*

When standing beside a freshly dug grave and putting a dear loved one to rest, the Lord of hosts is with us! While upon the sick bed and no longer able to be active, the Lord of hosts is with us. In a hospital room, standing helpless as doctors and nurses attend a loved one suspended between life and death, the Lord of hosts is with us! In any trial or storm of life, we may be certain, the Lord of hosts is with us! He is not only with us, but He is also our refuge! It is to Him that we can retreat when our hearts are breaking over the loss of loved ones, when we are languishing upon a sick bed not of our choosing, or when overwhelmed in emergency situations. It may seem that trials will consume us and the storms of life will overwhelm us; but remember, there is One with us, and He is the Lord of hosts! He is a refuge that will bring calm, peace, and grace to face the stormy blasts of life's trials and storms. Whatever the situation may be today, take solace in the truth, "The Lord of hosts is with us; the God of Jacob is our refuge."

# Do Not Forget

Psalm 106:13a

*"They soon forgat his works."*

How soon we tend to forget what God has done for us! Maybe a certain temptation has plagued us, but God was faithful, and He made "a way to escape" so that we would be able to bear it—I Corinthians 10:13. It may be that some trial so overwhelmed us that there didn't seem to be any hope of deliverance; however, our Lord did answer us when we called. He was with us in the trouble, and He did deliver us—Psalm 91:15. The Lord works wonderful miracles for us, but it doesn't seem to take us long to forget that He worked a miracle on our behalf. We aren't any different than the children of Israel were. God worked mighty miracle after miracle yet they soon forgot. We need to make a daily habit of remembering all that God **has** done for us.

*"When God brings any of His children into a position of unparalleled difficulty, they may always count upon Him to deliver them."*—*Streams in the Desert*

**Day 332**

# A Work in Progress

Psalm 138:8

*"The LORD will perfect that which concerneth me . . ."*

It is the Lord that began His work in us, and it is the Lord who will perfect that which concerneth us. This is our hope and confidence, that He is working in us. He is working to smooth our rough edges so that we may become more like the character of Jesus Christ. He does not expect us to change our old sinful nature, for certainly we never could. It is not a matter of us trying to be good enough, because that is not possible, for "as it is written, There is none righteous, no, not one . . . there is none that doeth good, no, not one"—Romans 3:10, 12b. *He* will perfect that which concerneth us! He, by His Spirit living in us, is able to conform us into the likeness of His Son. "For it is God which worketh in [us]"—Philippians 2:13a.

We cannot control our tempers in our own strength; however, the Holy Spirit is able to work a change in us so that our tempers do not flare like they did before we were saved. We do not have the ability to change any habits of our flesh, but God, by His Spirit, will perfect that which concerneth us as His children. All we must do is look to our Lord, rest in Christ, and yield ourselves to the Holy Spirit. We are a work in progress as we live our Christian life, and we can rejoice with confidence that "the LORD will perfect that which concerneth [us]."

# Thankfulness Is a Good Thing

Psalm 92:1-2

*"It is a good thing to give thanks unto the LORD, and to sing praises unto thy name, O most High: To shew forth thy lovingkindness in the morning, and thy faithfulness every night."*

It is a good thing to be thankful, and to be thankful unto the Lord. The Apostle Paul wrote to the Christians at Thessalonica: "In every thing give thanks: for this is the will of God in Christ Jesus concerning you"—I Thessalonians 5:18. Many Christians thank the Lord for the blessings, but sadly, they do not thank Him for the trials. If we truly believe that God is Sovereign—the Supreme Power and Ruler over all—then we will grow spiritually when we give thanks unto the Lord in everything. It is by comprehending and believing that God is sovereign that we come to "know that all things work together for good to them that love God, to them who are the called according to his purpose"—Romans 8:28. Everything has come from the Lord; therefore, it is a good thing for us to be thankful unto the Lord in all things.

The devil wants us to believe God doesn't care and that He isn't concerned about what we are going through. He wants us to question God's love by suggesting, "If God really loved us, why would He let bad things happen to decent people?" Anytime you are tempted to doubt God's love, remember, "He that spared not his own Son, but delivered him up for us all, how shall he not with him also freely give us all things? Who shall lay any thing to the charge of God's elect? It is God that justifieth. Who is he that condemneth? It is Christ that died, yea rather, that is risen again, who is even at the right hand of God, who also maketh intercession for us"—Romans 8:32-34. Our Lord is faithful; our Lord continually loves us; and He is praying for us. May we daily give thanks unto Him.

## *Day 334*

# All Joy

James 1:2

*"My brethren, count it all joy when ye fall into divers temptations."*

Have you ever wondered how you can count it all joy when you face devastating circumstances? How can someone be joyful when their spouse has suddenly been separated from them—either by death, divorce, or war? How can anyone be joyful when their child is deathly ill and the situation looks hopeless? How can anyone be joyful when the bank account is empty and the bills are due? How do we count it all joy like James exhorts the Christians? 1. Remember that no child of God is alone; therefore, instead of thinking of the difficulty, begin searching the Scriptures for God's promises, and "God, that cannot lie"—Titus 1:2b will be true to His promise. We must keep our attention upon the truths of God's Word as well as upon Christ Himself. The Lord Jesus Christ is our joy. 2. Like Christ, desire God's will above your own—Luke 22:42, and ask Him to help you. After all, He is our Helper—Hebrews 13:6. 3. "Sing unto the LORD, O ye saints of his"—Psalm 30:4a. Songs of worship and praise to God can bring joy to our hearts like nothing else can, because it focuses our attention on the Lord and not on the circumstance. The Apostle Paul and Silas demonstrated that in the jail at Philippi —Acts 16:25.

Satan doesn't want Christians to be joyful, because he knows that "the joy of the LORD is [their] strength"—Nehemiah 8:10b. We must realize that our enemy is the one trying to steal our joy; therefore, we must "be sober, be vigilant; because [our] adversary the devil, as a roaring lion, walketh about, seeking whom he may devour"—I Peter 5:8. We are going to face various difficulties that will tempt us to complain, to doubt, to fear, and lack joy; however, if we remember it is all a ploy of the devil to destroy our Christian testimony and rob us of our joy in the Lord, then we will be better equipped to "count it all joy when [we] fall into divers temptations."

# No Longer Servants to Sin

Romans 6:6

*"Knowing this, that our old man is crucified with him, that the body of sin might be destroyed, that henceforth we should not serve sin."*

God the Father has quickened us –made us alive together in fellowship and in oneness with Christ –Ephesians 2:5, giving us the very life of Christ Himself. Through Christ, we have access to His Spirit, which makes it possible for us to no longer be servants to sin. Our old man is crucified with him; therefore, our flesh is "dead indeed unto sin, but alive unto God through Jesus Christ our Lord" –Romans 6:11. "For in that he died, he died unto sin once: but in that he liveth, he liveth unto God" –Romans 6:10; therefore, the sins of our old nature, before salvation, will not have dominion over us if we are living and resting in Jesus Christ.

"Let not sin therefore reign in your mortal body, that ye should obey it in the lusts thereof" –Romans 6:12, for the sins of our old nature will continue in us only if we yield obedience to them. We will not be servants to sin if we yield ourselves unto God, if we obey Him "from the heart that form of doctrine which was delivered" to us –Romans 6:17, and if we yield our "members servants to righteousness unto holiness" –Romans 6:19c. As Christians we need to remember that the old man has been crucified with Christ, that the body of sin might be destroyed. Therefore, we no longer have to serve sin.

*Day 336*

# Not in Me

Genesis 41:16

*"And Joseph answered Pharaoh, saying, It is not in me: God shall give Pharaoh an answer of peace."*

Joseph knew that it is God who gives the interpretation of dreams. It is God who works. We are simply a vessel through whom He may work. If you have been given a voice that thrills an audience when you sing, then remember it is not in you to sing so delightfully; it is God who is using you to move upon hearts with His songs of praise. He gave that talent to you. If you are able to teach and compel the audience to desire to know God better, then remember it isn't in you; God has gifted you and is expounding His Word through you. If others look to you for advice and trust your insights and wisdom of God's Word, remember that it isn't in you. God is giving you the wisdom to answer them. If we, as Christians, would more fully comprehend that it is God working through us, we would be more likely to "do justly, and to love mercy, and to walk humbly with [our] God"—Micah 6:8b. May we remember that it is the Lord who gives, and it is He who takes away—Job 1:21b. It is not in any of us to do anything for Him, but when He has given us talents, may we remember where they originated, and that it is not in us, but in Him that we can do anything.

# Glorious Transformation

Isaiah 41:14-15

*"Fear not, thou worm Jacob, and ye men of Israel; I will help thee, saith the LORD, and thy redeemer, the Holy One of Israel. Behold, I will make thee a new sharp threshing instrument having teeth: thou shalt thresh the mountains, and beat them small, and shalt make the hills as chaff."*

The contrast here between a worm and a sharp threshing instrument having teeth is a glorious one. A worm is weak, fragile, defenseless, and can be easily bruised or crushed. An instrument having teeth is strong; it can break and not be broken. The glorious transformation is that Almighty God can take a person that is weak, fragile, and prone to becoming easily bruised or broken and convert them into a strong and enduring vessel by the power of His Holy Spirit. He transformed Jacob from being a supplanter, who took away his brother's birthright and his father's blessing—Genesis 27:36, into Israel—a prince with God—Genesis 32:28. He transformed Saul of Tarsus who "made havock of the church, entering into every house, and haling men and women committed them to prison"—Acts 8:3, into the Apostle Paul when "as he journeyed, he came near Damascus: and suddenly there shined round about him a light from heaven: And he fell to the earth, and heard a voice saying unto him, Saul, Saul, why persecutest thou me? And he said, Who art thou, Lord? And the Lord said, I am Jesus whom thou persecutest: it is hard for thee to kick against the pricks. And he trembling and astonished said, Lord, what wilt thou have me to do? And the Lord said unto him, Arise, and go into the city, and it shall be told thee what thou must do"—Acts 9:3-6.

None of us needs to live defeated, discouraged, despairing, or despondent lives, for the Lord is able to transform any who come unto Him through the redeeming power of the blood of Jesus Christ. He is able to make us to be what we cannot be on our own. "If any man be in Christ, he is a new creature: old things are passed away; behold, all things are become new"—II Corinthians 5:17.

*Day 338*

# The Day of the Lord

I Thessalonians 45:2

*". . . the day of the Lord so cometh"*

Mark it down – the return of the Lord is coming!  Generation after generation has been looking for His coming ever since the apostles saw Him taken up into Heaven –Acts 1:11.  The day of the Lord will surely come, but not until every one of His sheep has been gathered into His sheepfold.  Are you in that fold?  Does your heart yearn for that day to arrive when you will no longer serve the Lord by faith, but will see Him face to face? He said through the Apostle Paul, "The Lord himself shall descend from heaven with a shout, with the voice of the archangel, and with the trump of God: and the dead in Christ shall rise first:  Then we which are alive and remain shall be caught up together with them in the clouds, to meet the Lord in the air: and so shall we ever be with the Lord" –I Thessalonians 4:16-17.

You may be sure that the day of the Lord is coming, and it may even be this very day.  Therefore, "look up, and lift up your heads; for your redemption draweth nigh" –Luke 21:28 – "for the day of the Lord so cometh as a thief in the night" –I Thessalonians 5:2.  When He comes, there will not be time to get ready, for He will come "in a moment, in the twinkling of an eye" –I Corinthians 15:52.  Therefore, you will have to be ready.  The Bible not only tells us to be ready for His coming, but also tells us how to get ready for His coming: "That if thou shalt confess with thy mouth the Lord Jesus, and shalt believe in thine heart that God hath raised him from the dead, thou shalt be saved" –Romans 10:9.  Look up! "Behold, the day of the LORD cometh."  Are you ready for His return?

# Give Heed

Hebrews 2:1

*"Give the more earnest heed."*

"Give the more earnest heed" to all the Word of God. Follow God's Word so closely that you may say with the Psalmist, "Thy Word have I hid in mine heart, that I might not sin against thee" –Psalm 119:11. The Psalmist tells us in Psalm 19:7-10 that the testimonies of the Lord, the statutes of the Lord, the commandments of the Lord, the fear of the Lord, and the judgments of the Lord are to be desired more than gold and sweeter than honey to us. Give the more earnest heed when He is calling to you to come to Him for a time of fellowship. Do not let sleep keep you from Him, nor allow busyness to deter you from getting alone with Him.

Matthew Henry wrote, "Making excuses is making light of Christ." How often we grieve our Lord! We say we love Him, but we do not give heed to His commandments. Take the more earnest heed to "love the Lord thy God with all thy heart, and with all thy soul, and with all thy mind," for "this is the first and great commandment" –Matthew 22:37-38. Take heed that He is the first One you speak with in the morning when you awake. Take heed that your "mind is stayed on" the Lord throughout the day –Isaiah 26:3. Take heed that He is the last One you think of when you drift off to sleep at night. Take heed, "be sober, be vigilant; because your adversary the devil, as a roaring lion, walketh about, seeking whom he may devour" –I Peter 5:8. Turn off the television and open His Word. Get off of Facebook and seek His face. Hang up the telephone and "call unto Him." Build your relationship with the Lord by opening His Word and asking Him to open your understanding of all that He has written. "Give the more earnest heed" to God's Word, "lest at any time we should let them slip" –Hebrews 2:1.

## Day 340

# Adore and Reverence the Lord

Psalm 103:1

*"Bless the LORD, O my soul: and all that is within me, bless his holy name."*

Bless the Lord! Adore Him! Reverence Him! To bless the Lord is a way of worshipping the Lord! "O come let us worship and bow down: let us kneel before the LORD our maker"—Psalm 95:6. He is worthy of our adoration and our reverence. When we dwell on His goodness to us, His amazing grace toward us, His mercies that are always new every morning, how can we do less than adore our glorious Lord! Worship Him with abundant praise, and "sing unto the LORD . . . sing praise to the LORD God of Israel"—Judges 5:3. Worship Him in song, because "he hath dealt bountifully with [us]"—Psalm 13:6.

As we worship and adore Him, let us do so with reverence. He is the Creator! Almighty God is He! No one is greater than He, and no power can remove Him from His throne. He is the "most high God" in Heaven and in earth! Therefore, we need to humble ourselves and bow down before Him, giving Him the honor that is due Him. Acknowledge His greatness by bowing down before Him. When the Apostle John saw the Lord he "fell at his feet as dead"—Revelation 1:17a. When Daniel spoke with the Lord he was "on [his] face toward the ground"—Daniel 8:18b. Great men of God could not stand in His presence because of His awesome holiness, and neither can we. He deserves our humble reverence when we worship Him. "Bless the LORD, O my soul: and all that is within me, bless his holy name."

# Talk of God's Wonderful Works

Psalm 105:2b

*"Talk ye of all his wondrous works."*

If we talked more about our Lord's wonderful works and less about our complaints, we would be more joyful and rejoicing Christians. His wonderful works are plentiful; we could never speak too much about them. His wonderful work of salvation in us is glorious enough to keep us talking. Just think! His love for us is so great that He laid down His life for us and took our sins upon Himself, so that we could know freedom from sin and have eternal life with Him in Heaven: "Hereby perceive we the love of God, because he laid down his life for us" –I John 3:16. If you are saved, then "talk ye of all his wondrous works!" Salvation is a wonderful work that we should not be silent about; we should talk about it.

"Talk ye of **all** His wondrous works!" Talk to the farmer and tell him that God "giveth rain upon the earth, and sendeth waters upon the fields" –Job 5:10. Proclaim to the rancher that "the voice of the Lord maketh the hinds to calve" –Psalm 29:9, and He does care for them. Talk to those around you of the Lord's wisdom and might, of His wonderful Name, of His beauty and creation, of His great knowledge and deep understanding. "Blessed be the name of God for ever and ever: for wisdom and might are his: And he changeth the times and the seasons: he removeth kings, and setteth up kings: he giveth wisdom unto the wise, and knowledge to them that know understanding: He revealeth the deep and secret things: he knoweth what is in the darkness, and the light dwelleth with him" –Daniel 2:20-22. His wondrous works are abundant; therefore, "talk ye of all his wondrous works."

**Day 342**

# Praise the Lord

Psalm 106:1

*"Praise ye the Lord. O give thanks unto the Lord; for he is good: for his mercy endureth for ever."*

Praise the Lord for He is good! Joshua proclaimed to the Israelites, "Ye know in all your hearts and in all your souls, that not one thing hath failed of all the good things which the Lord your God spake concerning you; all are come to pass unto you, and not one thing hath failed thereof" –Joshua 23:14b. The same is true today concerning all of God's children. The Lord has never failed to accomplish for His children what He has promised; therefore, "praise ye the Lord!" Praise Him that He "is not a man, that he should lie; neither the son of man, that he should repent: hath he said, and shall he not do it? Or hath he spoken, and shall he not make it good?" –Numbers 23:19. "Praise God in his sanctuary: praise him in the firmament of his power. Praise him for his mighty acts: praise him according to his excellent greatness. Praise him with the sound of the trumpet: praise him with the psaltery and harp. Praise him with the timbrel and dance: praise him with stringed instruments and organs. Praise him upon the loud cymbals: praise him upon the high sounding cymbals. Let everything that hath breath praise the Lord. Praise ye the Lord" –Psalm 150:1b-6. As a Christian make it a daily practice to praise the Lord, for He is good!

# God's Strength in the Day of Adversity

Proverbs 24:10

*"If thou faint in the day of adversity, thy strength is small."*

When we become overwhelmed and allow troubles to consume us to the point that we fall under the load of them, then it is a sure sign that we are not resting in the strength of the Lord, but in our own strength, which is no strength at all. The Apostle Paul was able to do all things ***through Christ*** which strengthened him in the various days of adversity that he faced, because he went "in the strength of the Lord God" –Psalm 71:16. We have the same Lord as the Apostle Paul; therefore, we also are able to stand in the day of adversity in the strength of the Lord.

"The LORD is my rock, and my fortress, and my deliverer; my God, my strength, in whom I will trust; my buckler, and the horn of my salvation, and my high tower" –Psalm 18:2. We will never faint, give up, stumble and fall in the day of adversity if we will lean on our Lord who is mighty in strength, for "the weakness of God is stronger than men" –I Corinthians 1:25. It is only in His strength that we will be able to stand in the day of adversity and not faint.

## Day 344
# God's Word of Promise Gives Us Hope

Psalm 119:49

*"Remember the word unto thy servant, upon which thou hast caused me to hope."*

As children of God, we have been given "the word" of promise, but it is not just any "word"; "the word" we have been given is the **Word of God**! It is on His Word that we can depend with hope, regardless of circumstances. We may become faint and feeble, because our journey has been long and difficult; however, we have been given God's Word of promise which says, "He giveth power to the faint . . . the LORD shall renew their strength . . . they shall run, and not be weary; and they shall walk, and not faint" –Isaiah 40:29, 31. It may be that we presently are seeking Christ with a hunger and thirst for closer communion with Him. If so, we have His radiant Word of promise that declares, "Blessed are they which do hunger and thirst after righteousness: for they shall be filled" –Matthew 5:6. We may be overwhelmed because of sin, and burdened with the heavy load of our iniquities; however, God's Word of promise will give us hope when we remember that He said, "I, even I, am he that blotteth out thy transgressions for mine own sake, and will not remember thy sins" –Isaiah 43:25. It may be that we have walked at a distance from our Lord, preferring the lusts of our flesh and the enticements of the world for a season; however, God's Word reminds us that He said, "Return unto me, and I will return unto you, saith the LORD of hosts" –Malachi 3:7b. Whatever our present situation, we can take God's Word of promise back to Him, and ask Him to "remember the word unto thy servant, upon which thou hast caused me to hope."

# Rejoicing in Song

Psalm 33:1-2

*"Rejoice in the LORD, O ye righteous: for praise is comely for the upright. Praise the LORD with harp: sing unto him with the psaltery and an instrument of ten strings."*

Rejoice in the Lord and sing unto Him, for He is worthy. "The earth is full of the goodness of the LORD"—Psalm 33:5b; therefore, sing unto the Lord and rejoice in His goodness. Rejoice in the Lord, for "he is our help and our shield"—Psalm 33:20b. In our trials, regardless of the severity, our Lord is there to help us, and that should cause us to greatly rejoice. As Christians, we should be rejoicing in song, because we have been redeemed, and we are safe in God's hands. He should be our reason for getting up and facing the day, because He has given us eternal life. With Him we can face any hardship. There is nothing impossible for Him. He can part the seas—Exodus 14; calm the storms—Psalm 107:29; Luke 8;24; and keep His children safe in the fiery furnace—Daniel 3. Life is not always fair nor easy, but if Jesus Christ is our Saviour, then we have hope, and we can rejoice in the Lord all the time, singing songs of praise unto Him. Let us keep our focus on the Lord and not on our difficulties so that we will rejoice in the Lord and sing praises unto Him.

**Day 346**

# Controlling the Fire

James 3:6

*"And the tongue is a fire, a world of iniquity: so is the tongue among our members, that it defileth the whole body, and setteth on fire the course of nature; and it is set on fire of hell."*

With our tongue we can lift someone up with encouragement, or we can destroy someone with slander, gossip, and cruel words. The tongue is a little member, but it can do severe damage and destroy much, because "it is set on fire of hell." It is the devil's weapon and tool that he uses when we do not guard our hearts. "For out of the abundance of the heart the mouth speaketh" –Matthew 12:34. In a matter of moments we can greatly hinder or even destroy our Christian testimony with our tongue: "If any man among you seem to be religious, and bridleth not his tongue, but deceiveth his own heart, this man's religion is vain" –James 1:26.

So what is the solution to controlling this little member of ours called the tongue? Many would say we must be more disciplined and try harder to control it; however, James, inspired by the Holy Spirit, wrote, "But the tongue can no man tame; it is an unruly evil, full of deadly poison" –James 3:8. No man can tame the tongue; therefore, the solution is to yield the control of our tongue to God and allow His Holy Spirit to rule what we say. We must continually surrender to God on a daily basis and allow His Holy Spirit to guide and control all of our communication. We must pay attention to the Holy Spirit's warnings and yield to Him when He seeks to keep us from saying anything that would be displeasing to the Lord. When God and His Holy Spirit are in control of our tongue, then we will not speak words of "blessing and cursing" at the same time, which "things ought not so to be" –James 3:10. Instead, we will use our tongue to glorify God, our Father, and lift up His Son, Jesus Christ, our Saviour. We will speak kindly, gently, and encouragingly to others and build them up. We must be ever mindful that this little member of ours, the tongue, "is set on fire of hell"; therefore, we must yield control of our tongue to the Lord and let His Holy Spirit control it so that we may be an effective witness for Christ.

# Our Solid Confidence

Hebrews 1:10-11

*"And, Thou, Lord, in the beginning hast laid the foundation of the earth; and the heavens are the works of thine hands: They shall perish; but thou remainest; and they all shall wax old as doth a garment."*

Our life is always changing, but in it there is One who remains the same—the Lord God Almighty. He is the same as He was in the beginning when He laid the foundation of the earth. He has not changed, and He will not change, because He is "the same, and [His] years shall have no end"—Psalm 102:27b. The carefree days of our youth many times will change into heavy burden-bearing days as adults. Our joy-filled days may turn into heartache and sorrowful ones. Our house that was once so lively with children's happy voices may now be overwhelmingly silent as they have grown up and moved away. Whatever changes may come into our life, we can take comfort that there is One who remains the same, and He has never left us. He continues to be a comfort in sorrow, strength in weakness, hope in dire circumstances, and always the same. His love for us never changes. We may fail Him and fall into sin, but He is faithful and His love toward us remains the same. This is our confidence that when everything else seems to be changing, there is One—our Lord and Savior, Jesus Christ—who never changes, for He is "the same yesterday, and to day, and for ever"—Hebrews 13:8b.

When from my life the old-time joys
have vanished,
Treasures once mine, I may no longer
claim,
This truth may feed my hungry heart,
and famished:
Lord, THOU REMAINEST! THOU art stil
the same!
When streams have dried, those stream of glad
refreshing—
Friendships so blest, so rich, so free;
When sun-kissed skies give place to
*clouds depressing,*
*Lord, THOU REMAINEST! Still my heart*
*hath THEE.*
*When strength hath failed, and feet,*
*now worn and weary,*
*On gladsome errands may no longer go,*
*Why should I sigh, or let the days be*
*dreary?*
*Lord, THOU REMAINEST! Could'st*
*THOU more bestow?*
*Thus through life's days—whoe'er or*
*what may fail me,*
*Friends, friendships, joys, in small or*
great degree,
Songs may be mine, no sadness need
assail me,
Lord, THOU REMAINEST! Still my heart
hath THEE.
—J. Danson Smith

# Continuing the Fire of Prayer

Leviticus 6:13

*"The fire shall ever be burning upon the altar; it shall never go out."*

Keep the altar of prayer in private devotions ever burning. Do not let the fire go out upon secret prayer–being alone with God. Private prayer is the very essence of our Christian life. Family prayer and group prayer find their effectiveness from the times that have come from seasons of private prayer. Closet praying–alone with God–should be, if at all possible, frequent, regular, and undisturbed. "The effectual fervent prayer of a righteous man availeth much" –James 5:16b.

The question that people often ask is, "What should I pray for?" The Bible gives us many suggestions, such as "pray one for another" – James 5:16a; "Pray ye therefore the Lord of the harvest, that he will send forth labourers into his harvest" –Matthew 9:38; pray "for all men; for kings, and for all that are in authority" –I Timothy 2:1b-2a; "Pray for the peace of Jerusalem" –Psalm 122:6a. There is much that we can pray for; therefore, let us be on guard against allowing lukewarmness to invade our closet of secret prayer. If "the fires" of prayer in private devotions are waning, then be diligent to fan the flames so that they do not go out. Being alone with God in prayer is vital for the Christian to grow in grace and to walk with the character of Christ; therefore, keep the fires of secret prayer burning.

**Day 349**

# Daily Manna

Exodus 16:14, 15, 21

*"And when the dew that lay was gone up, behold, upon the face of the wilderness there lay a small round thing, as small as the hoar frost on the ground. And . . . they said one to another, It is manna . . . And they gathered it every morning . . ."*

As Christians, we must depend upon the Lord for our sustenance, our enjoyments, and our very livelihood. We cannot depend upon yesterday's allotment, for it will not be fresh and lively. Neither can we depend upon the world, for the world will never satisfy the soul of God's children. Jesus Christ is "the bread of life" –John 6:35. We cannot depend upon old anointing to provide unction for our spirit; we must "be anointed with fresh oil" –Psalm 92:10b.

Dependence upon God grows from searching the Scriptures daily. The more we learn about God, the more we want to get closer to Him; and the closer we grow in Him, the more we are aware of our need of Him. We are led to pray for "our daily bread" –Matthew 6:11, because the Lord desires that we be dependent upon Him on a daily basis. Seek the Lord daily for all the needs of life.

# That Which Only God Opens

Luke 24:45

*"Then opened he their understanding, that they might understand the scriptures."*

There are certain things that only God is able to open to us. Only God is able to open a heart to receive the Lord Jesus Christ as Saviour. In Philippi, on the Sabbath, down by the river, the Apostle Paul and Timothy spoke the Word of God to some ladies that were there. "And a certain woman named Lydia, a seller of purple, of the city of Thyatira, which worshipped God, heard us: whose heart the Lord opened" –Acts 16:14. It was not the Apostle Paul nor Timothy who opened Lydia's heart to believe upon Jesus Christ; it was the Lord. They presented the Word of God, but it was the Lord who was able to open her heart to believe. If God has opened our hearts to salvation, then let us open our mouths and proclaim the Gospel to as many people as we can, so that they too may have their hearts opened by the Lord to believe on Jesus Christ as their Saviour.

Only God is able to open our understanding of the Scriptures. "The natural man receiveth not the things of the Spirit of God: for they are foolishness unto him: neither can he know them, because they are spiritually discerned" –I Corinthians 2:14, for "the things of God knoweth no man, but the Spirit of God –I Corinthians 2:11b. If we are to understand the Scriptures, then God will have to open our understanding of them. He has given us His Holy Spirit to teach us the Scriptures, and He will open our understanding of them if we will take time to read and study the Scriptures.

## *Day 351*

# Working Together for Good

Romans 8:28

*"And we know that all things work together for good to them that love God, to them who are the called according to his purpose."*

All those trials that would cause our heart to sorrow, our faith to waiver or our hope to be destroyed are working for our good if we are saved through Christ. The betrayal of a friend, the death of a cherished loved one, the crippling of the body in some tragic way, the financial burdens of life are all working together for our good if we love God. In and of themselves they are not good, but God uses them to enhance the life of His Spirit in us in order to make us more like His Son, Jesus Christ.

If we are children of God, then we are "joint-heirs with Christ; if so be that we suffer with him, that we may be also glorified together" –Romans 8:17. It was through suffering that Christ learned obedience – Hebrews 5:8. And as joint-heirs with Christ, it will be through suffering that we learn obedience, which will be for our good. The devil does not want us to believe that suffering is for our good, because the more we conform to Christ, the less we will be under the devil's influence. If he can convince us to be servants to sin, then he can keep us from being effective for Christ. Therefore, when some kind of sorrow, tragedy, or trial enters your life, remember, all things are working together for good.

# God's Leading May Mean the Wilderness

Deuteronomy 8:2

*"And thou shalt remember all the way which the LORD thy God led thee these forty years in the wilderness, to humble thee, and to prove thee, to know what was in thine heart, whether thou wouldest keep his commandments, or no."*

The Lord leads His children into the "wilderness" and allows hard trials to enter our life so that we would learn humility and obedience. Pride can cause us to think more highly of ourselves than we ought to think. As a result, we could become like the children of Israel, who turned their hearts way from obeying God. We can become "desirous of vain glory" –Galatians 5:26, and forget that without Christ we can do nothing –John 15:5. It is in the "wilderness" experiences of our lives that we come to a greater understanding that our sufficiency is truly in Him to provide for our needs, to deliver us from our adversaries, and to safely lead us. As He brings us out of our hard trials, our wilderness experiences, we need to remember that God graciously led us through them in order to teach us to follow Him in obedience and humility.

**Day 353**

# My Light

Psalm 27:1

*"The LORD is my light and my salvation; whom shall I fear?"*

In a dark and evil world the Lord is our light; therefore we do not need to fear. The Lord Jesus is "the light of the world: he that followeth [him] shall not walk in darkness, but shall have the light of life"—John 8:12b. Because the light of Christ dispels the darkness of evil, His light can dispel fear; therefore, since we have the Light of Christ, there is no need to fear.

The Lord is a guiding light. His "word is a lamp unto [our] feet, and a light unto [our] path"—Psalm 119:105; therefore, when our path is uncertain, we can turn to God's Word for the direction we need. He will shine His light on our path to guide us through all the pitfalls of life. The light of the Lord is a personal light: "The LORD is *my* light." When we rest in Him and follow His light, there will be no need to fear.

# The Lord Looked Down

Psalm 102:19

*"For he hath looked down from the height of his sanctuary; from heaven did the Lord behold the earth."*

This is a tremendous thought that we Christians should take time to meditate upon: The Lord, mighty and wonderful, holy and pure, chose to look upon us. He who sits up high, condescended Himself, out of love and mercy, to look upon us down here on earth. Isaiah said, "In the year that king Uzziah died I saw also the Lord sitting upon a throne, high and lifted up, and his train filled the temple" –Isaiah 6:1. Have you seen the Lord high and lifted up, or is there some obstacle that is impeding your vision of your high and lofty Lord? It is to our benefit that we remove any obstacle obstructing our view of our Lord who is the highest, the grandest, the holiest, and the most marvelous. When we, like Isaiah, see Him high and lifted up, we also will be able to proclaim the words of Isaiah, "Woe is me! For I am undone; because I am a man of unclean lips, and I dwell in the midst of a people of unclean lips" –Isaiah 6:5, and we will bow in amazement that this high and holy God looked down upon us from the height of His sanctuary.

The Lord looked down to behold the earth, "to hear the groaning of the prisoner; to loose those that are appointed to death; to declare the name of the Lord in Zion, and his praise in Jerusalem" –Psalm 102:20-21. He looked down and, seeing our great need for a Savior, sent His only begotten Son to redeem us back to Himself. Hallelujah! God looked down upon earth.

**Day 355**

# Without Reservation

Luke 21:3-4

*"Of a truth, I say unto you, that this poor widow hath cast in more than they all: for all these have of their abundance cast in unto the offerings of God: but she of her penury hath cast in all the living that she had."*

This widow woman only had two mites (a very small amount of money), but she gave both of them to the Lord. But she gave far more than money; she offered up her faith, believing that He would care for her needs when the occasion arose. She offered to Him her love and devotion, desiring Him more than anything or anyone else. She gave without reservation, demonstrating her love as well as her confidence that God is able to provide, to sustain, and to care for her. She sacrificed that which she could live on to give back to Him that which He had given her. Her heart was filled with love and gratitude for her Lord, because she fully comprehended that every good and perfect gift came from Him; therefore, she was able to give all her living.

What a challenge of love, devotion, and trust this is to every Christian! This widow woman esteemed it greater to give back to the Lord rather than to keep any for herself to live on, for Christ was her living. May we Christians give back to the Lord with as much earnestness as this widow lady demonstrated.

# Fulfilling

Exodus 6:7

*"And I will take you to me for a people, and I will be to you a God: and ye shall know that I am the Lord your God, which bringeth you out from under the burdens of the Egyptians."*

We can fill our days with so many activities that we are on the go from morning until night. We can fill our lives with so much socialization that we are constantly with someone. We can fill our minds with all kinds of distracting thoughts in an attempt to keep from thinking of the emptiness we really may be feeling. However, none of these things will be fulfilling to us, because nothing can fulfill us like the Lord can. In sorrow, He is a comfort. In trouble, He is a help. In sickness, He is a healer. In need, He is our Provider. Joshua declared "that not one thing hath failed of all the good things which the LORD your God spake concerning you; all are come to pass unto you, and not one thing hath failed thereof"—Joshua 23:14b. Only the Lord can meet our every need in every circumstance of life and be fulfilling to us. He brought the children of Israel out from under the burdens of the Egyptians, and He is continuing to bring His children out from under their burdens today. Go to the Lord today, and you will find that He will fill the empty place in your life.

**Day 357**

# Mirroring Christ

II Corinthians 3:18

*"But we all, with open face beholding as in a glass the glory of the Lord, are changed into the same image from glory to glory, even as by the Spirit of the Lord."*

Does your face reflect the image of Jesus Christ? Can those around you see something different in you? Are they baffled at your patient response to their unruly outbursts causing them to take a closer look at you and wonder what makes you different from the general population? Are they quieted by your silence to their outbursts of rage? Do they seem incredulous at your kindness to their cruelty? What image are you mirroring today? Let it be the glorious image of our Lord Jesus Christ so that others will see a difference. "Blessed are the pure in heart: for they shall see God"—Matthew 5:8. Grow closer to Christ by spending much time alone with Him in prayer, and in reading and meditating upon His Word. Allow His Spirit to control your actions and reactions instead of letting your flesh control them.

The closer we get to Christ the more we will reflect His image and imitate His ways. He "went about doing good"—Acts 10:38. "When he was reviled, [He] reviled not again; when he suffered, he threatened not; but committed himself to him that judgeth righteously"—I Peter 2:23. "He was oppressed, and he was afflicted, yet he opened not his mouth"—Isaiah 53:7a. When we yield to the Holy Spirit within us and begin to take on the character of Christ in our daily living, we bring glory to His Name; "because as he is, so are we in this world"—I John 4:17b. We must spend time with Jesus through His Word and prayer, learn His ways, and get to know His character before we ever mirror His image in our own lives. It is not enough to be saved, though that in itself is glorious; we must walk, talk, and behave ourselves like the One who saved us, so that He can be glorified and those around us can be drawn to Him as well. Think about the image you are reflecting to the world. May it be the image of Jesus Christ.

# A Heart for Christ

II Chronicles 16:9

*"For the eyes of the LORD run to and fro throughout the whole earth, to shew himself strong in the behalf of them whose heart is perfect toward him."*

Is your heart perfect toward the Lord your God, or, in other words, complete in Him? Is your heart so surrendered to God that He has become everything to you; or does He still compete for your full attention and heart's love? George Mueller said this of himself, "I was converted in 1825, but I only came into the full surrender of the heart four years later, in July 1829. The love of money was gone, the love of place was gone, the love of position was gone, and the love of worldly pleasures and engagements was gone. God alone became my portion. I found my all in Him; I wanted nothing else."

Have you come to that place of full surrender unto God Almighty that your heart desires nothing but Him? "In all thy ways acknowledge him, and he shall direct thy paths" –Proverbs 3:6. Are you acknowledging Him in every aspect of your life and allowing Him to direct your paths? Do you desire His will over your own? Do you want nothing to come between you and your Savior? Do you pray before you venture to do something, whether a small or large venture? Search your heart, or better still, allow the Lord to search your heart to determine if your heart is perfect toward Him. "The steps of a good man are ordered by the Lord: and he delighteth in his way" --Psalm 37:23. Set your heart upon the Lord and seek to be one "whose heart is perfect toward him."

## You Are My Portion Oh Lord

You have given me of the grapes of Eschol
And sung to me the sweetest refrain
In all of Your glory
When You made me possessor of Jesus' Name

You are my portion
So full, so rich, so free
Of all that you are
You have freely given to me

You have opened wide the door
For me to come in and sup with Thee
Oh the joy that makes my heart to soar
That you wish to sup with me

You are my portion, Oh Lord
So grand, my heart does exclaim
I've been given more than I could ever afford
When given the glories of Jesus' Name

The riches of His grace
The abundance untold
May His reflection be seen in my face
And shine purer than silver or gold

You are my portion, oh my King
Such abundance I scarce can take it in
Of Your Name my heart will sing
In Your blood I'm cleansed from every sin

Rejoice, Rejoice, Rejoice
Lift up Christ Jesus' Name
With loudest sounding voice
To the entire world proclaim

He is our portion of grace, and mercy and love
He is our life, our strength, our joy
There is none greater than He above
The King of kings, the King of Glory

# Jesus Christ Our Example

John 17:4

*"I have glorified thee on the earth."*

The Lord Jesus Christ – our Rock, our Redeemer, our Strength, our Example – glorified the Heavenly Father while He lived on the earth. He glorified the Father by obedience, being "obedient unto death, even the death of the cross" –Philippians 2:8. In obeying the Father, He subjected Himself to the parental authority of Mary and Joseph on earth. When He was missing, as a twelve- year-old boy, Mary and Joseph searched for Him, sorrowing. And when they found Him in the temple, Jesus asked them, "How is it that ye sought me? Wist ye not that I must be about my Father's business? And they understood not the saying which he spake unto them. And he went down with them, and came to Nazareth, and was subject unto them" –Luke 2:49-52. He was the King of kings and the Lord of lords; yet, in obedience, He subjected Himself to them, that He might glorify His Father in Heaven and set an example for us to follow.

Jesus Christ glorified the Heavenly Father with His life on earth. When He was tempted, He yielded not. When He was hated by His very own, He continued to love them and forgive them, crying out from the cross, "Father, forgive them; for they know not what they do" –Luke 23:34. "When he was reviled, reviled not again; when he suffered, he threatened not; but committed himself to him that judgeth righteously" –I Peter 2:23. He was such an example for us that the Holy Spirit, through Peter, admonished us to "follow his steps" –I Peter 2:21.

Follow the example of Jesus Christ and continue to love those that hate you and despitefully use you, forgiving them for their unkindness. In so doing, you will glorify your Father in Heaven and make Him to be very pleased with you. The closer you get to Christ, the more like Him you will become. Saturate your life with Christ, for without Him you can do nothing —John 15:5. "Whether therefore ye eat, or drink, or whatsoever ye do, do all to the glory of God" –I Corinthians 10:31. Begin today, dear Christian, to glorify your Father so that you may say with Jesus Christ, "I have glorified thee on the earth."

## Christmas, Merry Christmas!

Oh Christmas, Merry Christmas!
Our Lord Jesus came to earth
Born in a lowly stable
His was an humble birth

Glory to God in the highest
The Heavenly host of angels did sing
Rejoice! Rejoice! Give praises to Him
Jesus Christ, the new born King

It's Christmas, Merry Christmas!
O come, let us adore Him
The holy Lamb of God who came
To heal the world of their sin

No greater gift has ever been given
Than this first gift which came from above
Our Heavenly Father's only begotten Son
He gave to the world with love

Oh Christmas, Merry Christmas!
Let us, everyone, remember
Without the birth of Christ our Lord
There would not be Christmas each December

# God Is with Us

Acts 7:9

*"And the patriarchs, moved with envy, sold Joseph into Egypt: but God was with him."*

Joseph was sold into Egypt, and then put in prison for a number of years; however, God was with him through it all. His enemies meant evil against Joseph, "but God meant it unto good" –Genesis 50:20. Those closest to us may do us harm, intending evil against us, but it just may be that, as in the case of Joseph, God will mean it for our good.

Joseph honored God as a servant in Egypt, as a prisoner in Egypt, and as he stood before Pharaoh; therefore, God honored him. Pharaoh put him in command over the land of Egypt and told him, "Thou shalt be over my house, and according unto thy word shall all my people be ruled: only in the throne will I be greater than thou" –Genesis 41:40.

Regardless of the situation or circumstance we face, God will go with us. He will use the trial to prepare us for further work He has for us; therefore, we should not despair or become bitter and angry. Instead, "Let your conversation be without covetousness; and be content with such things as ye have: for he hath said, I will never leave thee, nor forsake thee. So that we may boldly say, The Lord is my helper, and I will not fear what man shall do unto me" –Hebrews 13:5-6.

*Day 361*

# Let Us Worship and Bow Down

Psalm 95:6

*"O come, let us worship and bow down: let us kneel before the LORD our maker."*

Worship and pay honor to our Lord and render reverence to His position as Lord of lords over all. He is the Creator, and we are the created. He is pure and holy, and we are wretched and sinful. He has power in Heaven and in earth, and we are unable to do anything apart from Him; therefore, may we understand it is our privilege and duty to humble ourselves in His sight and kneel down before Him. True worship cannot occur without true humility. Humility demonstrates our nothingness before the Lord. He is Almighty, and we are weak and lowly. "Oh, worship the LORD in the beauty of holiness" –Psalm 96:9a.

Worship the Lord in humble adoration, abandoning every ounce of pride. Come before Him with a singular heart of devotion, giving Him undivided attention. Worship Him in songs of praise! Kneel down and adore Him. "Give unto the LORD the glory due unto his name; worship the LORD in the beauty of holiness" –Psalm 29:2. We, the body of Christ who make up the Church, would experience revival if we would humble ourselves before Him, worshipping and bowing down, kneeling before the Lord our Maker.

# The Name of Jesus

Acts 3:16

*"And his name through faith in his name hath made this man strong, whom ye see and know: yea, the faith which is by him hath given him this perfect soundness in the presence of you all."*

When we receive answers to prayer, whether it is for healing, financial needs, or some other request made to God, they come by way of the name of Jesus through faith in His name. The Apostles Peter and John were men of flesh like anyone else; however, they depended on the name of Jesus. Exercising faith in the name of Jesus, they prayed that the lame man who was "laid daily at the gate of the temple" would be healed—Acts 3:2b. "Peter said, Silver and gold have I none; but such as I have give I thee: In the **name of Jesus Christ** of Nazareth rise up and walk. And he took him by the right hand, and lifted him up: and immediately his feet and ankle bones received strength"—Acts 3:6-7. The Apostle Peter's focus was not on the lame man nor on the healing, but on the *name of Jesus Christ*.

If we desire answers to prayer, we must remember what the Savior said, "And whatsoever ye shall ask **in my name**, that will I do, that the Father may be glorified in the Son. If ye shall ask any thing **in my name**, I will do it"—John 14:13-14. Consider whether or not you are praying in the name of Jesus and for the glory of God the Father. Prayers will be answered when they are sincerely prayed in the name of Jesus through faith in His name so that He and the Father may be glorified.

## *Day 363*

# In Jesus' Name

John 14:14

*"If ye shall ask any thing in my name, I will do it."*

Here is a delightfully simple promise, yet it is as big as the great outdoors, and its expanse is as large as the glorious heavens above. ANYTHING that is asked of our Heavenly Father in the Name of Jesus Christ is given. If answers to your prayers are being withheld, it would be advantageous to examine your prayer and be sure you are asking in Jesus' Name and not in lustful desire of the flesh. The phrase commonly used at the close of prayers is "in Jesus Name." If it is simply a habitual phrase we use, it will gain nothing; however, if it is used in full belief of this verse, then all the inquirer needs to do is patiently wait, because the request will be granted. "God is not a man, that he should lie; . . . hath he spoken, and shall he not make it good?" –Number 23:19.

The name dearest to the Heavenly Father is His Son's Name, Jesus Christ. When Christians bring their petitions to the Father in the dear Name of Jesus, that precious Name will open the vault to receive "every good gift and every perfect gift . . . from the Father of lights, with whom is no variableness, neither shadow of turning" –James 1:17. Do not doubt His promise; examine your every prayer to see if you truly are asking in Jesus' Name, understanding that ANY THING asked in His Name will be given.

# Name Above All Names

Psalm 9:10

*"And they that* **know thy name** *will put their trust in thee: for thou, LORD, hast not forsaken them that seek thee."*

This is a wonderful promise! The Lord has not forsaken any that have sought Him, nor will He forsake any: it is a promise that cannot be broken. The Name of Jesus, our Lord, becomes sweeter to us as we learn more about Him. His is no ordinary name. His Name is excellent "in all the earth"—Psalm 8:1b, "far above all principality, and power, and might, and dominion, and every name that is named, not only in this world, but also in that which is to come"—Ephesians 1:21.

He is ***Jehovah-Jireh***, the Lord that will provide. He provided a ram for Abraham on Mount Moriah—Genesis 22:13-14; and He has provided us a Lamb, Jesus Christ: "For even the Son of man came not to be ministered unto, but to minister, and to give his life a ransom for many"—Mark 10:45. The Lord God has provided Salvation, because Jesus Christ *is* Salvation.

He is ***Jehovah***, the One who *is*. He never changes; His promises never fail. "[Our] days are like a shadow that declineth; and [we are] withered like grass. But thou, O LORD, shalt endure for ever; and thy remembrance unto all generations"—Psalm 102:11-12. He is present with us in all circumstances of life, and He never changes!

He is ***Jehovah-Rohi***, the Lord is my Shepherd. He will lead. He will protect. He will restore. He will comfort. He is the sufficient Shepherd; therefore, in Him our needs ***will be*** met— Psalm 23.

He is ***Jehovah-Shammah***, the Lord is there. He is our companion. "God is our refuge and strength, a very present help in trouble . . . The LORD of hosts is with us; the God of Jacob is our refuge. Selah"— Psalm 46:1, 7. When we begin to learn and know His Name we will be better able to trust in Him, for we will be able to confidently say, like the Psalmist, "Thou, LORD, hast not forsaken them that seek thee."

*Day 365*

# Victory Is Christ—Christ Is Victory

I Corinthians 15:57

*"But thanks be to God, which giveth us the victory through our Lord Jesus Christ."*

We often desire victory in our Christian life, and many talk about having the victorious Christian life. This verse clearly tells us that victorious Christian living isn't something we work toward; rather, it is something we receive the moment we receive Jesus Christ. We can have victory over our sinful flesh, because Jesus Christ "condemned sin in the flesh"—Romans 8:3b, making us "more than conquerors through him that loved us"—Romans 8:37. Salvation in Jesus Christ frees us from the penalty of sin. It also frees us from the power of sin over us by His indwelling Holy Spirit. "For [we] are dead, and [our] life is hid with Christ in God"—Colossians 3:3. "And if Christ be in [us], the body is dead because of sin; but the Spirit is life because of righteousness"— Romans 8:10. Therefore victory in Christ is not by trying, but by dying to self.

"Knowing that Christ being raised from the dead dieth no more; death hath no more dominion over him. For in that he died, he died unto sin once: but in that he liveth, he liveth unto God. Likewise reckon ye also yourselves to be dead indeed unto sin, but alive unto God through Jesus Christ our Lord. Let not sin therefore reign in your mortal body, that ye should obey it in the lusts thereof. Neither yield ye your members as instruments of unrighteousness unto sin: but yield yourselves unto God, as those that are alive from the dead, and your members as instruments of righteousness unto God. For sin shall not have dominion over you: for ye are not under the law, but under grace"—Romans 6:9-14. We fail to claim the victory in Christ when we fail to realize His victory is also ours. The Apostle Paul said, "I am crucified with Christ: nevertheless I live; yet not I, but **Christ liveth in me**"—Galatians 2:20a. Christ lives in and through us, always available, and we need to be continually going to Him. He is the victory for our Christian life, and our victory is in Christ.

# The Shout of Victory

The shout of victory
Proclaims God's promise done
Standing firm upon His Word
Faith's battle will be won

Why then dear saints of God
Do we struggle to believe?
When standing on His promises
We are certain to receive

The testimony of Christ
We know to be true
The disciple whom He loved
Wrote them down for me and you

And every act of Christ performed
The world itself could not contain
His every promise ever made
Today remains the same

We have but to ask our Father
In His Son's precious Name
All things are possible to them
Who by faith the promise claimed

So shout the victory
In Jesus Christ dear friend
He is Alpha and Omega
The beginning and the end

CPSIA information can be obtained
at www.ICGtesting.com
Printed in the USA
FSHW020813090420

9 781630 733230